"...*oots Cast a Shadow* is a fascinating exploration of identity and belonging, refracted through Caroline Topperman's research and imaginings of the turbulent, complex lives of her grandparents and parents. Using archival materials and personal correspondence, Topperman reconstructs her maternal grandparents' flight from Nazi-occupied Poland, not along the more usual path to Western Europe or North America, but eastward into Soviet Russia. This is a well-written book that reads in some parts like an action-packed thriller, and in others as an introspective search through history and ideology to uncover the truth about her family and herself. Readers will find much to learn and enjoy as they follow Topperman on this personal and multi-layered journey."

—**Dr. Nora Gold**, author of *In Sickness and In Health/Yom Kippur in a Gym* and *18: Jewish Stories Translated From 18 Languages*; editor of *Jewish Fiction.net*

"Caroline Topperman, a curious, bold, and compassionate writer, reinvents herself in new places, tells frank, well-paced stories about the living, and writes so powerfully about ancestors that they seem alive. She questions herself and readers: Can you guess? Are you able to imagine? Her historical and geographical imagination roams deftly across Canada, Germany, Poland, Sweden, Russia, and the United States. Her ancestors cast shadows but shed light on current questions: Are you communist, Jewish, Catholic, liberal, conservative? Do political, genealogical, religious and national categories make messes of human lives, or do they orient lives like a compass? Topperman's account of her family history is an alluring lead into global controversies."

—**Dr. Ronald L. Grimes**, author of *Deeply into the Bone: Reinventing Rites of Passage*

"Braiding together generational stories and memories, Caroline Topperman guides readers through decades of one family's hopes and struggles during harrowing political times and highlights the complexity of family relationships. *Your Roots Cast a Shadow* is meticulously researched and beautifully written with compassion and honesty. This memoir speaks to our interconnectedness and will have you reflecting on your own family story and its place in the world."

—**Liisa Kovala**, author of *Sisu's Winter War* and *Surviving Stutthof*

"Once I started reading, I couldn't put it down! *Your Roots Cast a Shadow* expertly connects the present with the past as the author takes you on an emotional journey of how historical events shaped the lives of her family over three generations."

—**Miranda Schell**, author of *Save Me a Dance* and *Paint Me a Story*

YOUR ROOTS CAST A SHADOW

one family's search across
history for belonging

CAROLINE TOPPERMAN

Health Communications, Inc.
Boca Raton, Florida
www.hcibooks.com

Library of Congress Cataloging-in-Publication Data
is available through the Library of Congress

© 2024 Caroline Topperman

ISBN-13: 978-0-7573-2542-7 (Paperback)
ISBN-10: 0-7573-2542-4 (Paperback)
ISBN-13: 978-0-7573-2543-4 (ePub)
ISBN-10: 0-7573-2543-2 (ePub)

Publisher: Health Communications, Inc.
          301 Crawford Boulevard, Suite 200
          Boca Raton, FL 33432-3762

Cover, interior design, and formatting by Larissa Hise Henoch

FOR MY FATHER,
WHO NEVER STOPPED TELLING STORIES

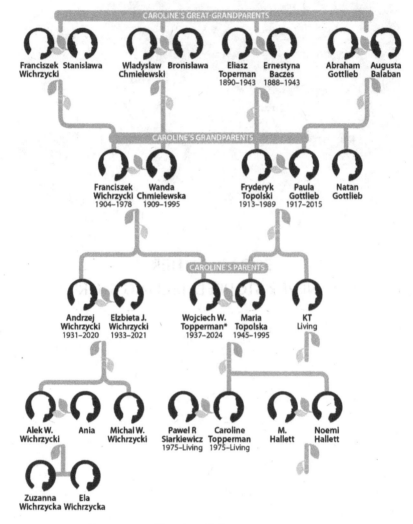

CAROLINE'S GREAT-GRANDPARENTS

Franciszek Wichrzycki — Stanislawa — Wladyslaw Chmielewski — Bronislawa — Eliasz Toperman 1890–1943 — Ernestyna Baczes 1888–1943 — Abraham Gottlieb — Augusta Balaban

CAROLINE'S GRANDPARENTS

Franciszek Wichrzycki 1904–1978 — Wanda Chmielewska 1909–1995 — Fryderyk Topolski 1913–1989 — Paula Gottlieb 1917–2015 — Natan Gottlieb

CAROLINE'S PARENTS

Andrzej Wichrzycki 1931–2020 — Elzbieta J. Wichrzycki 1933–2021 — Wojciech W. Topperman* 1937–2024 — Maria Topolska 1945–1995 — KT Living

Alek W. Wichrzycki — Ania — Michal W. Wichrzycki — Pawel R Siarkiewicz 1975–Living — Caroline Topperman 1975–Living — M. Hallett — Noemi Hallett

Zuzanna Wichrzycka — Ela Wichrzycka

*Name changed to Topperman

CONTENTS

CHAPTER 1

ARE WE REALLY DOING THIS? OUR MOVE TO POLAND

November 15, 2013, proves to be very cold and gray in Warsaw, and in leather jacket and tennis shoes, I am completely unprepared for the blast of arctic air. Winter came early to Warsaw that year, although it would warm up again by the holidays. We greet my cousin's daughter, Zuzanna, and stand awkwardly in silence, waiting for my cousin to arrive. For the past year and a half we have built a relationship around getting my husband and me to Poland. Zuzanna was our person on the ground, the one who sat in countless government offices to deliver our paperwork, and perhaps even forged my signature on documents when we didn't want to spend exorbitant sums of money on overnight couriers. So the fact that we don't have much to say seems strange, but then again, the last time we hung out, she was still a child. Now she is in her early twenties and thinks we are insane for moving all this way.

While we wait, we bond over Pixie, Pawel's and my eight-year-old blonde cairn terrier, who is uncannily the exact shade of Baltic Sea sand and who has made the transatlantic flight in the cabin, at my feet in her dog bag. We have her papers and official documents from the vet, but in contrast to the hoop jumping we have to do in Canada, no one stopped us at our point of entry. I can only assume that no one noticed a dog in a bag, and I certainly didn't advertise her presence.

Finally, my cousin Alek arrives and envelops us in a giant bear hug. Although he is technically my cousin, his kids and I are closer in age. His loud, barking laugh and steady stream of chatter are both comforting and familiar. When he sits with my father and his father, there is no doubt they are related. If I had to use one word to describe Alek, it would be *jovial*.

Alek puffs on the vape strung around his neck and points out landmarks as he drives us to our new home. What we see is a city reeling from the usual November 11 Polish Independence Day riot-filled celebrations, yet the streets are filled with pedestrians, trams, and bumper-to-bumper traffic. At one in the afternoon, on a Friday no less, everyone has somewhere they need to be. The main streets already have their elaborate vintage-inspired holiday decorations—swirly curlicues wrapped around lampposts, colorful bulbs hanging from lace umbrellas, and mini-waterfall lights—that even unlit contrast starkly with the gray day the sun forgot.

Along with its celebratory side, this day also sees the Nationalists march through the center of Warsaw. The chants and red flares settle on the city in an oppressive cloud that defines outright who is wanted and who is not. For now, the Nationalists are an abstract that are spoken about through gritted teeth or dismissed with the wave of a hand. We will come to learn that, unlike in Canada, where these kinds of groups are more or less underground, in Poland their voices are loud and clear. The country will hold their elections within a year of our arrival, and these are the early voices of discontent. They stand for God, country, and family. They stand against immigration, against any religion other than Catholicism, and against the LGBTQ+ community. Soon enough we will see this ugly underbelly gain an even louder voice. We will feel the dread of their angry, heated chants reverberating against our bones. While those who dress in pseudo military attire, with bomber jackets and heavy laced-up boots, make an imposing statement, it's the regular people, the ones you'd least expect to be filled with so much hate, who scare me the most because I don't know where they stand. For now, however, we are still protected by the excitement of our move.

Our drive takes us past communist-era concrete buildings intermingled with intricate prewar architecture and futuristic glass-and-metal skyscrapers. The mix is fascinating. You would never see this combination in Vancouver, which Pawel and I have just left, or in our hometown of Toronto. But here, many of the older buildings have been restored to their original pastel pinks, yellows, and blues. Those on the side streets, where tourists rarely venture, are still blackened from decades of pollution and neglect. Still, Warsaw is exceptionally clean compared to most European cities, many of which survived almost complete destruction in World War II. What it does have is what feels like a million roundabouts—all huge, with many lanes of traffic. For the life of me, I cannot figure out how they aren't one giant pileup all the time. Just when you think you are driving in a straight line, a roundabout takes you in another circle. Then there are the billboards. They are everywhere. Small ones and huge ones cover buildings, residential and commercial. They loom over the roads in a visual assault. It's like we've been thrown headfirst into a roundabout-driven billboard amusement park.

We squeeze by the police and military trucks that line our new home street with cops in riot gear enjoying a cigarette after a hard couple of days. Although we have arrived two days after the riot-like march, tension lingers in the air. Riots are tough on a city's morale. Routines are forced to change, and places that once were safe are no longer so. It will take another day or two for the police to clear out. The city is still in the midst of a cleanup.

Our apartment on 10 Smolna Street is in a seventies-era communist-style low-rise block. The ground floor bike shop offers a humanizing look. Inside the building, there is color and movement. My cousin's daughter had already warned us to prepare for a shock. She's right, and the peeling green paint in the hallways doesn't help. But our apartment has been completely renovated with hardwood floors and high-end stainless-steel appliances. In other words, happily, the inside does not match the outside. My dream of living in a charming Parisian-style flat oozing with character, with a pretty balcony where we can drink lattes and eat croissants, had long since evaporated. I feel like a contestant on one of those relocation shows where they want all modern amenities and local charm for the low price of $500 per month.

So, is this the romantic ideal? No, but it feels familiar, clean, and comfortable. The lattes and croissants will come soon enough. Besides, we are centrally located, and that's what really matters. We have no plans to buy a car, so easy access to everything is imperative. When I step out of my place in the middle of winter at 4 PM and it's already dark, I want to see people, stores, and restaurants. Try explaining this to local real estate agents. No one seemed to understand that I was not interested in a large flat on a quiet street—that I welcome noise, within reason, of course. In the end, this flat is the best of both worlds, on the park side of a busy intersection.

It's hard to give up your way of life. We had just sold virtually all of our possessions to move halfway around the world. The truth is that our decision to move was mostly because I was feeling claustrophobic in Vancouver. I didn't like how our lives were unfolding and felt that there was no real future for us in a city that never quite felt like home. Even though we moved to Warsaw by choice, we still want to maintain some level of normalcy. Everything is new and different, and I'm excited. The possibilities are endless, we have no idea what they are, but the immediate dream is to fall down the entrepreneurial rabbit hole. Start an online business? Sure, that would be great. Work in real estate development? I am always game to do that. For the first time in a long time, I do not feel stifled. The heaviness of the Independence Day riot aside, there's an energy to Warsaw. It's a city on the go.

Besides, people are looking out for us. My cousin thought ahead and brought us a large pack of toilet paper. Romantic ideals are one thing; practical everyday comforts are another. So yes, toilet paper, check. The flat is furnished, but we're missing towels and bedding. These aren't items we had thought to pack. Who would? This is our first time renting a furnished apartment; we aren't versed in the etiquette of the whole transaction. My cousin takes Pixie home with him so that she won't be alone in a new apartment first thing, and we head out into the bright lights of Złote Tarasy (Golden Terraces), the downtown mall.

The energy in the mall is electric. The place is loud and the lights a little too bright, just like any mall anywhere in the world. Zara Home has everything we need. My cousin drops us off. We could walk, but we'd have to navigate the warren of underground shops beneath the main street. Aboveground I can find my way in any city, but underground I am lost in an instant. In fact, it will take me close to a year to learn how to make my way through that maze. The very center of town is made up of wide boulevards. Aleje Jerozolimskie and Świętokrzyska run parallel to each other. They are joined by Marszałkowska. All are pedestrian friendly and lined with lots of trendy, oversized shops such as Zara, H&M, C&A, TK Maxx—TJ Maxx for all the North American tourists.

Are we tourists? I don't think so. What we are is outsiders, which is why several people will soon admonish us for not going to Hala Mirowska, where we could have bought perfectly good bedding and towels for a fraction of the price.

These are things you learn after the fact, the things that come to you in bits and pieces, as the days go by and you're settling into your new environment, and people are dying to tell you everything you should have done. We don't yet know about Hala Mirowska—that the large two-story market was originally built in the 1800s, then repurposed and rebuilt over the years. Or that now that it's back to its original purpose, stall upon stall of food products, homewares, and sewing supplies line the floors, while rows of flower stands crowd the entrance. We don't yet know about its sister building, Hala Gwardii, filled with higher-end wine stores and kiosk-style restaurants while the center is defined by long, wooden communal tables. A similar hall, Hala Koszyki, is a mystery to us, too. It stands at the other end of the city, a higher-end version of these two, and a sighting ground for the rich and famous of Warsaw.

What we do know is that on the way home, when our Uber driver swings by my cousin's so we can pick up Pixie, she apparently hasn't noticed we were even gone.

A few hours later, Pawel and I are sitting at our coffee table in our new apartment, with a bottle of fine French wine, gourmet cheese, fresh bread, and pickles we picked up at the mini-market on our street, where I let him do the talking. Yes, I know my Polish, but I'm still not comfortable using formal pronouns. Years ago, I was traumatized when I accidentally said "tu" to a waiter. I can still see his scathing stare as he turned to get my ice cream. I know that now, formal speech has to become the way I speak. Rules around language are taken very seriously here. Spoiler alert, the two-tiered pronoun system never becomes natural to me.

Pixie is lying on the couch, tongue poking out, comatose from jet lag. Our Internet won't be hooked up for a few days, which means that, for now, outside entertainment hasn't permeated the walls of our new home. When it does, I'll be shocked to find that almost all of it's in Polish. I will look in disbelief at Pawel. "I can't believe we just did this."

For now, though, reality doesn't matter; this just feels right.

This is a story of beginnings, but the story doesn't really start with me. It starts with my grandparents, and it could start even earlier, except that I know almost nothing about my great-grandparents. In an interview, my grandmother states that after serving in Józef Piłsudski's army, her father worked as a lawyer, but I've searched dozens of databases and haven't found anything close to that description. Another family member mentioned that he may have been a school principal, but that search also turned up nothing. It would not be fair to start with that generation and such a lack of details.

So, yeah, there are gaps. North Americans are used to gaps, so much so that we often forget where our roots are buried. It's easy to say, "I'm French Canadian or Irish American," but what does that even mean? Who are we really? Our society is one that constantly moves forward, sometimes at breakneck speeds. North Americans are the people of "What's next?"—a culture in which even taking a vacation is seen as weakness. At the same time, we think we can say whatever we want and do whatever we want. Really? Maybe we should look again because we aren't the center of the universe, and a lot of disenfranchised groups have never truly known war but are ready for a fight. There are some deeply unsettling things happening in the world right now. Scary people are using their bullhorns to talk about history and roots in dangerous ways that are clannish and exclusive.

This is a slippery slope. A dangerous process that threatens our humanity. Our history, our roots, is deeply planted. It's vital that we not let those roots be wrenched from the ground, let alone used to clobber others.

My father was unwillingly expelled from his family—their choice, not his—and about three-quarters of my mother's family was murdered during World War II. As a result, there weren't many people left to pass on the stories, to help us make familial connections. On my maternal side, almost everyone had some level of post-traumatic stress disorder. The few people, like my father, my cousin Alek and his immediate family, and my mother's brother, KT, are the only ones left who still remember the past generations firsthand and can pass on our history.

We need to understand who we are, and how we're all connected. This book is my contribution to that effort. I hope you'll think about your stories, and your roots, and what you know about your history. I hope then you'll think about how we can all live together, on even ground. This then is my story, braided with the story of my family.

CHAPTER 2

HOW HALF OF IT BEGAN, THE MATERNAL SIDE: MY BABCIA PAULA

Europe in the 1920s had begun with postwar recovery and chaos. This interwar period was marked by severe highs and lows, and a surge in populist and nationalist movements. Newly formed countries such as Estonia, Finland, Latvia, Lithuania, and Poland, which had gained their independence, were fighting to establish a national and international footing. Germany was bankrupt, forced to borrow money to sustain its economy. So, even with the Great War behind them, tensions between countries still ran high. Questions of nationalism defined the next decade. Multiethnic countries with regions that were ghettoized grappled with the question of how much autonomy individual communities needed. Hitler, who gained power in 1933, was ratcheting up world tension by making demands and breaking treaties.

But in 1935 in northern Poland on the Hel Peninsula—the popular vacation spot where Paula, or Babcia as I knew her, was enjoying her eighteenth birthday—trouble seemed a world away. This trip to the beach with friends—and free of parents—signaled the young woman's first taste of freedom. Finally, the girls were being treated like adults. The world and all its possibilities felt wide open.

The near future was uncertain, though. Paula was waiting to hear about university. She was sure she had the grades, but Numerus Clausus limited the number of Jews who could study in institutions of higher learning, and that made the odds of her acceptance slim. Chances were, it could be years before she'd be admitted.

Still, she had to try.

Uncertainty was a first for the girl who lived a privileged life, the girl who had shopped in Paris and fallen in love with artwork in Vienna, the girl who was the apple of her father's eye. Until now, her Jewish background had not been much of an issue, especially since her family was completely assimilated. They spoke Polish at home— no one knew Yiddish or Hebrew. True, in religion class, which was strictly Catholic, she joined the other Jewish girls on the ghetto benches at the back of the room, where they did their homework, but at home her parents didn't keep a Jewish household. Her uncle Majer Bałaban hailed from a long line of rabbis, and she knew her father's family was also quite devout.

Her dream was to be a doctor, to live on her own and travel, to see the world. At eighteen, independence could not come soon enough.

I picture Paula and her girlfriends flocking to the windy, sun-baked beach right after breakfast, spreading out colorful blankets, putting up wind blockers borrowed from the guesthouse. The Baltic never truly warmed, so the girls brought books to read, including Adam Mickiewicz's book of love poems, which I imagine Paula was devouring. But first, she'd pull off her wrap to show off the new bathing suit, complete with skirt and shoulder bows, that her mother had brought back from Vienna. None of the other girls would have anything like it.

Paula was the only daughter in a wealthy family, and her father, who was once an officer in Piłsudski's army, worked as a lawyer. Her mother oversaw an impeccable household, while Paula's younger brother, Natan, apparently kept to himself. As I heard the stories, my grandmother in her youth was the charmer. The statement "Dad, I'm dying for some fresh cookies" would send her father knocking on the baker's door. Her parents had a large circle of friends and acquaintances, and Paula loved attending parties where she'd be the center of attention. Well, mostly. Stanisław Lem—everyone called him Staś— the family friend who would go on to become an acclaimed science fiction writer, once thanked her for her birthday gift, then promptly told Paula she could leave the party. Staś was always working on stories he would sometimes read to her. He was also an eccentric, but because their parents saw each other frequently, Paula, at least, had to be nice to him.

Her relationship to Fryderyk—the man who would become my grandfather—was altogether different. To us kids, my grandparents were always simply, Babcia, Grandma, and Dziadzio, Grandpa. We were privy only to carefully curated glimpses of their lives. Shortly before she died, my babcia did an interview with my uncle KT. It was originally in Polish, but I only received a Google-translated version—the kind of version that is good enough to understand but also provides a certain level of hilarity. In a rough Polish-to-English my babcia shared,

> We met by chance on Hel. Me and two of my friends were spending the holidays there. We were then very proud, because the parents let us go alone, and those were the

days when the girls hardly were left unattended. It was
1935 and we just recently had our 18 birthdays. We were
planning on starting studies which also was the exception rather than the rule because the girls usually ended
education at high school and got married. We felt revolutionary, emancipated. However, during these holidays,
we all met our husbands, and the revolution ended for
us. We met them on the beach, even though there were
separate beaches for men and women. The girls were allowed to swim, but not to jump into the water from the
bridge. We were terribly protesting against it, so we went
on the men's beach to jump. I jumped directly onto my
future husband's head. And it all started.

That's right. Paula landed directly on Fryderyk's head. The tall,
athletic, handsome, twenty-two-year-old, blond-haired, blue-eyed
swimmer took notice of young Paula. Both were from Lwów, and
they started dating. So began the whirlwind courtship, or as Paula
recalls it, "From there things started galloping."

It was sometime between 1935 and 1937 in her hometown of
Lwów, and Paula had recently joined MOPR, the International Red
Aid society, a political Red Cross organization founded by Communist International that provided aid to political prisoners of the
"class war" around the world. She enjoyed the meetings, which often
featured interesting writers and intellectuals. Besides, here she had
the chance to mingle with her friends. Standing on street corners
handing out leaflets wasn't so bad either—chatting with passersby
was a good way to gather intel. Lwów was becoming an international
city, and while not as romantic as Vienna, it had its share of concerts,
plays, and so on. Overall, being a part of the revolutionary crowd
was stimulating.

When asked in an interview what attracted Paula, a young lady from a rich household, about working with the International Red Aid, she responded,

> My house was always fostered by the left-wing tenden-
> cies. My parents had socialist political views and me, as
> a teenager, I wanted to be more radical than them. What
> attracted me? The freedom; the faith in progress. We
> wanted to change the world, to get rid of the old, rigid
> customs. We saw the monstrous injustice and social
> inequalities.

As much as her parents tried to shield her, Paula kept up with international news, through underground newspapers—the kind her father did not want her to read. And, of course, the news was grim, like this 1934 report from the *New Republic* on political prisoners being held at Dachau:

> Each barracks consists of five connecting rooms, in each
> of which fifty-two prisoners are lodged. Each room is
> equipped with fifty-two berths, in tiers of three, rough
> tables and benches. The floor is concrete. The pris-
> oners sleep on straw sacks covered with a sheet which
> is changed once in two months. The walls are only a few
> inches thick, and the ill-fitting windows offer almost no
> protection against the icy cold, wind, or rain. For each
> fifty-two men a small washstand is provided, and the
> time allotted for washing, for the whole group, is only
> twenty-five minutes.

While Paula cared deeply about class inequalities and the mounting fascism, she was comfortable at home. Executing her duties as a revolutionary sometimes chafed. She didn't admit it to her

supervisors, but she was embarrassed to be seen asking for dona-
tions. So much for the romance of fundraisers and handing out leaflets in the town square. Instead of knocking on strangers' doors, she
ended up canvassing friends and acquaintances. Luckily, she had a
lot of them. Naturally, she did not want to telegraph the notion that
she needed the money herself. On one occasion when she was canvassing, her friend asked how much she wanted. Without thinking
she replied, fifty złoty—a considerable amount of money. Her friend
laughingly agreed and said he'd have it ready later that night. But
when he insisted on walking her home, she said, "I can go by myself,
thank you." She was indignant. Who was he, a man, offering to protect her?

In the city of Lwów alone, 30,000 people were registered as out of
work. Paula was beginning to get caught up in the excitement of attending rallies and protests. Not the illegal ones; those sounded scary.
They were also held in secret, in basements or behind public buildings. Raids were a common threat. The punishment, if she were ever
caught at such a rally, would be jail time. And of course, there was
the danger of a riot breaking out. Still, with a protest every weekend
and sometimes during the week, the whole city was in turmoil.

Bloody Thursday, April 16, 1936, galvanized the resolve of countless young revolutionaries. Most of Poland, like the rest of the world,
was still being choked by the Great Depression. Workers, especially
those in construction, were overworked, underpaid, and stuck la-
boring in harsh or inhumane conditions. Anti-government strikes
and rowdy protests, a common sight in all the major cities, were
often led by the biggest and the burliest, like those who carried the
heavy bricks for the bricklayers. When Kozak, one such worker, was

brutally killed by police during a protest, a huge funeral was planned for him in response. Paula decided to attend the rally. In fact, although she did not know it at the time, Fryderyk was one of the organizers of the whole event.

Mourners poured onto the streets. The protest grew in full force, much larger than expected. Soon the city became a sea of black. Bureaucrats had set out a short, official route that led from the morgue on Piekarska Street to the Łyczakowski Cemetery, so the mourners would skirt the downtown core. The crowd, however, broke through the police cordons, veering left through Bernardyński Square, Akademicki Square, and Legionów Street to the National Opera House, then winding through to Kazimierzowska Street all the way to the Janowski Cemetery. All the while, the anger kept building. A tram was tipped on its side. People were gathering behind it. A loud crack, and everyone started dodging police bullets fired into the crowd. More and more barricades appeared, the crowd using whatever they could find to shield themselves from flying bullets. A group of women carried a bullet-ridden coffin.

It depends on who you ask, but between 8,000 and 60,000 were in attendance that day, with 1,500 arrests. Upward of 19 people lost their lives. Paula never told her father she saw this all firsthand.

Pawel and I joined many rallies while we lived in Poland; most were calm, but a few stood out. A few that stood out were some seniors who remembered communist times and cried out, "Never again" and were physically carried off by police; women who were arrested for protesting some of the world's most oppressive abortion laws; and an artist who was jailed for painting a rainbow on a Mary and Jesus print. The protests became increasingly more desperate as the government imposed stricter laws on society. At first we didn't see how many of these rules would affect us, but as time wore on, the more I delved into my family history, the more I realized that it's easy for totalitarianism to sneak up on you.

When Paula finally accompanied Fryderyk to her first illegal communist political rally, she would have found the hall crowded and noisy, filled with speakers standing up for workers' rights, targeting the extreme injustices coursing throughout the region, and berating the social inequalities between classes.

You could never be certain about the outcome of a rally, but at least some of them proved to be uplifting, even fun. The most memorable one, perhaps, was the Kongres Pracowników Kultury (Lviv Antifascist Congress of Cultural Workers), which Paula went to with her mother, again, without her father's knowledge. Fryderyk aside, Abraham wasn't happy about his wife and daughter spending so much time with communists.

It was a time of controversy and upheaval. The previous month had seen huge clashes with police that ended in firefights and many wounded. Lwów was becoming a hotbed of Polish, Jewish, and Ukrainian intelligentsia, but it was also the center stage of the class struggle. A strong nationalistic undercurrent was rising, tensions were running high, and Paula's father, naturally, was afraid for the safety of his family. Paula would have been much too young to remember the pogroms of 1914 and 1918, but the sound of splintering wood as armed soldiers burst through doors and burned down homes was not lost on Paula's parents, along with the pitiful wails of women being forced to the ground.

The Lwów Antifascist Congress of Cultural Workers took place in May 1936, over the course of two days. The rally was inspired by the 1935 International Anti-Fascist Congress of Writers held in

Paris, where local unions came together with intellectuals to defend culture from the fascist plague. Coupled with the massive April clashes between city workers and the police, the Lwów rally became a culminating moment in the history of Western Ukraine's left-wing movement. The congress advocated for the cultural needs of all nationalities throughout the Polish state and called for national schools and equal rights for all local languages. The congress denounced pro-fascist government policies and condemned bourgeois nationalism and the capitalist oppression of the working masses.

The crowd that day was a sea of red ribbons, made by hundreds of volunteers. Everywhere, kids were carrying red carnations. In the main town square, hundreds of white doves were released into the sky. All so festive, so enticing—what, on an ordinary day, might have signaled a carnival in town. The streets were teeming as if all of Lwów had come out in force. For once, police stayed in the background, and no violence ensued. The crowd was big, joyous, calm. The speakers were well-known writers, artists, and intellectuals. Fryderyk was well-known to the authorities, and the Communist Party had suggested he lie low for the event. The first notable speaker was Wanda Wasilewska, the journalist, novelist, left-wing activist, consultant to Stalin, and founder of the Union of Polish Patriots. She had aided in the creation of the Polish First Tadeusz Kosciuszko Infantry Division and later, in 1944, helped influence the inception of the Polish Committee of National Liberation.

The main events were held in the Tramway Workers' building, a large redbrick structure with a huge meeting hall, which on that day at least featured a portrait of Maxim Gorky, founder of the socialist realism literary movement. The hall was standing room only, filled with leaflets with an excerpt from an editorial by Karol Kuryluk, editor in chief of Lwów's Sygnałów:

Wchodzimy w świat bez programu! Nie chcemy
wypowiadać szumnych słów i haseł ani stawiać
papierowych granic tężejących potem w mur, o
który musielibyśmy kiedyś tłuc bezradnie głową.
. . . Nie stanowimy ani lewicy, ani prawicy. Nie
reprezentujemy też złotego środka społecznie
czy literacko. Chcemy być po prostu ludźmi.

[We enter the world without an agenda! We do not
want to say blustering words and slogans, or create
paper borders, which would turn into walls that we
would inevitably have to bang our heads into. . . .
We are neither the left nor the right. We also do not
represent the so-called golden center, socially or
through our works. We want to be just people.]

Down with the class disparities, down with inequality and
nationalism—the shared economy that the Communist Party was
proposing was clearly the answer. This is what must have been going
through many young revolutionaries' minds. There was clearly a
disconnect with the younger generation who were trying to make
a change and their parents who had lived through the First World
War. Many notables rose to speak that day. Paula and her mother
heard some of her favorite writers, among them, Julian Tuwim,
Władysław Broniewski, Emil Zegadłowicz, and Henryk Dembiński.
The Congress ended with a loud, rambunctious rendition of the left's
anthem, "The Internationale." We can assume that they would have
been singing the Russian version. This is the literal translation:

Get up, branded by the curse,
The whole world is hungry and slaves!
Our mind is boiling indignant
And ready to fight to the death.
We will destroy the whole world of violence
To the ground and then
We are ours, we will build a new world,
Who was nobody—he will become everything!

Refrain:
This is our last
And a decisive battle;
With the International
The human race will rise! (2x)

No one will give us deliverance:
Neither God, nor a king, nor a hero—
We will achieve liberation
With my own hand.
To overthrow oppression with a skillful hand,
To win back your good—
Blow up the forge and forge boldly,
While the iron is hot!

Despite the political preoccupations of the city, romance bloomed. In Paula's Google-translated words,

> He [Fryderyk] came to our house, like any other day since we lived not far from each other, and he said he was fed up going back and forth in the rain or slush, so I either marry him, or it was time to say goodbye. I was terribly offended by that, but to be honest, I do not remember whether I was only pretending.

It was a really nasty summer. One day Fryderyk came all
soaked and said, "Do you see what you are driving me
to? I will get pneumonia and die and you will become
a widow."

I replied that if I was to become a widow, I had to be
married.

"Well, if you want to become a widow that much, then
let's get married," he said. Later he came with flowers
and put them on the table. I asked him to put them in a
vase, but he said that he'd just come to propose, and he
took back the flowers with him.

I am curious to know what my great-grandparents would have
thought of Fryderyk. Although he had a degree in engineering, his
ties to the Communist Party and his Jewish roots made it difficult
to find a steady job. No one would hire him. His views and passions
were a liability—and with political tensions running high, this was
not the time to be too vocal or too noticeable, either. As a result,
he spent much of that year searching for steady work in his field.
Luckily, he had been a high-achieving student, and that fact did not
go unnoticed. Thanks to word of mouth and a lot of networking, he
managed to work as a tutor while picking up odd jobs in mechanical
engineering. Would they have been able to see through all that and
let Fryderyk court Paula? Would they have wanted him to have a
high-paying job? I would love to know the answers to these questions. My parents loved Pawel, and it was important to me that they
got along.

My grandparents' wedding was held in June 1937, amid weekly
protests and rallies, at City Hall, not at a synagogue and with no

huppah. I can picture Paula in her white custom-made suit, just as I can picture her complaining about the hours of standing still at the dressmaker's. The handiwork, I'm sure, was stunning.

For their June honeymoon, Paula and Fryderyk chose the very fashionable Zakopane, a village in the Tatra Mountains frequented by intellectuals and artists. It was a place that already showed signs of becoming the kind of European ski village that North American resorts emulate today.

Zakopane even had its own local legend, the Story of the Sleeping Knight. Neither one of my grandparents told me this story growing up, but it's the kind of story I would have expected to hear while on one of the many hikes I took with my dziadzio (my grandfather). This would have been the perfect folktale for him to tell, but perhaps it did not come up because we were never in Poland together.

So the story goes, many years ago, in the village of Zakopane, there lived a blacksmith who was working in his forge when a stranger came one day, offering a bag of gold in exchange for a simple task. There was one condition. The blacksmith had to promise never to speak of what he saw. The blacksmith readily agreed and began making a horseshoe out of the gold block the stranger handed him. When the horseshoe was ready, the blacksmith then accompanied the stranger to a cave at the base of the mountain, where, to his surprise, there was an army of knights with horses, all of them fast asleep.

The stranger then requested a second task—that the blacksmith replace one horse's horseshoes. The blacksmith was surprised that the horse did not stir the whole time he worked. As they left the cave, the blacksmith could not help but ask the stranger about what he had seen. The stranger replied, "The knights you saw have been in a deep slumber for hundreds of years. They will wake when the time comes to fight a great battle. On that day the earth will shake, the sky will be filled with thunder, and the mountains will break open as the knights mount their horses and ride to protect Poland."

The blacksmith received his payment of a bag of coins, and the stranger went on his way. But the blacksmith could not stop thinking about what he'd seen, and soon enough the entire village knew where he had been. When he went to check on his gold a few days later, all he found was a bag full of dust. When he went to try to find the cave, it, too, was gone. The profile of Giewont peak is said to look like a sleeping knight.

Giewont is one of the most popular mountain hikes in Poland, and it has probably been that way for centuries. It seems like a natural place for my grandparents to have gone on their honeymoon. Old photographs with my grandparents in the mountains fill our family albums. My grandmother often wore a kerchief on her head, sometimes knickerbockers and other times a woolen skirt. My grandfather can be seen wearing wool trousers and carrying a backpack.

Thousands of tourists make their pilgrimage to the metal cross on Giewont's peak every year. There is a man-made stone staircase flanked by tall green grass and wildflowers that leads hikers single file to the top. The peak itself is stark gray stone, with a large metal cross that can be seen for miles. Looking back, the landscape is all peaks and valleys, and distant villages.

When Pawel and I did this hike, there was a steady stream of people on the trails and keeping our pace meant dodging the many groups. We were decked out in our high-tech hiking boots and day packs that we wore in the mountain ranges around Vancouver. The sense of accomplishment was real until we saw the throngs of locals making their way up in flip-flops. Even so, the magic of this mountain range captured our hearts, as it once did my grandparents'.

As their honeymoon was coming to an end, Fryderyk was surprised to get word that the Klein metal works factory in Dąbrowa Górnicza was offering him a position. He assumed that his reputation as a communist and a Jew had probably preceded him, but he was desperate for a full-time job that could propel his career. While Fryderyk headed to the factory, I assume that Paula was tasked with finding and setting up their new home. We have no way of knowing otherwise. As it turned out, the director of the factory was a liberal thinker who did know who Fryderyk was, and besides, the director needn't have worried because Fryderyk was under strict orders from the Communist Party to keep a low profile and not to get embroiled in illegal rallies. Lying low was key. Government personnel had infiltrated the party and were arresting members who then wound up in camps as political prisoners. After a quick visit back to Lwów, Fryderyk went straight to work.

On March 12, 1938, Austria became the first country to be annexed by Germany. Six months later, on September 30, Czechoslovakia was annexed. Poles had no idea what to expect for Poland. Paula was convinced that they would soon see a war, but Fryderyk said no, that was impossible.

CHAPTER 3

ASSIMILATION (OR NOT)
BY WAY OF FOOD

I am standing in the middle of the street, crying. "I hate this coffee. Why does everything taste so weird? Why is surówka served with *everything?*" To this day I don't get what's to love about a type of coleslaw. Why did we come here? What was I thinking? My poor husband stands helpless, watching my meltdown. He later tells me he was concerned by my extreme reaction, and worried that I was going to unravel. He felt bad, he said. He had no idea how to help me. We haven't found our support system. For now it is just the two of us trying to navigate our daily existence.

The honeymoon period in a new place lasts about a month. That's when everything feels new and shiny—before your new reality takes you by surprise. I have to wonder: Is this how my parents felt when they first lived in Baghdad or Paris, in Sweden or Toronto? No wonder they didn't hang on to the foods they knew. Or to the traditions. How could they? They learned it was easier to adapt than to blindly cling to old conventions. My father grew up in postwar Poland when food was heavily rationed. For years my parents had to be financially creative to put healthy meals on our table. Food was the bridge to our life in Canada and all the places my parents called home.

Adjusting to our new life in Poland is demanding. Having breakfast at Vincent's, a Parisian café in the heart of the city, helps, and in a couple of days we fall into a routine that leads us daily to this tiny piece of Paris, complete with flags, those iconic wicker chairs, and the best baguettes outside France. Each morning we leave our flat for a small park with sweeping views of Powiśle, an indie neighborhood bordering the Vistula River and the escarpment where we live. There are always lots of people, all walking dogs off leash, so we pick our way through dog poop and garbage left by partygoers, local drunks, and students. Pristine the park is not, but we have a prime view of the church grounds—one of the many, many churches in Warsaw—and a view of the river and the rooftops. Walking down a steep hill where kids toboggan in the winter, we come to the Chopin University of Music, where we're serenaded by students practicing the piano or violin or occasionally a flute, creating that alluring cacophony heard at the start of a classical concert, then make our way up to Nowy Świat, a part of the Royal Route.

This daily walk to Vincent's makes us happy. The general societal mood is electric, despite a certain heaviness that lingers. Warsaw is a city that displays its memories, especially those that contrast starkly with the modern world. Memorials and statues stand out on prominent streets. Buildings show off shell holes from World War II assaults. Every few steps there is a plaque commemorating a death or a war event, like the beautiful old library around the corner from our home that saw its books burned during the Nazi regime. Even with history at every turn, the pink, blue, and yellow buildings perk up the gray wintry feel of Warsaw.

Pixie, with her laid-back West Coast disposition, putters along at our side as we pass restaurants and cafés that will soon be bustling. Pixie loves Vincent's as much as we do. Why wouldn't she? The owner hand-feeds her fresh croissants, sometimes with jam. Those croissants are the best part of our mornings. Breaking apart the buttery flakes, each bite a delectable morsel, and washing them down with rich cappuccinos is the only sane way to start the day. Actually, there are three Parisian cafés to choose from on this street, each with its own flavor. Petit Appetit has vintage French music, and each baguette is named after a different city. A few meters away is Croque Madame, with whitewashed walls and bunches of lavender strategically displayed. Vincent's is my favorite because it reminds me the most of Paris, but each café is filled with the aroma of fresh bread. From flaky pastries to cream-filled macarons to warm, melt-in-your-mouth pain au chocolat to delicate madeleines, every day brings some new indulgence. In the weeks to come, when we finally rejoin society, we will drop by Vincent's on Saturday mornings to pick up a freshly baked baguette that is still warm to the touch, to pair with runny cheeses, fragrant meats, juicy red tomatoes, and crisp pickles. This is the meal that grounds us, that makes us feel we are home.

For now, walking to faux Paris every morning is our escape from the obvious. At some point, we will have to find work. At some point, we will have to eat healthier food. That means I will have to cope with grocery shopping.

When I finally try, some items really stump me. The tomato sauce tastes sweet, and the only milk I find is boxed, on a shelf. Eggs aren't in the fridge either, which makes for a confusing run around the market. It takes days of dipping into different stores before finally working up the nerve to ask a clerk about this strange new-to-me

milk. Actually, I have no idea what to ask, which is why the conversation goes as follows. "Przepraszam? Prosze pana, jakie to mleko,
czy można je pić normalnie?" This roughly translates as "Excuse me,
sir? What kind of milk is this? Can I just drink it normally?" Or at
least that's what I want to say. Whether it comes out like that, I can't
be sure.

"O co pani chodzi?" he scoffs. This term I will come to know in-
timately over the next four years. It translates roughly as "What are
you talking about?" said harshly. Dismissively. To be fair, I probably
sounded odd asking about milk I can drink "normally."

I went to Poland thinking I spoke Polish. Which I do. I speak
Polish fluently, but I was used to speaking Polish with my family
over dinner and throwing in the occasional English word or modi-
fying a Polish word when I didn't know how to conjugate. Conversations went like this, "Jak dzisiaj było w szkole?" (How was your day
at school?) "Okay. Miałam, science test i myślę że, that I passed." Do
I even need to translate? But in Poland, it will take a year before I
figure out that I should smile my biggest smile and say, "I'm sorry I
haven't learned that word yet," so people will laugh and possibly go
out of their way to help me.

This trick, or perhaps it is a coping mechanism, comes to me in
an unexpected moment. I have run out to a local business supply
store on Ordynacka, a small cobblestone-lined side street, because
we are in dire need of a printer ink cartridge. The store doesn't resemble a standard office supply store. Instead it's basically a hole in
the wall overstuffed with supplies tucked safely behind the counter. I
almost don't go in, but we really need the ink. I throw my shoulders
back, stand a little tall by way of a silent pep talk, and decide to enter.
I am, after all, an adult. I can do this. I have no idea what the word for

an ink cartridge is, but I know I can explain it. Also, I've been practicing what I will say for the five-minute walk. Guess what? It works.
The staff smiles at me, and I go home with what I need.

On another occasion, Pawel and I needed some cash, but we
couldn't find a bank machine. He left Poland at the age of twelve
before such a thing existed, and I've never lived there, so naturally
our families created their own words for these kinds of things. We
located a bank and asked if they had a *maszyna bankowa*, literally
translated to bank machine, the clerk looked at us for a few moments, then smirked and pointed out the *bankomat*.

Those first days in the markets, facing a cranky clerk, I turned a
bright shade of red, mumbled something incoherent, and rushed out
of the store.

A few weeks later we meet another Canadian expat. What are the
chances of meeting someone who grew up only blocks away from
Pawel, in Scarborough, a suburb of Toronto? Over coffee he laughs,
"I totally know what you mean, but you need to chill. Right up the
street from you, there's a great store called Food and Joy. They carry
food from all over Europe."

I know this store! I've passed it a hundred times. I just didn't realize I could afford to shop there. This piece of intel goes a long way
toward helping us get oriented and keeping our lives recognizable.
Adventure and change are generally good, but when your normal
is flipped upside down, it's important to hang on to some kind of
familiarity.

A few days after the milk fiasco, a friend from the United Kingdom
laughingly explains that the milk is heat processed, like canned milk.
The carton need not go in the fridge until after it is opened.

Not knowing the things that are obvious to locals is what makes
you feel like a foreigner. Like you so do not belong. It's the simple

things that get you, such as knowing how to accept change at a coffee shop. Do they hand you the money directly or place it in a tray? I have seen both. Friction is introduced into everyday tasks, and it's unsettling. Bluntly, I feel dumb much of the time, but the allure of new places and experiences is what makes me persevere. I assume that even if I embarrass myself, people will forget pretty quickly.

Day in, day out in Poland I think about food, and the importance of food, how it is that the right food makes you feel at home. When we first land, the new tastes and smells are exciting. They trigger bursts of memories. We can't get enough fragrant sausages, fresh kaisers, butter that tastes like butter, tomatoes that taste the way they smell, milk (once I understand it) that is creamy, inexpensive cheese that tastes expensive, and most of all, jam-filled pastries we dub "crack tarts" because they're so addictive. Sure, the wooden barrels of pickles and sauerkraut you have to fish around in do kind of gross me out, but the quality of the contents is undeniable. I'm no foodie, but here I can't help myself. At first, I want to try everything.

Food, I came to realize, transcends cultures and customs. Sit down to a meal, and suddenly you are bonding over the dishes on the table. My earliest memory is of food. I was standing at the stove, cooking a curry dish with my dad. I don't know if it was because of a lack of food when he was a child in postwar Poland, if it was left over from when he lived in Paris as an adult and had to ration food for cigarettes or metro tickets, or if it was simply an unfulfilled dream of being a chef, but the one constant in my memories of my dad involves food. In a different world he might have been running his own intimate restaurant with a continually changing menu.

Weekend mornings, after disappearing to share stories with the men at the local Filipino market in the Bathurst and Sheppard area of Toronto, he'd come home excited to use the exotic ingredients he had gotten. Any time he could experiment with different tastes, he would, and often his concoctions were delicious. Okay, one time he served lasagna with bananas. He said he thought the tastes would be complementary, but I'm betting it was time to use up bananas.

It was my dad who taught my mother how to cook. She made simple, everyday foods, and a few fantastic desserts. It was my father who conjured up the complex dinners. It was his dream to be a chef. And in our home, food did not go to waste. Saying, "Eww, that's gross," without trying the food first was tantamount to swearing at our parents. Years later, when I asked my dad why they were so obsessed with a habit that led to unhealthy eating for us all, he said, "I don't know. For a long time, we didn't have food, so we finished everything on our plates." That rule was extended to our little family.

"You don't have to like it, but you have to try it" was another rule. We were at a Chinese restaurant celebrating the end of the school year when Pani Irena, our live-in housekeeper, made a face at the lobster we had just been served.

Pani Irena was from a small village in Poland and didn't speak a word of English. My sister and I had no choice but to speak Polish with her and were her official translators whenever we were out. A short woman with a stocky build and mousy brown curls, Pani Irena took the place of the grandmother we never had. We had Polish grandmothers, actually, but that's another story. Always wearing an apron, she brought many Polish foods into our home that my parents would not have introduced to us.

I can still see her thick fingers deftly spreading flour on the kitchen counter, kneading dough and cutting perfect parallelograms to make kopytka. I remember exactly how to hold a knife to an apple without breaking the peel. Most of all, she taught me the importance of having new experiences. So, following her own advice, Pani Irena closed her eyes at the Chinese restaurant and took a bite of lobster. She then promptly ordered lobster for herself.

I was six or seven when Pani Irena first came to stay with us. While I remember her as an older grandmotherly figure, she was probably in her fifties, a typical illegal migrant worker who came to North America in order to send money home. Having lived behind the Iron Curtain for her entire life, Canada would have been an onslaught for her senses. I can only imagine how she must have felt in a country where everything was foreign. The one advantage she had over most immigrants was our family as a safety net. She was never on her own, her home was with us.

Before falling in love with lobster, however, she first learned how to cook vegetables. This detail might seem insignificant, but for my mother it was a vital part of our diet. Vegetables in Poland were always served overcooked, tasteless, and mushy, so when Pani Irena first learned to steam vegetables, she, too, had a minor revelation. As her comfort levels with new food grew, she began sending canned crab back in her care packages. She would stand in the small front room of our home on Holm Crescent in Thornhill and iron cash that she placed between two towels so as not to burn it. She would then slip bills individually into her letters in such a way that anyone checking the mail couldn't feel them. While there was no guarantee that the money would arrive, the cans always did, much to her family's annoyance.

When Pani Irena left and Maria came to live with us, we learned something new again. Maria was Paraguayan and often spoke to us in Spanish. Where Pani Irena used to dish up heavy dumplings such as pierogi alongside rich meats, Maria was the master of bread. She made the best pizza we had ever tasted. It was so good that before we knew it, every kid in the neighborhood asked for Maria's pizza for their birthdays.

Even with these amazing influences, today I am no great cook. I would rather just throw a few ingredients together and leave it at that. So, at some level, maybe there's also a disconnect with food. I'm even trying to remember food with my grandparents. My grandmother who came to live with us certainly wasn't the type to slave over a hot stove. She did make a great chicken salad using grocery-store roasted chicken and a wonderful tiramisu. Her specialty was a classic makowiec, a type of poppy seed roll. I can't even tell you what my grandfather liked to eat. I only remember his breakfast, always coffee with lemon loaf coated in chocolate.

When we first moved to Poland, finding that same brand of lemon loaf was like finding a corner of a security blanket. One day there it was on the shelf in our local Carrefour food market, in its yellow foil with Zitronenkuchen written in German across the packaging. It's not uncommon to see foods with foreign labels. The delicate spongy cake covered in a thin layer of milk chocolate did not disappoint. It tasted exactly as it had the first time my sister and I snuck thin slivers of the loaf when my grandfather wasn't looking.

Growing up, our home was filled with a variety of foods that got me used to lots of different kinds of things. Whether I like it or not, no food ever freaks me out. Of course, I still freak out over the ubiquitous surówka! The fact is that no matter how excited you are to try new foods, the time comes when you just want to eat something familiar. There's a reason we flock to comfort food. No one likes to feel uneasy. So, even with my fairly food-adventurous upbringing, there still came that moment in Warsaw when all I wanted to eat was what I knew and liked.

CHAPTER 4

THE OTHER HALF: MY MATERNAL SIDE, MY DZIADZIO FRYDERYK'S STORY

I had a close yet almost unspoken relationship with my maternal grandfather. Because we lived in Canada and my grandparents lived in Germany, we saw them every other summer. Beyond that, there wasn't that much contact. From stories, I know that my grandfather was a charming, effervescent man. But with us, he was quiet and steadfast. He spent much of his time in his office or hiking in the mountains near his home, and I remember his office as meticulous. Everything had its place and had to be replaced exactly. The Mexican jumping beans we gave him sat on his desk long after the larvae died. I fell in love with fountain pens because of the one he kept on his desk. But it was through walking and hiking that he and I communicated. Three or four of my steps to every one of his. I learned the names of trees from him. For many years I knew their names only in Polish.

I followed my grandfather on hikes in the Taunus Mountains around Bad Homburg, in the Swiss Alps, in the tourist village of

Torgon, and across golf courses after my grandparents moved to To-ronto. If Pani Irena can be credited with my fluent Polish, it's thanks to my grandfather that I can read the language. Of course, there was a big incentive, but I'll share that story later.

Fryderyk was born in Złoczów, a small city sixty kilometers east of Lwów, on the heels of the first Russian Revolution, which Lenin called the Great Dress Rehearsal for communism, and just before the start of the Great War. Fryderyk's father, Dr. Eliasz Toperman, was a linguistics teacher of German, Latin, and Greek, who had been raised in a predominantly German environment. He had moved the family to Vienna and then to Morawy in the Czech Republic after enlisting in the Austrian army at the start of the war. Fryderyk grew up speaking German and Polish, to which he would later add Yid-dish, Russian, and English.

When Fryderyk was five, the family settled in Lwów, and it quickly became home. As he grew older, he was tempted to return to the countryside where his family had a cottage. It was his fierce belief in fighting for equality that kept him in the city.

Fryderyk's passion was clear from the time he was in elemen-tary school. It made his blood boil seeing kids getting beat up after coming out of Cheder (Jewish Hebrew school), so he would jump in and fight the bullies every chance he got. As a thank-you, he would often be invited to dinner, and before long he learned to speak Yid-dish and to perform the Passover Seder. Even though his family was assimilated, being forced to walk by public signs that said, "Żydzi do Palestyny!" (Jews go back to Palestine) was difficult. The open dis-play of derogatory terms like "Bejlisy"—a reference to the notorious 1913 trial in the Russian Empire, when Menahem Beilis, a Jew, was accused of serial murder—fueled the young man's passion to fight for what was right.

Fryderyk respected his parents, but he was closer to his mother. His father was a teacher who traveled frequently and who ran a strict German-speaking household when he was home. He also demanded only the best from his son, and yet he took Fryderyk's side even when kicked out of school for misbehaving. Not surprisingly, the youth who spent so much of his time defending other students would soon become politically active.

In 1935, Fryderyk founded an interuniversity coalition that included the Independent Union of Socialist Youth, the Union of the People's Youth (Związek Młodzieży Ludowej), and the Legion of Left-Wing Youth (Legion Młodych-Lewicy). No longer satisfied with behind-the-scenes work, he summoned the courage to climb onto the stage at one of his rallies and speak about his past, about growing up poor and Jewish, having to fight to get an education. The speech ignited a massive brawl. The green-ribbon-wearing "heroes" of ONR (National Radical Camp), composed of far-right Polish ultranationalists, would have hated him simply because he was a Jew, meaning not a purebred Pole. This unrest pushed Fryderyk into the inner circle of the political agitators, and that summer, following Wanda Wasilewska's "Amnesty Action" campaign, Fryderyk and his comrades established an amnesty organization for political prisoners, with chapters throughout the country.

Although his political career was gaining ground, Fryderyk was proudest of the illegal press he founded, set up in his home, right under his parents' noses.

He was aware of the fact that his political leanings were costing his parents dearly, but he knew in his heart it was the right thing to do. Fryderyk and his friend Henryk worked diligently for an entire year, from May 1, 1934, to May 1, 1935, four nights a week, on a simple cyclostyle printing machine made by a friend. Another friend, Halina, who had put the crew together, did most of the writing, including translating articles from other underground presses. Their own work drew on the philosophy of Karl Marx and Friedrich Engels. The small group rounded up the funds to buy ink and paper. All work was done at night, and extra care was taken with organizing the various drop-off sites. By day, they hid their supplies in the baby grand piano. They knew if they were caught, each print run could easily land them five to eight years in prison.

The group managed to keep their work secret until one night, when Fryderyk's father walked in on them. He glanced scathingly at the propaganda his son was pushing. Defiant, Fryderyk said, "You can tell the police for all I care." His father, however, remained quiet, which was no small thing. His parents believed in civil liberties and national self-determination, having witnessed the disintegration of the Austro-Hungarian Empire. Now, here was Fryderyk, pushing for upheaval of the social order to achieve radical social equality.

During this time, while lying low so as not to draw attention, the students compensated for their isolation by reading all the Marxist literature they could get their hands on. Marx, Engels, Lenin, or Stalin—the young Communists devoured it all. Many nights were spent discussing the perfect socialist society, and how to achieve it. Occasionally, they were able to find other underground periodicals, including *Imprecory*, written in German. They also took this time to study the history and the pros and cons of the Communist Party of the Soviet Union. With the fascist movement gaining ground in Poland and the rest of Europe, Fryderyk was convinced that the only way to solve the ugly problems that come with fervent nationalism, including the persecution of groups such as Jews and Ukrainians, was to adopt a socialist system, like that in the USSR.

Years after his death, I found a book my grandfather had written, *Wspomnienia i Ludzie—Kronika Wydarzeń* (The times and the people: A chronicle of events). By that time I could read Polish well enough to know that this was an important document. The copy I inherited was dedicated to my mother. Just like the title suggests, it was a dense chronicle of events. Immediate family members were allotted a single sentence at most. Much of the text was simply his memories written for himself and his friends. While I never knew him as particularly political, I believe that without realizing it, he made several strong statements.

The first was his decision to call leaving Poland in 1969 a second immigration rather than an expulsion. The second was the choice not to choose Israel, which was the only easily available option at the time. He was adamant about moving to Yugoslavia, which was also a communist country but not under Moscow's rule. The condition to leaving was the renunciation of his Polish citizenship in order to get travel documents. My grandfather, dziadzio, in his mind was a Pole first. After many days of haggling with the government clerk, they agreed to use "of Jewish origin." In the postscript of his chronicle, he says he went on to regret this way of thinking and regret his remaining in the Party. My dad, though, is pretty sure that, like his own father, Fryderyk simply chose to ignore whatever conflicted with his beliefs. I would say they were all blind to what was happening. Blind to the atrocities committed by Stalin. Blind to the murder of hundreds of thousands. Blind to ensuring that millions more would starve to death. The young Polish communists of the 1930s clung to a steadfast belief in the ideals of the system. For whatever reason, they chose to swallow all the propaganda.

Willfully blind or simply stubborn, one thing about the young Fryderyk is clear. Once he chose a path, nothing would deter him.

On September 1, 1939, Fryderyk sent word to Paula, probably the only communication they had since he left, that the army had ordered him to a plane manufacturing company in Mielec, 200 kilometers from Dąbrowa Górnica. "At dawn on September 19, 1939, the German troops had moved out of the area, headed west, while the Russian forces had come within several kilometers of Lwów from the east." What should have taken a few hours, a day at the most, turned into a long, hazardous journey marked by constant bombardment from wailing Stukas dive-bombing the train tracks. Fryderyk ducked behind trees or dropped into the tall grasses of surrounding fields. He also lucked into farms and tiny villages that hadn't been evacuated, where for the most part people could still share food and water.

The train station in Mielec he found teaming with people but no trains. Chaos ruled. No one knew where to go. Fryderyk managed to hail a peasant who agreed to drive him to the airplane factory in a wooden cart smelling of potatoes and fresh-cut wood. They arrived at the factory only to see more Stukas flying in formation. Minutes later all the guards stationed at the factory were machine-gunned down. The villager then threw Fryderyk out of his cart and sped off in the opposite direction.

Who ordered the guards stationed out in the open? They'd been sitting ducks. Fryderyk jumped into a nearby potato patch and held his breath until the planes flew off. By nightfall all was quiet, and he could survey the scene of the massacre. By this time some of the factory workers were also out to survey the damage. Without a word they started digging graves. Some of the dead were barely recognizable, but each one was given a proper burial. It took most of the night.

As dawn broke, the workers reentered the factory—109 men and only one commissioned officer, Jablonski. He picked Fryderyk to lead the group and to be the first point of communication with the factory directors and military officials. It quickly became clear that they could no longer work. Most of the Łos bombers stationed in the clearing were damaged, and the rest were not in working order. Word was that the German army was approaching from Slovakia, in the south.

Given that the most important thing was to secure papers to ease their passage through the country, to get provisions and money, and to head east as fast as possible, Fryderyk convinced the factory directors to give him a lump sum of silver bullion, enough to pay the workers. The bullion was stowed in a large backpack while another worker and friend managed to fill a suitcase with bacon. By the time they organized themselves, the factory directors had fled south, for Romania, which at the time bordered Poland.

On September 8, to keep the factory from falling into German hands, the remaining workers set it on fire and headed northeast, in the direction of Biłgoraj. It took the better part of a week to reach the San River, but at least the weather held out as they hiked through the Molotov-Ribbentrop Zone, where there was very little fighting. The Molotov-Ribbentrop Pact, or the German-Soviet Pact of Non-aggression, had been created so that the Soviets and Nazis could partition Poland. The zone, then, was the part of Poland where there was minimal fighting at this time. Still, to avoid running into Hitler's army, the men mostly kept to the forests. At this point the group also separated. Most of the men joined the army under the command of Second Lieutenant Jablonski and headed back to Łodz. Fryderyk was sorry to see the hardworking men go. He would miss the camaraderie that had flourished during their brief time together.

The remaining thirty or so, including Fryderyk, were eager to lend their services to the military in other ways, so they decided to continue on to Włodzimierz Wołyński, a city some 133 kilometers (82 miles) north of Lwów. Their trek to the Bug River and Włodzimierz proved to be a challenge. The bridges had either been blown up or torn down by retreating troops and villagers. As they walked, the men passed hundreds of cars packed with officers and civilians, all heading to the Romanian border.

It was no better when they finally arrived in Włodzimierz. The commander of the unit was a drunk, profanity-spewing buffoon. At least when Fryderyk and the others advised him to lead his soldiers out of the barracks, where they were sitting ducks for a potential onslaught, he listened to their sound advice, and as a thank-you he gave Fryderyk the necessary papers for getting back to Lwów. That night they divided the silver bullion equally between them, and once again Fryderyk and a friend separated from the group.

The first village they passed had antiaircraft guns the entire length of the railway, which they were able to follow to the next town, where they were greeted with the call "Ukrainskyj korol jide" (The Ukrainian king lives). Suddenly, they found themselves surrounded by policemen and placed under arrest. Fryderyk showed the police chief their orders to show up in Lwów. The officer apologized and gave them a much-needed lift.

But in Lwów, the sudden detonations of falling shells made Fryderyk pause. The explosions got louder and louder. He arrived home to find his parents and Paula huddled together in the basement. In fact, when Fryderyk walked in, his father fainted. It's no wonder his family would have had that reaction. This was the beginning of the war, and communication would have been nearly impossible at best. Here is Fryderyk's account of his hometown's brave stand against the onslaught:

> Lasting a total of ten days the Battle of Lwów saw the vastly outnumbered and under-equipped rear troops and raw recruits who remained stationed around the city bravely hold back the enemy. Under the command of General Lagner, the Polish forces fought first against the Wehrmacht and then against the Red Army. They finally surrendered to the Soviet forces so as not to further endanger the lives of the men or the city and citizens of Lwów.

The following morning, on September 20, Paula and Fryderyk made their way through the streets to survey the damage and to try to find out what was happening on the front. Many buildings were already in ruins, and even more were pockmarked with bullet holes. The streets were littered with Russian leaflets calling for surrender. Still more, reminiscent of fresh snow, were falling from the planes that circled overhead.

Paula and Fryderyk were expecting the Russian forces to occupy the city, but it wasn't impossible that the Germans would return. In short, it was time to leave. Through back alleys, Paula and Fryderyk made their way out of the city, heading east. In the Łyczaków Forest that ringed the city suburbs, they met families who had fled the city when the fighting started. We can assume that there was chaos. This wasn't a time of cell phones and GPS. Rumors and word of mouth were the leading means of communication. No one would have had time to pack thoughtfully. No one would have been prepared. The path through the trees was dense, with roots that made walking difficult. On the outskirts of the forest, they saw Russian tanks head into the city. With that, Paula and Fryderyk turned back toward home. Their fate was sealed under Nazi rule. But there was hope for life, albeit a difficult one, with the Soviets.

On September 22, 1939, the city of Lwów surrendered, and the Soviet army entered without a fight. General Lagner managed to escape, but his officers were not so lucky. On that very same day, the NKVD—the Soviet political police—broke the terms of the peace agreement between Lwów and the Soviet military. The police officers were arrested, and many were sent to gulags in the Soviet Union. Others would be murdered in 1940 in the Katyn Massacre.

For now, and for the next few years, the Soviet regime was the lesser of two evils. Fryderyk was uniquely positioned to act. A loyal Communist Party member for many years now, he knew he could work within the Soviet system and with the troops stationed within the city walls. Lwów city officials had all fled, and the citizens were left to their own devices in a situation that was worsening by the day. When Soviet tanks rolled in, they found Lwów a badly battered city with no infrastructure. The power was out, there was no running water, and food was scarce. Fryderyk knew they would have to get the utilities up and running, or there'd be countless deaths and riots.

When hungry and scared, people take to the streets. With the onset of the Winter War between Finland and the Soviet Union, the troops were being deployed north. In other words, they weren't going to help rebuild the city's infrastructure. Fryderyk and some friends created the Komitet Inicjatywny (Initiative Committee) to set up a communal economy, and they called upon their fellow activists to help run the city. As a result, many workers mobilized and went back to their jobs. They rebuilt parts of the city and laid new tracks for the trams as well as building new ones.

Fryderyk, with his demonstrable ease and determination, was able to work his way up through the ranks. Within a year he was able to leave his job as deputy director of the Tramtrestu, the tram and trolley bus department, to become district chief for the metal, power, and chemical industries.

For now, the Soviets and Germany respected the Molotov-Ribbentrop Pact, and while it wasn't always easy under the new rule, the citizens of Lwów were able to go about their lives in a moderately normal way. Meanwhile, Germany was busy fighting Britain and had troops in North Africa and Crete. Croatia had declared itself an independent state, and there were rumors of atrocities against the Serbs. But all of that seemed so far away.

At vacation time, Paula and Fryderyk, hoping for a break, headed to Truskavets, an hour and a half to the southwest. At daybreak on June 22, 1941, a week or so after they'd arrived, bombs started falling on the nearby army airfield. Nazi Germany had broken its pact with the Soviet Union and was fast approaching.

At precisely 10 AM, the voice of Molotov, the Soviet foreign minister, came crackling over the air, "Vrag budet razbit, pobeda budet za nami" (The enemy will be defeated, victory will be ours). With great difficulty under a hail of bombs, Paula and Fryderyk managed to catch the last train out and make their way back to Lwów on June 24, which now was also under heavy fire. There was complete chaos, including guns firing from rooftops, as the two made their way to Fryderyk's sister's house, ducking into stone entryways and cowering in open basement windows.

When they finally arrived, they found Nula sick in bed and unable to travel. Her husband was in nearby Kharkiv with a group of his students from the Polytechnical University. Paula and Fryderyk made sure Nula had enough supplies to last the next few days, then left for their own apartment. On the way they passed countless people fleeing the city with nothing but the clothes they were wearing. With the Nazis on their doorstep, there was no time to pack.

Except that Paula did pack—in her own special way. In an interview she said, "Some people left the town exactly as they were, taking nothing with them. I managed to pack my backpack, but completely without any deeper thought. I packed the wedding outfit and my favorite high-heeled shoes. It would [have been] a shame to leave them."

At the train station the couple were given papers and told to enumerate their abandoned property. They were also given two spots on an evacuation train heading for Kiev. At the old Polish-Soviet border in Volochisk, soldiers appeared and started separating out the younger men, among them Fryderyk, who was herded onto a truck bound back to Lwów, where he received orders to join the military. Paula, meanwhile, stayed on the train. She had planned to meet up with friends in Kiev.

Life is made up of a series of events. It's not like the movies, which are paced specifically to keep our interest. In reality, life is full of filler pieces that happen but aren't all that interesting to read about. Do you really want to read about the day when I woke up, took a shower, brushed my teeth, took the dog for a walk, went for coffee, and kind of hung out for the day? Definitely not. I imagine that, even though people were living through a war, there must have been lots of days that just kind of happened. The goal was to get through another day, to survive, to live, to make it to the next day.

In some ways I think those days of 1941 might have been the hardest for me to read about. Can you imagine waking up severely underweight and starving, with no hope of getting enough food? Can you picture standing in long lines to get rations—of what, you don't know. You'll be wearing whatever clothing you own, trying to keep things as normal as you can, but not knowing what normal even is anymore. If some of what you are reading sounds fragmented, that is because it's how my grandfather, my dziadzio, documented it.

At daybreak on June 27 the trucks finally rolled into Lwów. Fryderyk was exhausted; the trip had been long and arduous, with rations nothing more than a small piece of bread and a cup of watery coffee twice a day. On route, the trucks kept getting stuck as well, and the men had to clamber out to push them. Thanks to constantly dropping bombs, no one got any sleep either.

Paula was presumably on the train heading east. She was probably terrified, doing her best to survive, and hoping that her friends would be at their meeting point in Mariupol. Finding them would have been a long shot, but it was either stay and face the Nazis or flee and face the unknown. She was now on her own. This was a story she never told.

The city was much quieter than when Fryderyk and Paula had left only five days before. The few people who were still there on the

streets hugged the sides of buildings as they walked, or stayed in
the shadows, heads down. No one dared look up. Every few hours,
bombing shook the city and sent everyone scurrying inside. Un-
locking the door to his apartment on Kochanowski Street, Fryderyk
was shocked to find his terrified in-laws at his kitchen table. They
had been evicted from their home and had nowhere else to go.

It would be another two days before Nazi troops would occupy
the city.

Fryderyk had to report to the district headquarters at 10 AM the
next day, June 28. For now, he could walk through town and survey
the damage. As he made his way over the cobblestone streets and
darkened entryways, he ran into several of his friends. Some had
also been drafted but were waiting to report to their units, others
were still planning to evacuate, and others were gathering supplies
and planning to stay.

When Fryderyk ran into his sister, Nula, he learned that her husband had sent a note saying he would return once things quieted
down. She told him she was feeling better and would wait this all
out in her flat. Nula also told Fryderyk that, thanks to some work
acquaintances, their parents had managed to rent a small cottage in
Brzuchowice (Briukhovychi), a nearby village. It was quieter there,
and with their father not working, it was also more cost-effective.
Fryderyk asked Nula to get word to their parents to let them know
that he was safe and would be in touch as soon as he could. As far as
I know, he never did and never spoke with them again.

That night, despite the occasional bombardment and a call for
all residents to shelter in their basements, Fryderyk slept soundly in
his own bed. The next morning, he woke early, put on fresh clothing
and a new pair of well-soled shoes, pocketed some basic documents,

bade his in-laws goodbye, gave them the keys to his home, and made his way to the makeshift army barracks to report for duty. But before he could get there, he ran into an already mobilized small, unarmed plainclothes unit standing in formation. The Soviet officer in charge barked at Fryderyk, ordering him to join the line.

The plan was to march east by way of Winniki (Vynnyky) toward Tarnopol (Ternopil), but Fryderyk barely fell into a rhythmic step before the men realized that the officer in charge had abandoned them. Now at the edge of town, at the entrance to the Łyczaków Forest, they broke ranks, wondering what to do. Some of the younger boys and many of the Jews turned back toward Lwów. Fryderyk tried to warn them about going back, but his efforts were in vain. With no one making the decisions, he took charge.

Choosing back roads and the forest for cover, a route well-known to Fryderyk from his youth, he led the men. Along the way, they saw German planes bombarding retreating Soviet troops, leaving countless dead and wounded soldiers and their horse carcasses.

On June 29 at 6 AM after a seventy-two-kilometer trek, the men arrived in Złoczów, Fryderyk's birthplace, where they were able to catch a train to Tarnopol. The men crammed themselves into a compartment, and when the bombardment of the railway began, Fryderyk lay down under a bench. By now, as he writes in his book, he was completely numb and no longer felt any fear.

In Tarnopol the group dispersed, and Fryderyk unexpectedly ran into Paula's brother, Natan, who had also been drafted. Together, the men received their new orders to go east and join the Trudarmia, the Soviet forced-labor army, as was the general order for all displaced people who weren't called up to join the Red Army or who were not immediately deported.

Everyone knew what it meant to join the Trudarmia, where everyone between the ages of fifteen and sixty, other than pregnant women and women with children under the age of three, was subjected to hard labor—working in the coal mines, refineries, and ammunition factories or in building and clearing roads. The conscripts also lived in camps that were little better than penal labor camps.

On June 30, 1941, six days after Paula and Fryderyk evacuated Lwów, the Wehrmacht officially occupied the city, and on July 1, the pogroms began. The infamous waves of persecution drove Jews from their apartments, forced them to clean the streets on their hands and knees, and targeted Jewish women for humiliation—stripping, beating, and raping. These violent riots that succeeded in killing thousands of Jews were carried out by locals, Ukrainian nationalists, and by German death squads.

Fryderyk and Natan began the trek, walking and occasionally catching a train, all the way to Kiev (Kyiv), where Fryderyk reported to the civilian communist authorities. At the local Party headquarters, they found a note Paula had left for Fryderyk, saying she was safe, she had met up with their friends, and together they had left for Stalingrad (Volgograd) via Dnipropetrovsk (Dnipro). Their destination was to be Mariupol, some 780 kilometers (484 miles) southeast.

Fryderyk managed to obtain papers both for himself and Natan so that they could report to the civilian authorities in Mariupol, where a steel factory was hiring workers. Fryderyk was an imposing, charismatic man. We can safely assume that whatever meeting he'd engineered to secure those papers had involved a lot of stories and drinking. And from that moment on, the two men were on their own. They set sail on a barge down the Dnieper, headed to Dnipropetrovsk—a trip that many years later Fryderyk would recall as filled with "fantastic adventures on the way while traveling with a colorful crowd. It was a beautiful July."

As soon as they hit the ground in Mariupol, Fryderyk was surrounded. Someone behind him whispered, "Look, someone's being arrested," but before he could hear the rest of the sentence, who did he see right there in front of him, standing in complete shock, but Paula?

At the police station they explained that the Western-style knickerbockers Fryderyk was wearing had been given to him back in Kiev. In other words, he had not been Westernized. He was not a spy. His papers confirmed his story, and he was released.

That night, Fryderyk celebrated reuniting with his wife and friends, and the next day he showed up for work at the Illich Steel and Iron Works factory. As an engineer, Fryderyk's talents would have been in demand. Under the circumstances, and even though the factory was run by the local mafia, the couple's living conditions were nominally acceptable. For the next three weeks, he kept to himself and collected his salary at the end of each day.

Mariupol was a beautiful city, and the young couple adapted quickly to their new circumstances, thanks to some much-needed assistance. Paula wrote, "We looked different than the Soviet people, but the Russians helped us. Our neighbors could see that we completely could not cope with such things as doing the laundry or cooking, because we had never done it before. What is more, I have never even heard of using wooden paddles to do the laundry." Fryderyk would not have known how to cook or take care of a household.

That would have been his mother's domain. And most likely, Paula's family had domestic help, leaving her free to pursue her education instead of being tied to working in the home.

Skip forward two generations to my childhood and experience of this same woman. When I think about it, I don't remember my babcia doing much around the house, but she was always up for a hike or, in later years, to play canasta. But spending time in the kitchen? Never. It's no surprise, then, to read her account of looking back on that time: "We did not even know how to cook a soup. The Russian neighbors discreetly showed us how to do it. Trying to follow their steps I took to cooking a soup. I put everything I could think of into a pot—peas, beans. I was proud of myself while I was giving the soup to my husband."

Apparently, Fryderyk took one look at the soup, ostentatiously crossed himself, closed his eyes, and took a sip. "This is the ultimate proof that I love you," he said after the first swallow. "I'm going to eat this soup, but it will probably kill me."

This stability of Mariupol was short-lived for Fryderyk and Paula. It was now early July, and the Nazis were approaching, having launched Operation Barbarossa on June 22 to conquer the western Soviet Union and ultimately repopulate it with Germans. For Paula and Fryderyk, as for countless others, it was time to uproot and keep moving deeper into Soviet territory.

From Fryderyk's book, a short summary of the brutal facts:

> The Germans began their invasion of Soviet territory through the Ukraine. As the Soviets retreated, they shot their political prisoners, destroyed industrial plants,

burned crops, disposed of food reserves and flooded mines. Almost 4 million people were evacuated east of the Ural Mountain range, some 2,500 km east of Lwów. By the end of November, Ukraine was under Nazi rule.

As my grandparents continued their journey, more people joined them. This time, instead of only Paula and Fryderyk, it was ten friends who left together. Among them was the young son of Paula's friends, the Koszutskis. Fryderyk and Paula did the organizing. They brought only what they each could carry, everyone pooling what little money they had left, and Fryderyk was tasked with organizing transportation.

First up, they boarded a small, motorized boat on a calm sea and headed for the port city of Taganrog, on the Sea of Azov in southwestern Russia. Fryderyk writes that he "would always remember the full moon reflecting brightly on the smooth surface of the sea that night."

Once the group arrived in Taganrog, they haggled with local fishermen over selling their boat for a few coins and some dry bread before making their way to the train station, which was overflowing with thousands of evacuees, all just like the ten travelers—clamoring to get on any available transportation. There were no rooms for any amount of money, and it seemed that basic sanitation was now a thing of the past. The stench of unwashed bodies filled the air. Everyone was dirty and exhausted, and the young child in the group had to be fed.

It took three days before Fryderyk finally found room on a train: "The conditions of the evacuation were extremely difficult. Roads and all means of transport were crowded with refugees. It took force to find a place at train stations and on trains. People rode on train steps, buffers and roofs. At the station we had to wait for several days before a train arrived. Luckily the summer weather was warm, albeit with cool nights." Right before reaching Rostov-on-Don, some seventy kilometers (43 miles) east of Taganrog, they found shelter in an old, abandoned watchtower.

Even though their whole world was in chaos, they still needed official evacuation orders to travel deeper into Soviet territory. Fryderyk, who spoke Russian fluently, was charged with going to the city for the official papers. No papers, no passage. That meant standing in long lines and signing countless documents, patiently waiting to cut through the red tape.

Finally, just as the August days gave way to September, the group was granted room on a barge heading up the Don River to Kalach, where they hoped to catch a train to Stalingrad. What they found was a nightmare—a partially destroyed rail station and total pandemonium. The frenzied energy was palpable, with over a million evacuees flooding a city that normally housed half that number. They made their way to the port, where the Koszutskis' only suitcase was promptly stolen and with it the vital sustenance needed for their son. Fryderyk headed to the local constabulary to report the theft, and with no place to stay, he spent the night at the police station, using his shoes as a pillow. He awoke to find his shoes gone.

For the sake of the child and the women who were sick, the group decided it was best to find spots on a barge for the 400-plus-kilometer route southeast to Astrakhan, a city on the Volga River in the southern Soviet Union. To continue on land, mostly by foot, would have been just too much.

Only the madness they encountered in Astrakhan made the chaos of Stalingrad look tame. By now, all ten in the group had succumbed to the lice infestation plaguing all evacuees. Even chopping off their hair didn't do much good. Everyone's skin was crawling with the microscopic parasites that covered the body with red, itchy bite marks. At the train station Paula sold her last gold ring and a few trinkets to buy passage for all of them to Tashkent, Uzbekistan, via the border city of Orenburg.

She might also have been pregnant at the time, so, yes, there was a lot going on.

Passing through the independent German republic of Engels, for the first time on their journey the group was met with total silence. Empty homes lined the tracks, and fruit trees hung low to the ground, weighed down by unpicked fruit. Rotten vegetables were piled high in wheelbarrows. It looked as if the villagers had simply disappeared. As it turns out, that was not far from the truth. These villages belonged to the Volga Germans, ethnic Germans who lived along the Volga River, who had colonized Russia in the eighteenth century. They retained their culture, language, and traditions, but on September 3, 1941, the Soviet Union forcibly transferred them to Siberia and Kazakhstan.

They didn't know it at the time, but Paula and Fryderyk—my babcia and dziadzio—were one step ahead of the Nazis during their journey east.

I read my grandparents' accounts in amazement. Unlike my travels with Pawel, which we could pick and choose, my grandparents were forced to keep moving. And yet these nightmare scenarios from their youth did not end up dampening their love of travel. For as long as I knew my grandparents, they remained avid travelers and adventurers. And amazingly, their luck held out. After Fryderyk's shoes were stolen at the police station, he somehow managed to obtain a pair of shiny black dress shoes that looked ridiculous and were of course completely impractical, but with no other footwear, he had no other choice but to wear the fancy shoes. Wouldn't you know it, but they fit him like a glove.

It was sometime in September 1941 when Fryderyk and Paula's group finally arrived in Tashkent. The road to Uzbekistan had been rough, especially in Orenburg, but they made it in one piece, although everyone was extremely exhausted. The first few days were spent wandering through the crowds, trying to find a place to stay and, with any luck, some work. Fryderyk estimated tens of thousands were living at the train station alone. It took a few days, but thanks to his old contacts in the Party, he secured jobs for the others in a factory just outside the city, and after two weeks, the group of ten was able to shed their displaced persons status. They set up house in an old schoolhouse on Tachtapulskaya Street, where they crammed, along with ten or so other evacuees from Rostov-on-Don, into one classroom. The women shared the wrought-iron beds with paper-thin mattresses while the men slept sardine-style, side by side, packed tightly on the floor.

By a complete fluke during this time, Paula and Fryderyk also ran into old friends from Lwów. That was a joyous reunion. Young couples with big dreams, with their whole lives ahead of them. This is how my grandfather remembered the moment. Romantic and vague? Perhaps. I think for that time, and in that moment, that is how it had to be: It was a brief escape from the reality of war.

After several weeks of finding odd jobs whenever possible, Fryderyk was offered the position of head of the metal and machinery department in a nearby factory. At least, as he says in his book, his reputation from Lwów had preceded him.

The general mood among the refugees in Tashkent varied. Some, terrified that Hitler's armies would win the war, were planning another escape, across the Turkish border. Others, including Paula and Fryderyk, were optimistic, and this optimism would help them survive. One moment in particular gave Fryderyk hope for the future. It also gave him faith in the Red Army—although at the time, he didn't know that faith was displaced.

Walking down the street, Fryderyk heard Stalin's voice over the radio in a local restaurant saying, "Budiet jeszczo prazdnik na naszej ulicy" (There will be celebrations on our streets again). That sentiment filled his heart, and as the year wound down, the group that was staying in the schoolhouse lit a small fire in their paltry stove and sang patriotic songs late into the night.

During World War II, over a million Jews fled or were evacuated from the western Soviet Union and annexed territories into the Soviet interior, escaping the advancing German forces. This mass exodus also involved the execution of civilians by the NKVD.

In 1941, Operation Barbarossa triggered the evacuation of approximately 16 million Soviet civilians eastward, including over a million Jews, alongside the relocation of industrial facilities to secure them from enemy capture. Many evacuees, including Jewish families, found refuge in Central Asian countries like Kazakhstan and Uzbekistan. An estimated 300,000 perished due to harsh conditions while others died in combat, but none fell victim to the Holocaust.

This is important history to take in. We mostly hear about the Jews who fled to North and South America, but many also fled to the East, where they did not die in the Holocaust. What then happened to them?

In November, Fryderyk was delegated to travel to Samarkand, a nearby Uzbek city on the Silk Road that is renowned for its mosques and mausoleums. At the very last minute, just as Fryderyk was boarding the train, Paula jumped on, too.

The details of this time were largely undocumented, and mostly retold with knowing looks. I am assuming that Paula wanted to go with him because she had probably recently lost a child. This is an educated guess on my part. I've heard several versions of her losses, but I never heard her speak of them.

During the day, while Fryderyk was inspecting the factories, Paula was able to distract herself by visiting the famous buildings of the ancient imperial Mongolian capital, and as the weeks went by, the two slowly adjusted to their new surroundings. Knowing my grandmother, I think that Paula would have been aching to work, but this was wartime, and nothing like that would have been available to her. My grandfather was under enormous pressure, overseeing the building of a key canal that would bring water and sustenance to the starving population of Uzbekistan.

As 1942 wore on, Paula could see that Fryderyk was working much too hard. The weather was damp and rainy, their rations were meager, and not only was he constantly on the go, but he refused to slow down. Then, one day he woke up almost paralyzed with nephritis, an inflammation of the kidneys. At the time, the couple were temporarily living in a dugout, and with no medical care he spent the next couple of weeks in feverish semidarkness, falling in and out of consciousness.

Paula did her best to care for him, but he was in desperate need of medicine. By the time he had stabilized enough for villagers to transport him back to Tashkent, his condition had worsened. At that point, he contracted meningitis.

Once again, Fryderyk's connections in the Communist Party came to the rescue. He fell under the care of a visiting military doctor who immediately sent him to the hospital for infectious diseases. Placed on a cot in a chilly hallway, he was injected with sulfamide every four hours. That lasted three days straight. When he wasn't sleeping, he lay staring at the sliver of blue sky through a window just above his head. When one of the doctors came by to do a spinal tap and Fryderyk heard him say, "Sanguina pura [clean blood]," he managed to impress the doctor. For one thing, since he knew Latin, he also knew what the doctor said, and for another, he was still alive. The doctor took Fryderyk under his wing. His care grew remarkably better.

Even after he left the hospital Fryderyk still had a long way to go, so Paula and their friends went into action. They began to donate blood in return for white bread, which they then traded for sugar, apparently an essential ingredient for Fryderyk's recovery. This was no easy feat, since Paula herself weighed less than ninety pounds, but as she would say years later, she was accustomed to the hunger, and her body was strong and resilient. Still, Fryderyk wasn't out of the woods quite yet. The sugar caused an intestinal disorder that then led to months in a convalescent center, where he lay on the roof of a hut beneath a canopy of trees. I guess if there was a plus side to that, it was that he enjoyed full sun, and had as much fruit as he could eat.

When Fryderyk had finally recovered enough to go home in June, he went to work for the Department of Mine Launcher Armaments. He was also able to secure a job for Paula, and they both enjoyed a larger daily ration of food.

Shortly after this time, Paula and Fryderyk discovered that MOPR (International Red Aid) was still active, and they began receiving substantially more food. While they were still poor, their constant hunger became a thing of the past. Finally, they had better living conditions. A sparse room in a Russian family's home meant that at least the necessities were taken care of, and Paula was happy not to be cooking dinner every day. I can assume that Fryderyk was thrilled to have someone else preparing the meals.

The work in the factory, though, was backbreaking. It was also performed largely by Russian women, given that most of the men were fighting at the front. Later, Fryderyk would say he was convinced that it was women who had won the war because they'd done all the factory work needed.

Then one cold February day, more good news. It was winter 1943, and the Soviets had annihilated German forces at Stalingrad. An entire army of the best German soldiers had been wiped out. Work momentarily stopped as everyone took to the streets, cheering and hugging. Fryderyk notes what happened next. "Over the next few weeks, the victory did prompt a mass evacuation but this time in reverse, with many evacuees choosing to return West immediately."

The young couple did not go west, however. Instead, later that year Fryderyk was transferred to a larger division in Factory N808 as a construction engineer, where he continued working and rehabilitating. Being his enterprising self, Fryderyk also joined the local branch of the Polish Patriots Union, where he became deputy chairman.

Come the following February, as the refugee evacuation continued their resettlement, a call went out for qualified candidates to help grow already established industrial plants in the central Soviet Union. Fryderyk jumped at the chance to sign up. His transfer orders sent him to Factory N825, in Szczółków, a small village nearly fifty kilometers (31 miles) outside Moscow, where he and Paula found a tiny stone house. It wasn't much, but it was all for them, and it was nice not to have to share with another family.

By day, Fryderyk worked as the factory's chief technologist in charge of construction, while evenings saw him commuting to Moscow as a member of the postwar economic planning committee. My grandfather writes extensively about this part of his life. He threw himself 100 percent into work, and there is basically no mention of my grandmother.

It was now 1944, and I think that those three years on Soviet territory would have flown by for them. My grandparents were driven people, and I can only imagine that their drive to not only survive but to succeed was in high gear. The future was a big unknown, so there was only the present. This feels like a strange thing to say. The war was still raging. People were being murdered in concentration camps. I can't help but think, would they have known about this then?

During this time, Fryderyk was busy founding the Association of Polish Engineers and Technicians in the USSR. That entailed publishing a call to all Polish engineers who had been dispersed by the war. It was convincing enough that some 300 wrote in, requesting to return to Soviet-occupied Poland to start rebuilding their country. Yet at the same time that Poles were mobilizing to return to their homeland, Fryderyk was given orders to move to the organization's new Moscow headquarters.

It is here that Paula finally reappears in his account. Apparently, she was stunned at the level of luxury they were granted in the

Moscow Hotel. Each couple had their own room, complete with a private bathroom. They also got regular care parcels filled with food and clothing. Quite the novelty, after wearing the same things day after day, plus it was nice to finally have something new. Although the rooms lacked full kitchens, each one came with a hot plate, and while Paula still hadn't mastered the art of cooking—meals began with everything thrown into one large pot—at least they were no longer starving.

But her real appetite was to continue her medical studies, and so, in her words, "I went to a class; I sat down and started listening. I did not have any documents; I was there illegally. However, because I came in regularly, they got used to me. Later, officially they admitted me to the school."

It seems crazy that Paula could walk into a classroom and just start taking a class. In North America you need top marks in school and in your MCATs and possibly some connections to get into medical school. How did Paula just sally into university and get accepted? I can only guess. This was wartime. Doctors were desperately needed, and there were no transcripts as we know them today. The Polish university where she studied briefly was now in Nazi territory, so she had no way of proving to the Soviets that she had in fact once been a student. If, however, she was keeping up with the course load, then technically at least, why shouldn't she attend?

There was one document, though, that my father found among my mother's papers. A document that shocked him when he first discovered it but that sounded vaguely familiar to some longtime family friends when he asked around about it. Typewritten on an unofficial-looking slip of paper was the testimonial of my mother's birth certificate.

Mrs. Paulina, the wife of Director Fryderyk Topolski, gave birth to her daughter, Maria at 4:00 PM on July 27th, 1944, in Stalowa Wola on C-X street, building 2 apartment 4.

20. VII.1945
Stalowa Wola

J—H street, building 2 apartment 16
Certified Midwife Maria Hendzel

This is a signed birth certificate, but it is also full of holes. For one thing, Paula and Fryderyk were still living in Moscow, and for another, their last name was still Toperman. The second "p" would be added decades later by my parents, courtesy of Swedish authorities, and yes, there's a story about that, too. Then there is the matter of the date. I was raised with the uncontested knowledge that my mother was born on January 4, 1945. So, why all the discrepancies? As it happens, accidentally "losing" or changing children's birth certificates was not uncommon in the war, for many reasons. For my grandparents, it would have been important that their daughter be born on Polish soil, as a Polish citizen. So somehow, at some point, they managed to find a "certified midwife" who would say as much. This then is the official government-issued abbreviated birth certificate, dated three years after the fact:

I testify that Maria Augusta Topolska was born on the fourth of January in nineteen forty-five in Stalowa Wola, to Fryderyk Jozef Topolski engineer and Paula Topolska (nee Gotlicka).

Stalowa Wola 30 June 1948

Presumably, the other birth certificate was hidden away and largely forgotten. While military records may have been more precise, civilian records would have been patchy at best. Since the timeline is murky and I am piecing it together, my sequence may be wrong, but I can guess that this paperwork switch would have been relatively easy to do. Entire cities were decimated; no one would have questioned a "lost" birth certificate.

All this time, Fryderyk was quickly moving through the ranks in the Soviet Communist Party. He was now deputy chief of military production. Still, he wanted to go back to Poland. He could have easily stayed in the Soviet Union; at one point later, he's even invited to a meeting with Stalin, but Poland would always be home. The problem with relocating easily was that the NKVD—the People's Commissariat for Internal Affairs—thought him too valuable. The NKVD had jurisdiction over both the secret police and the regular authorities—in short, sweeping powers—and they did not want him to leave.

Still, Fryderyk looked for ways to get to Poland. When he realized that the USSR was putting together a Polish army Kościusko Division, he presented himself to the Russian military command. They sent him to the army base. The Kościusko Division was to be formed and based out of Lublin at the end of August 1944. Turning on the charm, Fryderyk convinced a young officer on the night shift to give him written orders to join the Regional Commission for Army Reinforcements—where else, but in Lublin.

Orders in hand, Fryderyk boarded the plane, expecting the three-hour flight to be uncomfortable at best. He didn't expect, as he later told Paula, for the one and only time in his life to believe in God. The plane was carrying cigarettes and alcohol, and everyone on board, including the pilot, was drunk. Somehow they managed to land at the Lublin military airport forty kilometers (25 miles) or so outside the city, and when his feet touched Polish soil, Fryderyk knelt and kissed the ground. At last, he was back in his homeland.

I know the date of August 1944 does not jive with the official end of the war, which was on September 2, 1945. But the German retreat and the division of countries took time. The Soviet army needed about a year and a half to make it from Moscow to Berlin—the Battle of Berlin took place between April 16 and May 2, 1945, at which time Berlin was divided into east and west. Lublin—including the Majdanek concentration camp—had been liberated on July 23, 1944, at the same time of the Lwów uprising. That meant Fryderyk found himself in Poland only a few short weeks after the Wehrmacht was pushed back.

Yes, it is complicated, and it is difficult to explain. It is not as if everyone lays down their arms and goes home. There are many displaced persons, and records are in disarray. Countries are being portioned, borders can be fluid, and much of this is being done by forces that are not on the ground. As such, the average individual, like my grandfather, is focusing on carving their path forward as best they can in an otherwise chaotic time.

For more perspective: The Warsaw uprising lasted from August 1 to October 2, 1944, but the city wasn't liberated by Soviet forces until January 17, 1945. Auschwitz was liberated ten days later, on January 27. In other words, there was no single day when everyone simply dropped what they were doing, and peace ensued. It was Japan's surrender to the Allies that ended the war officially.

What is important for my grandparents' story is that, for the most part, the cities in the European theater were now piles of rubble, with no infrastructure. Some buildings still stood, yes, but they were shells, good only for keeping their inhabitants safe from the worst elements. There was no running water, let alone electricity.

For the next month, Fryderyk traveled throughout Poland touring factories, many of which had been looted by the German and Soviet soldiers. The good news was that many of these factories had been built shortly before the start of the war and could quickly be repaired. In September he was finally able to pay a visit to Lwów and his hometown of Brzuchowic. There he had a joyful reunion with his sister.

Nula had survived the war, thanks to hiding in an attic three meters by three meters, most of that time lying down, since there was no way to stand. She had spent three years in this windowless room with a man who was not her husband. Although she'd married just before the war, and her spouse had survived in the northern Soviet Union, she felt too much had happened, and she could not go back to him. So she chose another partner—a sympathetic neighbor who took her in, and the two of them hid out in the attic. It was during this long stay that Nula learned that their parents, as well as Fryderyk's in-laws, had been sent to a death camp sometime around August 1943.

Having reunited with his sister, Fryderyk knew it would be safe for Paula to return as well. He caught a military plane out of Lwów for Moscow, where two plainclothes secret police were waiting for him. This was actually the second time he'd been mistaken for a spy, but luckily, he still had his Soviet-issued government papers and was quickly released. Even better, the future wife of the Polish ambassador to Moscow worked in the office where the police had taken him. She knew Fryderyk well and could vouch for him—an alliance Fryderyk also used to his advantage for an official offer to run the largest steelworks factory in Stalowa Wola, Poland.

Without delay he collected Paula and flew her to Brzuchow for a brief stay with Nula. They then drove to Lwów to try to find answers about their parents and friends. News was slowly trickling in, and no one was yet aware of the extent of the damage. If anything, the bits and pieces they did hear were so terrible, they couldn't—or didn't—want to believe them. They wanted to know what had happened without actually knowing. Paula shares,

> When I went to Lviv there were no more Jews. I wanted to have a look at our old apartment. It was already occupied. These people living there did not let me in, even though I made it clear I did not want to take anything. I just wanted to have a look. We spoke through [a] half open door, secured with a metal chain. They said I cannot come in and they did not explain why. These were not some ordinary people, but the family of a Lviv University professor. My husband's family home was also occupied by some rabble, they also did not let him in. We never came back to Lviv. I had absolutely nothing after my family.

Paula remained with Nula while Fryderyk moved to Stalowa Wola to run the factory and restore the utilities that the Nazis had destroyed while retreating. Almost immediately the mechanical plant and repair workshops were made functional, which meant that the production of spare parts for tanks and cars then began. During the next few months, he took over production in the cities of Łodz and Cracow.

At thirty-two years of age, Fryderyk then became the head of the national board of the coal industry. Five months later, in December, he sent for Paula and Nula as well as other friends he planned to help find work.

On her first day in Stalowa Wola, Paula decided to visit Fryderyk at work. Unbeknownst even to him, several months earlier, his superiors had decided to change his last name from Toperman, to erase any reference to his Jewish origins. The other reason for the change was that there had been a German official with the last name Taperman, and they didn't want Fryderyk associated with him. The trouble was, Fryderyk forgot to tell Paula about the change. As a consequence, after making some innocent inquiries for her husband, she found herself sitting behind bars in a cold jail cell accused of being a German spy.

The question of names in my family is a big one. Later, Paula even changed her maiden name from Gottlieb to the Polish-sounding Gotlicka. *How was it so easy for them to simply change their names?* I wonder. A name is a big part of someone's identity, and the outwardly Jewish part of theirs was formally erased. Years later I struggle with my identity, and I cannot help but wonder if that is partly because my grandparents' identity was ripped away from them. Is this something that can be passed down?

By this time, although Paula accepted Fryderyk's continued belief in the Party, she was finished with politics. She could see communism's actual effects on the population—the war had made her a realist. Being Jewish still wasn't safe, and many Poles blamed Jews for everything that had happened in their country. The few Jews left lived quietly and unassumingly, hoping not to draw attention to themselves. Paula's uncle Meyer Bałaban had died in the Warsaw ghetto. The rest of her family, as well as Fryderyk's, had been obliterated. It was as if these people had never existed.

Not surprisingly, given all this trauma, even though the young couple's lives had begun to settle, the memories remained. Paula was constantly afraid. Friends of theirs who survived Auschwitz came back as hollow shells of their former selves. Sitting together in the evenings, they tried to talk of other things, but the subject of the Holocaust was always bubbling beneath the surface.

There is nothing simple or straightforward about any of this. I'm not sure that Fryderyk and Paula really understood yet what had happened. I don't know if anyone on the ground did. Millions had been tortured and forced to witness unspeakable atrocities. And then it all ended. There weren't armies of psychologists waiting in the wings; there was just the sheer will to rebuild, to move forward. All I know is based on my most vivid memory: my mom telling me that three-quarters of her family perished in the war.

After my grandfather died, my mother and my uncle found a suitcase filled with letters from his mistress. As far as I know, Fryderyk and this woman did not have any children, but since he was traveling extensively throughout the 1940s, it would have been relatively easy to have a family and a woman on the side—and there *was* another family he was close with. My father says it was widely known that Fryderyk was having an affair with his secretary, but that his communist comrades had told him it would be unbecoming to get a divorce.

At this point in the story, Fryderyk was reluctantly staying in their marriage, while Paula was staying despite knowing, I assume, that it was probably a broken marriage. In her words,

One did not want to remember certain events, tried to erase the memory of the tragedy, get away from the past. We had friends in Poland who survived the Holocaust, who were prisoners in Oświęcim. They evaded talking about it, afraid of being misunderstood, but at every chance the topic surfaced somehow. We felt that they have gone through something unimaginable. And yet, the anti-Semitism did not end after the war. We were still not certain that being a Jew is safe. We have tried to deny this. We were afraid that we would not bear the weight of this disaster. That was beyond any words. We preferred not to say anything and not to develop some sort of inferiority complex in our children.

While my grandparents were trying to protect their children from the horrors of the war, it seems that they unintentionally also erased part of their roots. Only once they started school did my mother and her brother, KT, who was born in Katowice in 1947, discover they were Jewish. Communism clearly wasn't going to fill in the identity blanks. Paula writes,

We had a villa with a garden, servants, my husband had a chauffeur. At the same time I saw what was happening around us. People lacked everything: housing, shoes, carts for children [strollers], food; they still lived in extreme poverty. The women spotted it first, as they were closer to everyday life. Much sooner than my husband I began to have doubts as to whether this best of regimes was in order. I even signed up for the Party to make him feel better, although the political activity in my case was not in question. I respected the work of my husband because he was not just any political commissar. He was doing specific things and devoted everything to the cause. When he revived Polish mining, they degraded him. . . . That was terrible for him. We had to move to Warsaw. I was glad because I could finally finish medical school. But I was terribly afraid that they would imprison him, there was a high probability of that happening. Yet he still believed in the system. Sometimes I even wondered whether he was only joking. But no, he was a naive optimist just like a boy scout.

As for Party politics, Fryderyk was still dragged into them when one faction or another was losing prestige. Many of his relationships became strained, and he was recalled from his position after he and his peers were forced to criticize themselves publicly at the Warsaw headquarters.

Following the demotion, his immediate superior, Hilary Minc, offered him a position in Prague, but Fryderyk, determined to remain in Poland, accepted an offer in Warsaw. He had set up trade deals in East Germany and in 1949 joined the National Committee for Economic Development.

With the start of the Cold War, the economy across the Soviet Bloc turned away from reconstruction to rearmament. Fryderyk, tasked with setting up ammunition and weapons factories, was also given the authority to override local planning. With a shortage of qualified workers, rather than simply hiring up-and-coming communists, he pulled in competent engineers and specialists who had previously been blacklisted. Things moved along until Fryderyk hired Colonel Grajworonski, who, as it turned out, was an NKVD informant. Everything he reported was then added to a file that Moscow had on Fryderyk, dating back to 1944.

It was only years later that Fryderyk realized this was most likely the reason he had rarely been invited to Party gatherings. That information, coupled with the anti-Semitic wave pouring out of the Soviet Union, got Fryderyk dismissed from his committee post.

CHAPTER 5

CHOINKI AND MENORAHS: A CLASH OF HOLIDAYS IN WARSAW

Hanukkah comes early in 2013, starting on November 27. Most of our things are still in boxes somewhere on the ocean. It's at this moment that it hits me. Where do I buy a menorah and candles in a Catholic country? In Toronto or Vancouver, it was easy. But in Poland? I finally realize that the only place to find a menorah and candles is in the general store next to the Nożyk synagogue on Twarda Street, in what was once the Jewish part of town.

Entering the courtyard, I feel the same way I do when I first see the boundary marker embedded in the sidewalk on Swiętokrzyska depicting the wall where the Jewish Ghetto once stood. The friend I'm walking with, a longtime resident of Warsaw, admits it is the first time she has noticed the marker. I don't say anything, but I want to yell out at everyone mindlessly stepping over the metal plaque, "Do you know what you just walked over? Do you know what happened here? How can you go about your day and ignore history? At least take a second to acknowledge it." This isn't about religion; it's more about humanity. I am frustrated. I am terrified that this is ignored. Why isn't more being done to educate the public? I know that there is a good chance that the Holocaust will be forgotten in the near future, and that will be dangerous for the entire world. I feel paralyzed with my thinking, and I'm not entirely sure what I can do to relay my fears to anyone who will listen.

A uniformed soldier cradling a large gun stands guard out front. This is a very common sight around most European synagogues. The main synagogue in Berlin stands behind a ten-foot fence. The main synagogue in Florence has concrete barricades spanning a six-foot perimeter around the entrance. Paris, Prague, Venice—if the city even has a synagogue, then it's most likely behind some sort of wall, populated with armed guards. Churches on the other hand are easily accessible, with doors that are open to the public.

We approach a man sitting behind a large glass wall. "What do you want? Why are you here? Are you Jewish?" I say that I am, and my husband is not. We have to hand over our passports and with much skepticism he allows us, finally, to enter. I am more welcome in the general store, and when the man behind the counter learns I'm in the market for a menorah, he is thrilled to show me everything they have. I also buy some candles and a few other treats that will get us through the holidays.

As we leave, after he tells me that I'm always welcome, he says a few words in Hebrew. I smile and mumble something. I hope he doesn't guess that I have no idea what he said.

Our first holidays in Poland, a month and a half after we arrive, are stressful because we don't know what to expect. Up until this moment we have been busy getting settled. In addition to a brief visit at Alek's home with his wife, Ania, and their two daughters, Zuzanna and Ela, who still live at home, we visited Pawel's aunt on his father's side, and his uncle on his mother's side. We have also spent a memorable evening with my uncle KT that will set the tone for our relationship in Poland. Shortly after our arrival he invites us to a party hosted by a local radio station. I scramble to find an appropriate outfit to walk a red carpet, spending more than I want on a pair of navy patent heels with gold detailing, which I have to this day. Much of that night is hazy, but I clearly remember being introduced only as "My sister's daughter," and people's amused confusion as they turned to me and asked my name.

That is more family than we are used to, and the traditions are unfamiliar, too. Growing up, my family always had a Christmas tree and a menorah, and that was it. We opened presents on Christmas Eve instead of Christmas morning like many of my friends, but it wasn't an elaborate event. Growing up we didn't have a lot of money, and my parents had to make do. There weren't complex dinners or big parties. There weren't days or weeks of food preparation, or piles of presents under the tree. There were no gifts for Hanukkah either. Instead, we each got one present on Christmas Eve, and that made the holidays more special—like the time I got the Sony Walkman I was dying to have. I treasured it until it fell apart. So, for us, the holidays came and went, with the rustic menorah I'd made in Jewish kindergarten. We had dreidels and Hanukkah gelt, those golden chocolate coins you can find at every drugstore, and occasionally we would celebrate with cousins. Still, it felt as if the games and accessories were for show. None of us really knew what to do with them.

So, our first December in Warsaw, my cousin messages me on the sixth, wishing me a happy *dzień świętego mikołaja*. I have no idea what that means, and I have to look it up. It's Saint Nicholas Day when apparently kids get token gifts. Come to think of it, I do remember learning once in school that in France kids wake up on the sixth to find presents and sweets in their shoes. Around this time, tree lots start appearing all over the city, claiming to have the best Choinki (Christmas trees). I don't get excited about the trees, but I like the way the word looks in Polish. People buy them early, although most of the trees won't be dressed until the twenty-fourth. That, I learn, is the tradition: Christmas Eve dinner, tree decorating, then opening the presents.

Trees don't only appear in these lots for sale but are found dressed and for sale in the flower kiosks on every street corner along with wreaths and other Christmas decorations. We opt for a small pre-decorated tree, as they are really pretty. Kilometers of lights are strung through all the major town arteries and squares. Interestingly, for a predominantly Catholic country, most of the displays are non-denominational. Vintage parasols along Krakowskie Przedmieście complement the old-style architecture leading to the grand thirty-foot tree in Old Town. Along the way, dancing snowflakes are projected on the buildings. Weeping light fountains line the streetlamps on the Soviet-style Świętokrzyska Boulevard, softening the angular buildings. In the distance, as pedestrians walk through lit archways, is the ever-present Pałac Kultury (Palace of Culture), glowing in whites, reds, and greens. Street after street has its own magic that will brighten the night sky during the darkest, coldest days of winter.

Dinner on the twenty-fourth is important to my husband, although he's not terribly attached to the food itself. This is good news because the traditional cabbage rolls, pierogi, and *ryba po grecku*—a

Greek-style whitefish in a carrot, celery, and tomato sauce that I'm fairly sure doesn't exist in Greece—are all foods I can live without. Besides, this is shortly after my middle of the street, food breakdown, so I'm extra vulnerable in that department. The trick is that we need twelve vegetarian dishes. Since it's just the two of us, small quantities will do. We buy cabbage rolls for Pawel, along with crepes, eggs, caviar, smoked salmon (since fish is allowed), and hummus with vegetables. Sushi is our compromise. He can get as many traditional foods as he wants so long as I get sushi. For Hanukkah the only traditional food we serve is potato latkes.

Pawel takes care of the menorah and the candles. That, along with all the food, is fun and makes this time more special, but where I am not prepared to compromise is assimilating to traditions that I don't agree with. *Traditions* is a word that people hide behind when they don't want change.

My babcia, Paula, doesn't invite us to spend the holidays with her and my uncle KT, which is a relief. I have no idea what they celebrate, I'm assuming Christmas, for his adopted kids. That's one down. My cousin Alek invites us for dinner, thankfully not on Christmas Eve. They aren't traditional anyway, so I probably wouldn't have anything to worry about. I think my husband declines his uncle's invitation, all in all, the first holiday goes by smoothly. Easter will be the next hurdle, but that's not for a few months.

This whole religion thing confuses me, and the older I get, the less I want to have anything to do with it. I simply cannot understand why anyone would want to believe in a higher power. I grew up knowing I was Jewish on my mother's side. In Jewish kindergarten, we learned the Hebrew alphabet and all about the holidays, all of which were celebrated. The clay menorah I made that year is the one my father uses to this day. Bits of Jewishness crept in around the edges even after that, so I guess I was culturally Jewish, although that's a term I don't really like. Judaism has always had a place deep in my bones, it has always been a part of my identity, but it's qualifying the relationship that has always bothered me. Can I be Jewish without believing in religion?

Growing up, I don't remember ever celebrating Easter except decorating eggs, but we certainly celebrated Passover with extended family. It was always a traditional celebration involving readings by the youngest child (usually my sister), the appropriate questions asked, and the table laid out exactly as it should be. But that's it, no explicit religious instruction. Religious icons on our walls were art pieces to be enjoyed rather than religious messages beaming down on us. The only piece of religion that was in our home on Bathurst Street in Toronto was a mezuzah at the side door, and that was left over from the previous owners.

When I was ten or so, my mother gave me an Old Testament and said that I should read it and come to her if I had any questions. She told me I should know the stories, but that's all they were: stories. If I decided that I wanted to believe in God when I got older, I could. But, she said, she and my dad did not believe.

We were still living in Thornhill, a predominantly Jewish suburb of Toronto at the time, on Porterfield Crescent, and right outside my bedroom was an old white Ikea bookshelf filled with books my sister and I shared. The Old Testament lived there, as did a number of other works, including the Qur'an and several other religious texts. What I devoured were the Greek myths. I couldn't get enough of them. The stories and characters were wonderful, and for many years that's all I read. At some point, though, I got my hands on *Sally J. Freedman as Herself* by Judy Blume. I read it over and over again and then again. It stars a young girl growing up in a secular-ish Jewish family right after World War II and talks about some of the horrors of the war. When my grandmother saw the book she was horrified. She wanted my mother to forbid me from reading it. Luckily, my mother declined. After that book, it was *The Silver Sword* by Ian Serraillier, then *Davita's Harp* by Chaim Potok, and then almost everything written by Isaac Bashevis Singer. That's how I slowly started getting my religious education.

So my education in Jewishness was mostly based on history—not ancient history, but history tied to World War II and what happened after. My mother liked to say that she felt Jewish from a cultural perspective rather than a religious one, but for a long time I had no idea what that meant. You were either a believer or you weren't, right?

At my elementary school, a secular public school, the split was about 40-60 Jews and non-Jews, and I didn't really feel like I fit in. Most of the Jewish kids had bar and bat mitzvahs; they celebrated Hanukkah and other Jewish holidays. At my home, we did bits and pieces—whatever worked at the time—minus the actual religion part. My dad has a Roman Catholic background, but other than Christmas I never felt connected with that side. Is that because I didn't know his family growing up? Or because he made such a concerted effort to understand Judaism that, apart from Christmas, we didn't celebrate any other Christian-based holidays? Somehow there was always just this understanding, this underlying knowledge, that we were Jewish.

Then, in the eighth grade, getting ready for our school's holiday pageant, I stood staring at the stage split in two, with one side celebrating Christmas and the other Hanukkah. I had no idea which side to join until my friend grabbed me by the hand and said, "Your mother is Jewish, so that makes you Jewish." She gave me a vintage headkerchief, and I chose my side.

CHAPTER 6

IN SEARCH OF ME: OUR FIRST YEAR IN POLAND

When people ask me where I'm from, I say, "How much time do you have?" I'm never from where I happen to be living. We assume that identity is rooted in your birthplace, but what if you left a place before you knew where you even were? I was only a few years old when my parents emigrated from Sweden. We then spent half a year in Germany with my grandparents before moving to Toronto. Other than my military-issue dog tags—which everyone received around the time I was born, and which will let me into a Swedish bomb shelter should there be a nuclear attack—I have zero connection to that country.

"Oh, so you've come back to your homeland." I hear this over and over whenever I tell people I have moved to Poland. Inevitably, they ask if I plan to stay forever. My response is a nervous laugh. "Forever is a big commitment," I say. What I'm really thinking is, *Are you crazy? Live here forever? Uh, no.* Poland is cool, I like living in Europe, but given the choice, hands down it's going to be London or Paris. Pawel and I chose Poland because we could get passports, because we speak the language, and because we could live without immediately blowing through our savings.

Is it okay to say we didn't really consider much past that?

Once we arrive, it hits me every day that, while I have Polish heritage, growing up in Canada has made me a Canadian by nature. In Poland, I'm a foreigner in a not-so-foreign land. Although my roots run deep in the soil of this country, I do not feel Polish. I don't resonate with Polish culture. I have no childhood memories of Poland, like I do of Germany, where my grandparents settled after being forced out of Poland in the sixties. Really, I am a Canadian with Polish roots. I am a Canadian with Polish roots. I am a Canadian with Polish roots. How many times do I have to repeat that?

Poland is a country that belonged to my grandparents and parents. My father was okay with Pawel and I moving, but my mother, who died when I was in my teens, was probably rolling in her grave. Yes, she had an attachment to the country. She even wrote radio plays for the Canadian Broadcasting Company (CBC) that were broadcast in Poland, but her feelings for the place did not extend to embracing the people. You can believe that she wasn't thrilled when I started dating Pawel. After she got to know him, she liked and respected him, but at first, she was upset. All Polish men are losers, she said; only my father was a good man.

There was a lot to reconcile when it came to how my parents viewed Poland. They left years before I was born, with mixed feelings about their country of origin, and the home of my not-always-welcome, aka Jewish, ancestors. By the time they arrived in Canada, my parents had lived in so many places, their worldviews were drastically different from that of the Polish immigrant community in Toronto.

These differences trickled down into things like social life and language. I didn't grow up with Polish friends, for instance, so casual slang escaped me. I spoke a version of the language that made me more comfortable with older adults. When we first landed in Poland, I was acutely aware of this discrepancy between how people my age spoke, and how I was speaking. Plus, Pawel doesn't have an accent, but apparently I do. I hadn't realized that until what feels like every single person points it out and discusses my accent as if I were not there.

It turns out that a large number of people have left Poland in the past few years and completely forgotten the language. They then come back with accents. Over and over again I explain I've never lived in Poland. "Spoko," people say. I take "spoko" to be a short form of "spokojnie," which means be calm, and that feels insulting. *Stop telling me to calm down!* I want to say. After a while I realize that what "spoko" actually means is, that's cool, or no problem. Cue eye roll. Who knew?

For once I understand how my husband feels in Canada, always struggling with people butchering his name. Pawel is pronounced Pavel. Don't get me started on his last name. Only here, now I'm the one explaining my name. Caroline, which in Polish is Karolina (Karolinka, Karolcza), has diminutives I absolutely hate. Topperman is also a mystery to people, and I laugh the first time I hear Pawel spell it out.

Actually, I'm surprised no one asks me why I didn't take his name. When we married, it never occurred to me to change my name, and he didn't seem to care one way or another. In Canada, having different surnames is no big deal. Here, it's, why don't you two register as a married couple? If we do want to register, I will have to write a formal letter informing the government of what our hypothetical, nonexistent child's last name would be, and I refuse to do that.

This accent business makes me realize that for the first time in my life, people cannot place me. I don't fit into their boxes. When Uber drivers see my English-looking name, then hear me speaking Polish, they're confused. I tell my story so many times, I might as well create a handout. A lot of times people want me to counsel them about getting to Canada and finding jobs. Later, I learn that a segment of the population left to work in other countries where they went on to forget the language, and that's what makes the stayed-put Poles angry—unreasonably angry. That's why they're rude to me.

When I'm not being insulted, I am answering myriad questions about Canada and what could have possibly brought me here to Poland. People think I have lost my mind. Canada is the land of milk and honey. Poland is the place where dreams go to die. That's what they try to tell me. Suddenly I find myself on the defensive. Why wouldn't I want to have an adventure in a new country? We don't have children, and life should be about taking chances. Pawel and I are extremely fortunate to be able to uproot and move to a different country with no concrete plan. When we were leaving Canada, most of our friends were all for our decision. Poles here look at us incredulously. The truth is, before we left, we were overworked and overtired. Vancouver is a great city for some, but it never fed my soul. Warsaw is far from perfect, but the galleries, the museums, the coffee shops, and the arts scene are all accessible. And let's face it, Warsaw is at least close to a lot of world-class cities.

This accent business also makes me realize just how much I have taken language learning for granted. Growing up in Toronto, almost everyone I met spoke with an accent. Both my parents spoke with accents, and it was no big deal. They spoke Polish, English, Swedish, and some Russian. My mother could also speak some Italian, Spanish, German, and Yiddish. She had an amazing talent. She would start speaking a language after being in a country for a day or two. My father spoke some Farsi from his time in Afghanistan. Language was always a way of making borders dissolve wherever we traveled. So, naturally, our parents wanted my sister and me to speak more than just one.

I learned English once I started school; Polish was spoken at home. Thanks to that, my sister and I could easily communicate with my parents' friends and with our grandparents. Growing up, that was a luxury my cousins didn't have. For whatever reason, their parents did not ensure that my cousins learned Polish. This made it hard for them to communicate with that section of the family. I know they felt our grandparents didn't even really love them as much.

After a year in a Jewish kindergarten, where I learned some Hebrew—all I remember is eating apples and honey during the holidays—I was sent to a French immersion elementary school, and after that, a French high school. Living in Canada, our parents knew that French could only help us. Plus, I think Paris was lodged deep in their hearts.

My family celebrated the fact that I could easily navigate English, Polish, and French. "Stop" and "wait," the first words I learned in English, are probably the words that, as an adult, I listen to the least.

As part of our effort to inject ourselves into Warsaw society, Pawel and I go against our natural instincts to hibernate. Instead, we venture out. Our first foray, in January, is joining a business club. Appropriately named SkyClub, it sits at the top of a tall office tower in the heart of the city. SkyClub is owned by a British businessman and is totally pretentious and overpriced, especially by Polish standards. It has a nineties vibe, and a lot of people walking around as if they are important. The hostesses' skirts are a little too short, their button-down blouses a little too tight. The breakfast, however, is delicious, and the views cannot be beat. The bathroom stalls have floor-to-ceiling windows, which make going to the toilet an exceptional event. We decide to become members.

The club will be a great place, we think, to make connections. I think my husband secretly likes the idea of getting properly dressed in the morning and heading into an "office." He is not as comfortable with this whole working-from-home thing as I am. Before long, he meets some people, and I wind up getting hired to write their web copy.

Pawel pushes forward with online work while I get serious about my blog and working with international brands. I have some income, still, from my old job in Vancouver, but I decide that I can make it as a blogger. So I begin contacting brands that want more North American exposure.

In March, we make a quick return visit to Canada to see our new nephew, then purchase two one-way tickets back to Poland. That's it. Bye-bye, safety net. For now, Warsaw will be home.

CHAPTER 7

THE PATERNAL SIDE, MY FATHER: WOJTEK'S STORY

Just as one set of my grandparents was fleeing east, into Soviet Russia, the other set was in Central Asia, in Afghanistan. Unlike Fryderyk and Paula's story, which I've pieced together from Fryderyk's chronicle of events and an interview that Paula gave a few years before she died, I know my father's story from the stories I heard growing up and from interviews I did with him and his brother, Andrzej. If my maternal side seemed fragmented, then my paternal side is an even bigger gap. Even I need to step back to see how the puzzle pieces fit together.

Briefly, Franciszek Wichrzycki, the man who would one day become my paternal grandfather, was born in imperial Russia, in 1904 in Czuchor, a tiny village near Kamieniec Podolski (Kamianets-Podilskyi)—a place so small I have yet to find it on any map. The woman who would become my paternal grandmother, Wandeczka Wichrzycka, née Chmielewska, was born in 1909 in Kiev, in the heart of Ukraine.

Somehow, in 1916—in the midst of the Great War—Franciszek's father received a piece of land in Radość, a Warsaw suburb. Poland, as we know it now, did not exist; at the time the land in question was in a German neighborhood, and when my great-grandfather arrived to claim the land, he was shot and killed. A few months later, his wife, my paternal great-grandmother, who was now a widow with three sons, arrived as well, and in time, she met a man and remained in Poland.

Around this time, in 1917 with the start of the Russian Revolution, there was an exodus of Poles from Kiev, and Wandeczka's whole family fled to Warsaw. They settled in Dom Kolejaza (the Railwayman's House) on 70 Targowa, and her father worked at the ministry of communications, in the railway department.

At the start of WWII, when the first bombs fell, Wandeczka's mother was in a hospital that was destroyed, and she was found among the dead. But by this time, Wandeczka and Franciszek were already living in Afghanistan with their sons. Thankfully, Wandeczka's father survived the war, in Warsaw.

The man who would one day be my dad, Wojtek, was born to Wandeczka and Franciszek in Warsaw on April 11, 1937, at the Dom Kolejaza on 70 Targowa, two years before the war's outbreak. That made Wojciech Władyslaw Wichrzycki—Wojtek for short—a prewar, pre-move-to-Afghanistan baby.

From the time my father was three years old until he was seven, he and his family lived in Kabul, Afghanistan, with their staff in a big twelve-room villa surrounded by a great stone wall. Hazar-Ulam Hussein, a devout Muslim, cooked for the family. His mother would come down into the large kitchen, and they would discuss the menu at great lengths. Wojtek loved Ulam's Afghan meals. He could make anything. Sometimes Wandeczka managed to obtain ham from the

Polish Consulate, which, naturally, Ulam cooked under great protest and got around the situation by using long tongs, so he wouldn't have to handle the meat. Then, after the meal, he'd approach Wandeczka and say, "New pot need," showing her the hole in the bottom of the pot that needed replacing, because he refused to even wash pork-tainted pots. The family loved Hazar, and for the seven years they lived there, he was a constant presence.

Despite the luxury of there being a gifted cook on the premises, there was no running water. Instead, every day, a Bacha Sak/ow, a boy who carries water, would arrive with a big goatskin bag filled with water for bathing, washing dishes, and cooking. The bathroom was an outhouse in the yard, and once a week or so a man would come with a donkey to clean out the waste.

It was thanks to a nanny whom the family employed when they arrived in Kabul that Wojtek also picked up quite a bit of Russian. But it was at preschool at the French Embassy that he learned French with a Parisian accent. There were only five or six kids in the class, and their teacher, Mme. Beaudoin, would sit in the corner and knit using metal needles. Whenever Wojtek misbehaved, which happened often, she would crack a needle across his hand. One day she hit him across the face, and that night Wojtek told his mother.

The next day Wandeczka went straight to the school to discuss the situation with Mme. Beaudoin, who asked, "Where would you like me to hit him?"

"If you have to hit him somewhere, give him a spanking," Wandeczka said.

"Hit a child on the behind?" Mme. Beaudoin was visibly shocked. "But that's like a sexual proposition," she sputtered in disbelief.

This response floored Wandeczka, who let Mme. Beaudoin know in no uncertain terms that if she ever hit Wojtek in the face again, she'd pay for it in blood. With that encounter, his education at the French Embassy came to an end. From that day on, he was taught at home.

Franciszek, my grandfather, was away a lot, but when he was home, he'd show Wojtek and Andrzej pictures of the highway he was building. Franciszek was the head engineer for part of Afghanistan's AH1 Highway, specifically Khyber Pass, the stretch of road that would one day join Kabul to Jalalabad. Although the highway would not be finished until the 1960s by the Americans, even in the 1930s, it was a huge project.

Effectively, my grandfather had been contracted by the League of Nations, the precursor to the United Nations, as part of an aid package for developing countries. On one occasion when he brought the boys along to show them the great road, they walked on the rough yellow terrain, stumbling under the beating sun, staring at the mountains and seemingly impassable rivers. Altogether, with the help of several thousand workers under his command, Franciszek completed hundreds of kilometers of the road, including tunnels and bridges. Wojtek remembers hearing that the governor offered his father a great deal of money and a statue erected in his honor in Kabul, if he would just change his mind and stay rather than return to Poland.

For all the enjoyable moments, though, living in Afghanistan could not have been easy. Wandeczka, for instance, was at risk in certain circumstances. When staff warned her that one of the men should go to the market, she brushed them off, grabbed her basket, and left the house. She returned a few hours later covered in rotten fruit and bruises from the pelting stones. She refused to accept the situation and, in response, made an effort to learn Farsi, one of the local languages. A few months later, when Wojtek accompanied her to market, he was proud to find she was the only woman trading with the men.

During that time, she also began teaching. With her pedigree in tennis and sports in general she was the perfect choice for teaching gym at the local school. And because he was so young, Wojtek was allowed to accompany her. He liked school, moderately, but found it much more fun to kick the ball around with girls during the break. Once again, Wandeczka got her way. When the general came to check on the school, and under her watch, the girls were permitted to wear shorts while playing sports.

In 1944, Franciszek and Wandeczka joined the Union of Polish Patriots, which in turn helped the family return to Poland. After seven years in Afghanistan, as a part of the movement to get Poles to come back to their homeland, Franciszek and Wandeczka returned to Lublin, which had already been liberated from Nazi control by the Soviets and the Moscow-formed Polish army.

As memories tend to be, my father's stories of that time are disjointed. What I'm left with are bits told to me at different times, fragments that paint a picture of the family returning to Poland while the war still raged nearby. Combined with the way borders have shifted through history, things can get confusing. In this account, my father's family journeyed from Kabul to what was then the Soviet city of Termez, but is now part of Uzbekistan. Looking at a map now, you might be confused. I know that I was. Termez is now in Uzbekistan, but back then it was the Uzbek Soviet Socialist Republic. With some prodding I managed to extract this memory:

When we left Afghanistan, we left Kabul for the
Afghan-Soviet border, specifically Termez, which was on
the Soviet side, on the other side of the Amu Darya River.
There was the Aral Sea, which later dried up, and there
were two rivers, Amu Darya, which was on the border,
and Syr Darya, which flowed south. We crossed the Amu
Darya, which was only a few dozen, no, a few meters
wide. There were planks set up across the deep water of
the river. There was no other way across, so these men
carried our things while the planks bowed beneath their
weight, but they had to because that's where the railway
was. Afghanistan didn't have a railway. Then we sat in
Termez for two or three days waiting while the authorities looked at every document and searched every single
one of our belongings. They took all of my father's home
movies. Six years' worth of documentation, all the neg-
atives, and a few dozen films made on his 8 mm Kodak
camera. They took everything they could, and of course
they exchanged our money for their benefit, they gave us
one ruble for a bag of afghani, when it was the other way
around. Much later, they accused my father of building
roads against the Soviet Union during the war. From
Termez we caught the train to Tashkent, then circled
north of Kijów [Kiev] to Moscow.

There we were in the metro, which was as tight as hell,
and the trains were stuffed, overstuffed with people. I
was little back then, I was just a squirt, and Engineer
Okienski would hold my hand. When the crowd became
too much, he would squeeze my hand, and I would make
a loud grunting noise. A cry would surface, "Rebenok,

rebenok mal'chik, detskoye mesto, chtoby sdelat' dlya nego." "Chłopak, dziecko miejsce zrobić dla niego" [Small kid, boy, make room for him]. The crowd would shift and compress itself even more.

At the time, we were living at the Polish Embassy in Moscow and traveling daily to a hotel for dinner. Those were the restrictions. There would be some soup, maybe a little bit of meat, but my mother would collect the bread in her bag and bring it home for later or the next day. We were always able to find some fat or jam for the bread. At the embassy, about a dozen of us in total received a bag of rice, some salt and pepper, and a blanket.

Later, in '58 or '60 when I was in STS [Student Satirist Theater], I met up with a writer, Fedecki, who was translating texts from Russian—his Russian was excellent. We started speaking, and suddenly I looked at him and said, "We know each other." He had been sleeping on the steps at the Polish Embassy in the Soviet Union. He was a journalist reporting on the war, twenty-two or twenty-three at the time. It was cold, and my mother gave him a woolen Afghan blanket. He had a Japanese girlfriend, and they received some food as well. They were trying to obtain papers for travel. And here we were remembering each other from 1944. We spent a month in Moscow. We wanted to go to Poland but there were no trains.

My father often remembers parts of his childhood in bits and pieces. I never know when a conversation might set off a slew of memories. I mentioned earlier that we always had a Christmas tree at home. I don't know whether my mother's family celebrated with one. I imagine they must have since they were hiding their Judaism. I did not, however, realize how important having a tree was to my father until he told me this story:

> It was 1944, so I was seven and Andrzej was thirteen.
> We went out into the city to comb the area looking for
> anything that could be a tree. Lublin was a small town,
> an old town with old walls, and finally we found a bush,
> it wasn't a tree, but the shape was sort of like one. So
> we brought it home, and found some chocolates covered
> in foil. We quickly ate the chocolates and crushed the
> paper to make colorful balls. We also had small candles
> that we affixed to the tree. You know, the worst kind, the
> ones that make trees catch fire. That was our tree. We sat
> with the first voivode of Gdańsk [before he was officially
> appointed], he was the one who had brought Poles to Af-
> ghanistan. The tree stood in the corner and a neighbor
> brought over some nuts. We made holes in them and
> strung them on our tree. That no one had a camera back
> then to take a photograph, tragedy, tragedy.

The problem with memories is that they don't always have clean transitions. I know I was asking a lot when I questioned my father about his first months back in Poland immediately after the war. He was a young kid at the time, and how much can anyone really remember in great detail from their childhood? While I understand that not everything may be 100 percent accurate, I can tell that he's seeing everything he recounts. This is the family's time in Warsaw, right before they fled north to Sopot, where food was more readily available.

It was November 1944, in Lublin, and we were living about eighty kilometers (49 miles) from the front [which was near Warsaw at this point in time. A few weeks later, on January seventeenth, Russian troops would cross the Vistula River into Warsaw]. We were waiting for the fighting to stop; we were waiting for Russia to push the Germans out of Warsaw. The new communist government was governing out of Lublin. I remember being in the park and seeing German planes flying overhead, and whenever I heard bombs falling, I searched frantically for somewhere to hide. It was cold, but there wasn't any snow—that would come later. January was cold, and the Vistula froze, but there wasn't any bridge into Warsaw, so they [the occupants of the city] quickly built a floating bridge because people were coming home. People were walking back to Warsaw from the surrounding areas.

We were back in Warsaw on January twenty-fifth. We crossed the river, and I remember walking around with my grandfather. The rubble on Chmielna Street was two stories high. There were bare walls just standing on their own. Warsaw was 90 percent destroyed, systematically destroyed. A tank would roll down the street shooting at the buildings, then a second one would follow and throw fire at them. Let it burn, let it crumble, and so on. Sometimes the front of a building would be gone, and all you would see were apartments with their contents, it almost looked like someone could be living there, except all the people were gone. Often they were hiding in basements.

That's the small piece of the war memory I have. In Sopot it was different. It was better, except we had a strict curfew. At 9 PM everyone was home, and no one ventured out, no one was allowed out. This lasted until 1947. The forests around the area where we lived were full of gangs. They would come out of the forests and kill communists. But these were rogue gangs, they were demoralized ex-army.

By May 1945, food was still scarce. Franciszek tracked down work in the north, in Sopot, on the Baltic Sea, and so the family packed up and moved. Picture a caravan of three flatbed trucks, with Wojtek, Andrzej, their cousin Elżbieta, and her mother seated atop woven bags filled with millions of złoty. My father's parents rode up front in a car with a young soldier nicknamed Pepesha after his PPSh-41 submachine gun, who was tasked with getting them to Sopot safely.

This was deliberate, their trying to look like a group of refugees, resettling. The woods were filled with paramilitary bandits, and no one was really fooled by the group. In fact, it was pretty obvious this was a group of communists. This seems to be a running narrative in my family. Everyone subtly changes their identity to fit in.

Sopot, a beach town on the Baltic Sea, is a magical place reminiscent of Vancouver, with that relaxed you-are-on-vacation air that comes with the pungent smell of salt water. The first time I saw Sopot was in winter, its pristine shores free of the cacophony of tourists who descend in summer, leaving Pixie free to run, dig in the sand, and bark at the waves. The next time was with my dad, when he came to Poland in 2015 to visit his brother. It had been fifty years since

Wojtek had last seen Sopot, but he remembered it as if it were yesterday. And even though he was disappointed to find his old home renovated and the fence they used to run across gone, he could still point at every house on the street and say who used to live there.

In 1945, the family had first landed in a hotel near the *molo*, on the beach—today those are premium spots costing hundreds of dollars a night—before securing the house at 30 Mickiewicz Street, at the corner of Abraham—the house that, in 2015 at least, was still standing. This trip brought back a flood of childhood memories for my father.

The entrance to the flat was a comfortable room with a staircase off to the side, and beside the staircase stood a large wooden dresser, where Wojtek loved to hang out and spy on his brother and his friends. Andrzej had hated this, of course. It was bad enough having to share a room with his younger brother and look out for him. The kid needed to be taught a lesson, so Andrzej got inventive, and one day he put metal thumbtacks on the dresser. When Wojtek jumped off the banister in his bare feet and landed on the tack-ridden dresser, he yelled so loud the neighbors rushed in to see what was happening.

Sometimes, however, Andrzej played nice, and the boys hung out together. They loved swimming in the freezing waters of the Baltic, although they had to watch for unexploded mines and leftover ammunition on the beach, the same as in the forests. When the two found old shells, Wojtek watched as Andrzej would remove the powder and then, back at the house, pour it carefully along the beams in the attic before striking a match. It was exciting, watching a trail of flames light up the room! Luckily, they didn't burn the house down since the wood was fresh and couldn't easily catch fire, and their parents never found out what they were doing.

If anything, routine mornings were hard for the young Wojtek.
He liked school well enough but often got in trouble. Plus, the boys
were always rushed out the door, now that their mother worked as
the secretary to their father, who had been appointed head of the
Department of Transportation, in charge of roads and bridges. Wandeczka, in other words, was needed at the office. She had no time for
dawdling.

After school then was the best of times, with Wojtek and his best
friend, Ryszard, left to their own devices, stealing chestnuts or li-
lacs from neighboring trees and selling them back to the owners.
Everyone knew what the boys were up to, but Wandeczka's excellent
homemade pies helped to mollify the neighbors.

But on the heels of the war, things were tight, so hand-me-downs
from father to brother to Wojtek were the norm, or long pants made
into shorts with knitted suspenders. In the summer Wandeczka attached strips of fabric to pieces of wood to make shoes reminiscent
of Japanese sandals. In the winter, when there wasn't enough coal
to heat the house and keep it warm, she repurposed a large leather
travel bag Franciszek had made in Afghanistan. Carefully cutting out
leather soles and poking holes in them, she joined knit leggings to
the soles to make Afghan socks. It gets to me, when I hear this detail.
Coincidentally, I used to wear Afghan socks to warm up before ballet
class.

CHAPTER 8

MY FIRST TIME IN POLAND: MY FATHER INTRODUCES ME TO HIS ROOTS

I wasn't raised in a typical Polish household, or perhaps I should say that I wasn't raised in a typical Polish immigrant household. I learned a lot more about Polish culture when I went over to Pawel's house than when I was around my parents at home. Our traditions were all over the place. I think my parents took what they wanted and threw out the rest. My mother hated Polish culture. She wanted nothing to do with it. Many immigrants dream of going back home. My parents never had that dream. They were happy to adapt to Canada.

There were some traditions that they did hang on to, mushroom picking being one of them. Come to think of it, any tradition we did keep revolved around food. Anyone who has any connection to Poland has eaten smoked mackerel and gone mushroom picking. I'm not sure you're allowed to get a passport without having experienced these things. No trip up north to Ontario cottage country was complete without a cooler full of smoked fish, usually mackerel, and if we

went away for Thanksgiving, my dad would disappear into the forest
to search for mushrooms. "I think I'll wait to see if you guys die or
not," said the youngest kid on one extended family trip as she stared
at the fragrant pot of creamy mushroom stew. We did not die. We did
not get sick. In fact, all these years later, I still remember how good
that stew tasted.

Warsaw in 2013 is a new, made-to-look-old-but-shiny-and-
extra- clean city, compared to many of its counterparts. Warsaw
1995 was a different story. My mother died on March 6 of that year,
and that summer my father decided it was time my sister and I were
introduced to our homeland. That was when I first met my cousin
and his daughters. I also started reconciling with my uncle and my
babcia, Paula, although it would take many years before I'd be comfortable around her.

This sounds like a strange thing to say because for a long
time, my babcia was my best friend. We were the two musketeers. I'm not sure when it all started to go wrong. Maybe it was
after they moved to Canada on my mother's insistence, and my
dziadzio—Fryderyk—died in Toronto. Shortly thereafter, when I
was thirteen, Paula moved in with us, and I first witnessed how un-
believably selfish she was. It feels like an odd thing to say, wrong
even. Her husband of fifty or so years had died, and here I am calling
her selfish.

Yet her behavior was exactly that. Seemingly out of nowhere
she began monopolizing my mother's attention. My grandmother
moved into the spare room in our home, and she promptly took
over. One time the piercing wail of the fire alarm jolted me from
reading. Running down two flights of stairs, I arrived just in time
to yank a melting pot off the stove and throw it in the sink. I then

ran furiously upstairs. "What the hell?!" I yelled at my grandmother. She barely looked up from her game of solitaire. There she was lying on her bed, in her pink bathrobe. "Didn't you hear the alarm? Why wouldn't you even come down to check that everything is okay?"

No answer. She just kept on with her cards.

That night, when I told my parents what happened, my mother promised to have a talk with her mother. The thing is, I know, we all knew that she did the whole thing on purpose. She was subtle in the way she operated, but she wanted all the attention, good or bad, and if she got it from my mother, so much the better.

March break 1990, after my grandmother had been living with us for four months, my mother decided it would be good for her to go away with my sister and me. My grandmother's friends vacationed in Fort Lauderdale, so that's where we went. She then spent the entire week drinking cognac in her room while my sister and I sallied back and forth between the apartment and the pool.

The sad part about my grandfather's death was that it was not only a blow to my grandmother, but it also cemented my mother's guilt complex toward her mother. None of us really understood why, but like seeing the elephant in the room, we could all sense its presence.

I don't remember how long my grandmother lived with us until my mother finally reached her limit and told her mother outright that she would need to move back into her own apartment. Either that or sell it. They did look for a house with an in-law suite, but nothing was ever good enough for my grandmother. The truth was none of us wanted her to continue living with us. I'm surprised my father didn't put his foot down and demand she leave. While she did not admit it to us, I believe that my mother was secretly relieved that they could not find anything suitable. So life moved on, and my grandmother went back to living on her own. Six years later my mother was diagnosed with cancer, and six months after that, she died. It all happened very quickly. There was no time to prepare, barely any time to say goodbye. This is not a cancer story, but one incident I cannot forget.

One day, early on in her illness, the two of us were home together alone when my mother appeared in the doorway of the room where I was sitting. I thought she was asleep, but no, there she was ordering me to call people who I knew were deceased. It turned out that she had accidentally taken too many pain meds, but it's telling that in that moment her focus was reconnecting with friends and family who lived in Poland. I was in my first year of university, and looking back, much of all I see is a fuzzy memory. Mostly I remember being numb.

What should be a surprise to no one, it also tore my family apart. My father wasn't demonstratively affectionate, so in an effort to help us heal, his way of reaching out was to introduce us to our roots. Somewhere deep down he probably knew that it was now or never. This was the time for us to meet his side of the family, and to see where we came from.

What we saw in 1995 was not the Warsaw of today. Picture those movies set in Eastern Europe, where everything is gray all the time. That's what we encountered. Also, Poland was in the process of transitioning from the old złoty to the new one while also accepting the euro. So everything had three prices. Anytime you wanted to buy anything, you had to do the math. Factor in exchanges like this: "Yes, I would like to buy a pair of black Puma sneakers."

"You will have to go across the street to get the other shoe."

I'm not kidding. That was Warsaw for you, in 1995.

The main reason for our visit, however, was to connect with family who up until this point were surreal entities who weren't even present in our photo albums. My father was home, but I felt as if I was an outsider meeting key players on his side of the family for the first time.

It wasn't until after my mother died that my father's family began to have a role in my life. Even then, they didn't have any impact until after I moved to Poland. My father was a steady and stable presence in our home, but our lives revolved a lot more around my mother's side of the family. I didn't even learn about my father's side of the family until much later when I inherited old letters and the fascinating account of my grandfather's time in Afghanistan.

In my case, everyone here came into my life at a much later date, and so I have to work backward while getting to know them. Alek, Andrzej's son, is my first cousin but a generation older, meaning I'm closer in age to his two daughters. He has, however, an undeniable connection to my father. The way he speaks, his mannerisms—they are exactly like my dad's. Comfort in the familiar was not lost on me, and I took to Alek and his daughters right away. His older daughter, Zuzanna, eventually played an instrumental role in helping me get my Polish passport, so I suppose I made a decent impression on her as well back in 1995. At the time, she was still a cheeky kid who wanted to eat fries at the first McDonald's in Warsaw, a luxury they couldn't afford. Not exactly exciting for us, but this was still only a few years after the fall of the Iron Curtain. Years later we chuckled over how, for our first meeting, we had brought spending money for the girls, and in order to keep everything straight, I kept their money in separate pockets. The only problem was that I kept forgetting which was which. Zuzanna, however, knew exactly how much each of them had spent.

It was not as easy with my father's mother, Wandeczka. She was not babcia or any other variant of grandmother, just Wandeczka, a diminutive of Wanda. That's what she wanted to be called. I was nineteen years old when we first met. Put another way, she waited nineteen years to meet her granddaughter. She never reached out. Her home was in Warsaw, but I never saw it on that trip with my father. She may have already been living with Andrzej and his wife. I imagine her home would have been a lot like his. It would have been filled with artifacts from Afghanistan and the Far East—perhaps a cabinet overflowing with miniature statues carved out of wood and stone, rubbings of architectural carvings in Bangkok, and wooden masks on the walls. Our first meeting was odd. She greeted us warmly and exclaimed, "I love your nose ring. It's beautiful." She was a tiny but very feisty woman. I remember that she kicked my dad at one point. She died not long after we met.

Franciszek was the grandfather I never knew. Though he had been deceased for over two decades when we made this trip, that was not the reason I did not know him. He had been angry when my parents married, and he was too stubborn to reach out when I was born, causing much of the family discord. I felt his presence on this trip, though, and I knew him from family stories. The first time I "met" him was when I was shown artifacts that he and Wandeczka brought back from their travels. The handmade jugs, the plates, the trinkets, these are his memories, ones that I can share. My dad's only, and older, brother is Andrzej. I don't have any real memories of my uncle from our 1995 trip, but we went on to grow very close after I moved to Poland with Pawel. Andrzej is important to me, however, because he is the gateway to Franciszek and Wandeczka. He was able to talk about them from a different perspective than my father could, and he provided me with a wealth of papers and photographs. I think that my father felt the rift between him and his brother even more strongly than the one with his parents. Andrzej was his rival, his ally, and his protector. When I finally saw the two of them interact, after I had moved to Poland, it was delightful to watch my father turn into a little kid who hung on his older sibling's every word.

My second trip to Poland was in 2011 when my husband and I decided it was time for a honeymoon some ten years after getting married. This took us driving through Poland, which is an interesting experience all on its own. Some villages consisted of only a few crumbling houses; others were simply one long, narrow, winding street. Others were proper small towns. Whatever their makeup, each one had a sign showing that you were entering a built-up area and a sign indicating that you were leaving. With that came a quick and drastic speed change, sometimes with little warning.

On one of our adventures, when I was driving, the car suddenly started beeping loudly. "What the —— is that?!" I yelled and swerved off the road. "Did I drive over a bomb? Are we going to explode? Should we get out of the car?" Good thing my husband approaches things calmly. We started to investigate and finally figured out that this heart-attack-inducing noise was merely a friendly warning that there was a speed camera up ahead.

Even though the back roads were sometimes slow, especially if you got stuck behind a farm vehicle, I much preferred them to the highways. Stone or stucco houses line the roadways, gardens are filled with bright flowers, and many streets display wayside shrines featuring the Virgin Mary or an elaborate cross. Stork nests pepper the landscape. If you're lucky, you might see one making its home on a tower specifically created and cared for by local townspeople. Summers in Poland are glorious. At the first sign of warmer temperatures, tables and chairs sprout in front of restaurants, and the streets are flooded with families out for walks. Then the formal patios appear, and the population's demeanor relaxes in anticipation of the holidays. Tourists and locals spend every spare moment outside, meandering over cobblestones, photographing the colorful buildings in Old Town, or enjoying a drink.

All this is in stark contrast to the invisible weight that seems to fall in the winter months, a weight that makes it hard to forget Poland's tumultuous history. Poland is advancing rapidly and in many ways is leaps and bounds ahead of Canada with regard to technology and infrastructure, but, especially in small towns, people still burn trash as a means of staying warm. The air thickens with the smell of garbage. You feel your lungs burn as you inhale, and an aftertaste lingers in your mouth. Instead of meandering down streets and enjoying evenings out, most locals cover their faces and hurry home. The towns of Lublin and Cracow were especially bad. In Cracow several people yelled at us for walking outside. In Lublin, what should have been a really fun weekend turned into a game of ducking inside as quickly as we could.

Walking around Warsaw, you often see specific graffiti on walls. One that stands out is a *P* merging into a stylized *W*. At first I think the image refers to a band or a gang, you know, like the graffiti one sees splattered on any bare wall in any city in the world. What I learn is that this image is a kotwica (anchor) with a long, fraught history. During the Second World War, the *W* was an emblem for the Polish underground resistance, representing Poland's struggle to reclaim its independence. The kotwica then resurfaced during communist times and was used by those fighting the regime. Over the years the meaning of the emblem changed, depending on which group chose to use it. It was always a sign of resistance, but I notice who is using it now. The nationalists use the symbol to exclude everyone who isn't like them while others use it to demonstrate national pride.

The kotwica is displayed prominently, for instance, at the entrance to the Warsaw Uprising Museum, a place Pawel wanted to see. I tag along, only mildly interested because, as much as I enjoy museums, ones like this can be depressing. We venture to the back to find a large stone memorial wall erected in honor of everyone who died during the uprising.

I thought that by this time I knew my family's story, so I don't expect to see any names I recognize. Still, just for the hell of it I check the large index books. Sure enough, I don't find anything. But when we start walking, roughly halfway down I turn my head to the left, and there—right there where I happened to look—three Wichrzyckis are listed. My dad's family. People I never knew, people who were never spoken about.

Later, when I ask my dad about them, he is just as surprised as I was.

Another offshoot of our roots, another mystery.

On this trip, one of the places Pawel and I both wanted to visit was Auschwitz. My husband had never been, and I strongly believe it is a place that everyone should see. We hadn't yet mastered the art of

booking train tickets, so we found ourselves on a very slow train in
a six-seater compartment heading south, toward Cracow. I don't remember every detail of that trip, but I can guarantee that at least one
of our fellow travelers was digging into a homemade sandwich with
a side of pickles. Also, I vaguely remember that we were stopped
on the tracks for several hours for some unknown but important
reason, which made it late when we arrived at the Queen Boutique
Hotel.

This was probably the nicest hotel we had ever stayed at, and I
was shocked that we could actually afford it. The rooms were big and
modern, and the price included a gourmet breakfast complete with
fresh salmon, a wide array of high-end cheeses, freshly baked breads,
and other a la carte items. All of this in an old history-packed brick
basement. My only complaint was the oversized glass door. "This is
dangerous," I remarked on our first day, "someone is going to crash
into it." Of course, on our third day I smashed face-first into that
door. My sympathetic husband laughed so hard he couldn't breathe.

So, yes, there was a disconnect between this neat hotel and the
reason we had gone there—like the pink and yellow buildings in
Warsaw that can sometimes feel as if they are masking a dark history. It's easy to get caught up in the colors and forget what happened
on the streets. I found this to be true of many European cities. They
have complex historical layers that we don't see in North America.
Cobblestones, plaques, and intricate architecture all highlighted
to attract tourists, and it can be easy to forget that people live with
these traumatic histories every day. Take Dachau, a concentration
camp outside Munich, Germany, which has homes backing onto the
cider brick walls topped with barbed wire that surround the camp.
Then there is the residential street from Auschwitz to the death camp

Birkenau, lined with pretty houses and flower-filled gardens. Beneath the facades there is a world of politics.

While there have been proposals on the table, Poland does not have any laws to provide restitution for property plundered by the Nazis. One part of the population is fighting for what was stolen from them during the war. The other is fighting because they believe that the government is paying too much attention to Jews.

To visit Auschwitz, we joined a tour group of ten or so. Some were from other European countries, and a couple from the Middle East caught my attention. Right from the start they asked questions that made it clear they had very little knowledge about the war and even less about the Holocaust. Our guide was patient and answered everything with no judgment.

We snaked our collective way through the low-rise brick buildings, looking at the piles of human hair, eyeglasses, and children's toys displayed behind large panes of glass. We walked through barracks where the prisoners slept stacked one on top of the other. We looked at old photographs, the occasional one with a flower tucked behind the frame. I watched the questioning man get quieter and quieter, but it wasn't until the end of the tour when I saw his transformation.

We were about to enter the gas chamber when our tour guide stopped us and said, "Inside you will see a flame that burns twenty-four hours a day in memory of those who have died. We ask that out of respect you do not speak or take any photos."

As we walked in, I saw the questioning man's companion pull out her camera. Before she could open it, the man grabbed her arm, harshly shook his head, and took it from her. I could see that he got it. He understood the magnitude of what had happened. This was his life-changing moment.

As important as it is to visit Auschwitz-Birkenau, an overwhelming feeling of sadness and despair enters your heart. And it just won't leave. We tried to shake the feeling by taking a bus to the Wieliczka Salt Mines. Walking down the 380 steps to the first level of the salt mines delivers us to a different world. All in all we descended to a depth of 135 meters, where miners lived in underground caverns linked by three kilometers (1.9 miles) of tunnels and several small lakes. The miners lived this way for weeks on end, chiseling religious and political statues out of blocks of salt, and creating intimate chapels. One chapel still hosts weddings to this day. Everything is made of salt. It takes half a day of wandering through this strangest of worlds to find some release from the weight of the previous day.

Even though our visits to the memorials happened a few years earlier, they were permanently circulating in my thoughts when we moved here in 2013. A slow transformation is happening. I don't yet know how, but those experiences are starting to shape how I see the world.

As we slowly adjust to life in a new country, I continue to struggle with health problems I had before we made our decision to move. It started in 2010 when I could barely get out of bed in the mornings. We had just rented out our Yaletown condo and were renovating a Vancouver Special, a common style of house found in the immediate city suburbs—basically, a really ugly, boxy home designed to maximize floor space.

The Vancouver Special was on a charming street lined with mature cherry blossom trees in East Vancouver. We thought this would be a great decision—until we found ourselves sitting on the sidewalk, watching all our things being stacked in the garage. With no working bathrooms, no heat, and minimal electrical service, there was no way we could move in anytime soon. Then, out of the blue, our ballroom dance teachers offered us an apartment—her mother had passed away, and the place was vacant—and a client-friend lent us a second car.

And that's how it came to be that we moved into a retirement home for two months. I won't lie; it was a very pleasant apartment, and if it hadn't been for the emergency alert button by the front door, you wouldn't necessarily know you were in a long-term-care home. Strangely, no one questioned our being there, even though we were forty years younger than the youngest resident.

It was around this time that my energy started waning. Between running my Pilates studio, overseeing the house renovation, and studying for the real estate exam, I'm not sure how I made it through some days. As time progressed, I felt worse and worse. It finally reached a point where I couldn't take it anymore. I went to a walk-in clinic and demanded blood tests. I was met with the dreaded and now well-known response, "Oh, it's probably just stress. You're fine."

"No, I'm not fine, I am gaining weight unexplainably, I feel like shit, and I want to know why. Also, my dad has high cholesterol, and my mother died of cancer." That did it. The magic "C" word and suddenly the doctor took me seriously. Less than twenty-four hours later I got a panicked phone call from the clinic: my iron levels were so low they weren't appearing on the test.

Six months later I had ten iron injections, which stained my skin a dark rust color for the next two years. By that time, we had sold the house and moved back to Yaletown. It turns out that quiet residential streets are not my cup of tea.

A year later when I told my new doctor I still wasn't feeling well and that my sister was diagnosed with hypothyroidism, he glanced at my blood tests, didn't show them to me, looked me straight in the eye, and said, "You're fine."

Do you know what it feels like to be told, "You're fine," over and over again? After a while you do begin to think it's you, that you are quite simply going mad.

Arriving in Poland, that feeling didn't magically go away, but the excitement of our new situation allows me to put my health on the back burner for a little while longer.

And that's how the first part of our year in Warsaw passes. It's life, but it is starting to move along nicely. That job I mentioned has panned out, and I am now working for OpenBooks, a start-up funded by Michał Kicinski, a well-known player in the video-game world. The job consists of my writing copy that will be attractive to American audiences. Canada doesn't really count, so I get busy dropping all the *u*'s and shortening the Polish text. Poles have a tendency to overexplain; what takes one sentence in English takes a paragraph in Polish. And of course I was making all the text generally more punchy.

Except my efforts do not go over. Again and again I'm told that they can't "feel" my text. What does this even mean? What exactly do you want to feel? We are building a pay-what-you-want website for books. My copy is straightforward. I look over the letter being sent to authors who are mainly in the United States and put together a "welcome to our website" text as well as a "how it all works" section. I'm still not exactly sure what they want to feel. Do they want to laugh or cry, or maybe both?

By the end of my first week in my new job, I'm sobbing. Things get worse. The guy managing the project seems to be more interested in our process than our productivity. When I announce that I've gotten a well-known book reviewer onboard, he has no idea what I'm talking about. What he wants is a detailed process of how it will work. Then the "lawyer," I use the term loosely because I'm certain that this is the kid's first job, can't read his way through an English contract and has to enlist my husband, who is not a lawyer but has experience with legal documents, to help him.

Not only that, but because they are so afraid of . . . well, actually, that's just it, I'm not 100 percent sure what they are afraid of. . . . The lawyer is given too much control, and everyone is forced to sign non-disclosure agreements, even the potential authors we want to host on the site. It's crazy. And I don't have the heart to tell them no one cares enough about their project to steal it.

In his work, too, my husband comes across this same kind of obsessive secrecy. On several occasions he witnesses first-time beginner entrepreneurs requiring major US investors to sign multiple-page NDAs before even disclosing what the project is, never mind providing any details. It seems to be a thing and happens over and over again. I can only guess that this is some sort of leftover communist police-state paranoia, which was justified then but reads differently now.

A lightning trip to Toronto in March to meet our new nephew helps us with a reset, and we come back to Poland with a renewed spark. One day, we meet up with our friend who saved me from my initial food meltdown and learn that one of his jobs is to teach English. We spend some time commiserating about the differences between British English, which is the go-to in Poland; American En-glish, which is the "native speaker" English everyone seems to want to use; and Canadian English, a mashup of the two, with which we are both familiar. We also despair that many companies seem to

accept their English copy when it is "good enough" instead of properly written. An idea is born, and we decide to cofound a native-En-
glish copywriting company called SayWhat.pl.

We are all excited, but when we go to register our business, almost everyone warns us that it will be horrible, that the process will
be unbearable, and so on. There seems to be a built-up perception
of what horrible things might just happen. Fine, so we prepare ourselves. There are pep talks, we make sure to have a good meal and
lots of coffee. Finally, we are ready. What happens next is disappointing. After all, we were gearing up for a fight. The person behind
the desk is very helpful, even fixing some of our mistakes, and before
we know it we are done. The whole thing takes, well, minutes.

Native English speakers are highly sought after, so setting up an
English-language company seems to be an ideal move. I'm not always sure if people are looking for American or British English; either way, not once does anyone ask for Canadian English. I, however,
am in a good position, because I can write in all three styles. I am
stopped on the street and in cafés with requests to teach English. It's
difficult to explain to people that I am in no way, shape, or form an
English teacher, nor do I want to be.

Unfortunately, even though we have eternal Canadian optimism,
our business doesn't go very far because of a small but persistent
problem. We are constantly outbid. There are many people who have
ESL—they simply pass a test, then proceed to teach and write or
translate English passably and for very little money, much less than I
would ever dream of charging. It's not proper English, but it is good
enough that no one wants to pay more for English-language services.
The businesses that settle for "good enough" are simply unwilling to
change. We come across this problem over and over again until we

both decide that we've had enough.

Somewhere during all this, Easter is upon us. This is not a holiday I have ever celebrated, save for painting eggs with our Polish live-in nanny, Pani Irena, and I have completely forgotten about Easter until one day when I see a little girl skipping down the sidewalk ahead of her parents, carrying a doily-covered Easter basket. I freak out. I have never seen anything like this, although Pawel assures me this is done in Canada as well. Now I begin to notice other changes, including multicolored Easter palms at every flower kiosk.

Pawel has become my cultural translator. Before we married I told him that Easter was a holiday I wasn't prepared to celebrate, so naturally here, now, we are both wary of dinner invitations. My aversion isn't abstract either. A friend once invited me to Easter service at her church, where we packed ourselves into a pew, and I was half listening when I heard the priest say, "We must forgive our fellow men, the Jews who killed Jesus."

Did I just hear what I think I heard? My friend turned to me in shock and mouthed, "I had no idea. I'm so sorry."

No idea? There was no way this sermon was suddenly different from previous years. I thought this was simply the first time she'd heard what was being said. I looked around the room and saw people nodding in agreement. No one spoke up, no one shifted uncomfortably, no one looked around. At that moment I decided for good that Easter was a holiday I want no part of.

Poland is a study in contrasts. One day we are sitting at a French-themed café on Nowy Świat having fresh baguette sandwiches when the usual city noises change. There is an ominous chanting. A crowd of mostly young men with a police escort is making their way down the street. The pink and blue buildings fade against their black and green flags. Some of the men wear scarves covering their faces, many are shaved bald, and almost all of them wear bomber jackets and combat boots. This is the Polish Nationalist-Socialist Party marching proudly in the streets, aching to silence more than one voice.

Just down the road is Mysia Street—part public walkway with designer floral shops and clothing stores, part political statement with the free speech memorial sitting center stage, taking over the entire space. The huge black strip ending in a flick that rises several meters into the air is meant to represent the line that a censor's pen would make during communist times.

Walk a little farther and you wind up at Plac Zbawiciela, where a giant rainbow is displayed, the same rainbow that gets destroyed every year. Its very existence is an affront to the militant wing of the family-values crowd. It's a very busy square with a giant roundabout. On one corner is a large church flanked by restaurants. One of them is Charlotte, a dreamy bistro. Pawel says this is the reason I wanted to move to Poland in the first place. He's not completely wrong. I fell in love with this spot the very first time I saw it. In the summer Charlotte is so busy, their tables spill out onto the square. For breakfast you can order a bread and pastry basket with jars of fresh honey and chocolate. Trust me, there is nothing better, and it's the one breakfast I would break my gluten-free diet for. In the evening the square is teeming with people all out to have a good time.

Midyear of my first year living in Poland, I find out that you can walk into a clinic and just ask them to give you blood tests. My Canadian mind has a hard time wrapping its head around this new development. "So you are saying that I can just walk into the clinic by my home and ask for whatever blood tests I want?" I repeat while my husband's aunt laughs. The next day I walk into Centrum Damiana with my passport for ID in hand. I pay the equivalent of about forty-five dollars and leave after a full set of blood tests and the promise that my results will be available within the next few hours. My mind is blown. I have just come from a country that touts itself as being at the forefront of medical services, and yet my medical records aren't readily available to me, and doctors are vague with their responses. My home country is a reactive approach to medicine rather than a proactive one.

But Poland is the opposite? Who knew?

I have no idea what to expect, but I'm pleasantly surprised. The building is spotless. It doesn't look or feel much different than a medical building I'd find in Canada. There is a reason for this. In a nutshell, Poland has a two-tiered medical system. NFZ is the government-sponsored side, and it's not great. Then there are the private clinics, open to anyone who has the money to use them. Think of them as being à la carte centers. While someone might not be able to afford an expensive procedure, taking a simple blood test is likely within reach.

Two days later I am sitting in a sunny office in front of an endocrinologist clad in a white lab coat. Yes, two days. No, not two months but two days later, and with an apology that they couldn't get me in sooner. I am in shock, but not as much shock as the endocrinologist who can't believe I'm not taking medication. She peers at me over her gold wire-rimmed glasses, "But in Canada they didn't give you any medication? In Canada?" she splutters repeatedly, much to my amusement. She can't quite believe it when I say no.

So begins my road back to health. I am immediately sent for a slew of tests, including a thyroid ultrasound. If I need something, there is a doctor who is going to help me.

This whole process will take about a year and a half before I finally settle on an endocrinologist I can work with long term. In any case, the changes in my health are almost immediate.

Feeling more myself, I start looking around for business opportunities, and the truth is that I would love to buy a place in Poland that we could rent out. Even though I've been dealing with health issues, and Pawel has been detoxing from a very stressful few years, we are still excited about opportunities. It must be our general enthusiasm or our willingness to think big, but one of the first things the owner of Vincent's, our favorite breakfast place, said to us when he found out we were from Canada, was "Ahhhh, la poutine!" and we immediately started making plans to procure the necessary ingredients. That spurs the idea of opening a poutinerie in Old Town Warsaw.

We are convinced this is a business that cannot fail. Poutine is close enough to Polish comfort food, which consists of potatoes and meats. There are dozens of hole-in-the-wall waffle places with giant lineups. A favorite pastime for people in Warsaw is to go for a walk, and a great place to walk is along the Royal Route and Old Town. A mix of cobblestones and sidewalks, stores filled with art and jewelry, restaurants, coffee shops, and a bunch of churches line the street. Then you arrive at the edge of Old Town, and the square opens up in greeting. On the right is the Royal Castle, now a museum, and on the left are the narrow cobblestone streets that wind their way to the center of Old Town. In the middle is a large square, usually packed with tourists and locals. Balloon sellers call out to children, and rubber-band-powered plastic toys fly high up into the air. Even on a normal day it feels like a party.

During the summer months, the road leading up to this spot is closed to traffic, and people spill out onto the street enjoying themselves, enjoying life. During the holiday season this part of town becomes a winter wonderland. All of which is a long-winded way of saying, what is better than just walking? Walking with a snack. It could be a coffee or a waffle doused in powdered sugar or a cup of the famous liquid chocolate from Wedel. Now I ask you, wouldn't a poutinerie fit right in here? It would!

I continue to look around for opportunities while working at OpenBooks, the start-up, and we settle into a slower-paced routine. We are used to the North American rat race, where people live to work. If you aren't busy, you aren't being productive. Here, we are shocked when the city seems to go into slow motion as soon as the weather warms. The sun doesn't set until late, and the whole city is either outside or heading to cottages. Every day feels like a celebration.

Sometime during that summer, along with one of my coworkers, we decide it would be fun to produce a range of fitness T-shirts with slogans like Last2Quit, iStretch, and Effortlessly Chic, and head to Łódź on a recon mission. Roughly 130 kilometers (80 miles) southwest of Warsaw, Łódź was a textile-industry metropolis before the war but it is still the place to go when looking for textiles and manufacturing. We have an appointment at one of the many clothing fulfillment centers and get fabric samples and the cost for embroidering our slogans.

Afterward, we take a walk through this town, which is a mix of postwar rundown brick buildings infused with a strong dose of hipster everything. Prewar factories have been turned into chic shops, and crumbling brick buildings seamlessly blend with ultramodern glass-and-metal structures. What was once a bustling multiethnic city is now a city that is searching for its identity. There is a stark contrast from one street to the next, some bustling shopping districts, and others displaying rundown, overgrown shells of what once was. I regret not spending more time in Łódź. "Hmm, maybe we could get a place here?" I muse to Pawel as we stare at an abandoned building. True, true—real estate is one of my weaknesses.

On the first day of August, we are wandering up our street when we notice an unusually large group of people congregating on the sidewalk near the roundabout, where two main city arteries meet. Rondo de Gaulle'a, or the Charles de Gaulle Roundabout, is big, noisy, and on any given day backed up with cars, buses, and streetcars. Communist-style gray buildings surround it, and in the very middle sits a huge palm tree art installation, *Greetings from Jerusalem*, a tribute to Warsaw's deep connection to its lost Jewish community. It is worth noting that the palm stands in the center of the intersection of Aleje Jerozolimkie and Nowy Świat, which translates to Jerusalem Avenue and New World. We walk over to check out what's happening. The air is tense, and it's unusually quiet. We can sense something is brewing, but we have no idea what is going on. Pixie is in full flight mode and trying desperately to get home. Then an eerie silence descends on the street. It's quiet—and by that I mean not a sound.

All of a sudden someone calls out, and a bunch of kids dressed in period costumes run out into the street carrying flares. Within seconds the air is dense with smoke, and then all the stopped cars start one long uninterrupted honk.

One minute later, conversations resume, and everyone moves

along like nothing has happened. We are still standing, completely in shock. We are certain Pixie is considering moving back to Canada and away from the madness. Later that evening, after a little digging, Pawel figures out that the August first is the Warsaw Uprising Memorial Day.

The following year we know what to expect and leave Pixie at home. The minute of remembrance ends, and we resume our conversation in English when suddenly a kid, likely a student at Chopin University, runs up to us in a panic. He's very polite, but his voice is shaking. We can absolutely relate to his fear. He's an Asian foreign exchange student who is wondering if World War III has broken out and if he needs to be running to his embassy. Pawel calms him down, and we go our separate ways.

CHAPTER 9

MOVING AND ADAPTING: UNPACKING THE HARD PART

While I can't really understand what all my family went through, I do understand the act of starting over. When Pawel and I announced that we were going to move to Poland, a lot of our friends were shocked. Even after, they couldn't understand how we managed to do it. The truth is, because we've moved so often, I can pack up our place in a day, a day-and-a-half at most. Every time I move, I can't help thinking about my mother and grandmother—my babcia, who took only what was necessary, including a pair of heels. Moving is tiring and scary, but it's also thrilling, filled with opportunity. In fact, when it comes to the actual buying and selling of homes, my mother is truly my inspiration.

As a young girl, I moved with my family from Sweden to Canada with a few months in Germany in between. I was young, so I don't remember this in great detail, but I think the experience must have imprinted itself on my psyche. When my parents and I finally joined my uncle KT in Canada, we moved into a two-story apartment on Elgin Street just north of Toronto. After that we moved closer to KT, living on Porterfield Crescent, then came Holm Crescent, and finally the infamous house with the blue garage, on Bathurst Street.

When Pawel and I moved 4,362 kilometers (2710 miles) west to Vancouver as young adults, I continued that trend, moving every few years. First, we lived on Nelson Street, then Haro, then Richards and East Tenth, and finally on Mainland. We couldn't stay put in one place. In Poland, we moved three times in four years. I don't know what compels me to move. One day I wake up and really see my surroundings, and I know it's time for a change. By this time, I've usually made all the changes to my home that I can afford, I know the neighborhood, and I'm no longer inspired. In other words, it's time to go.

I do know I get this from my mother. As the story goes, she sold our flat in Sweden to a couple she met in the parking garage. Even if we weren't actively looking for a new home, one of her favorite things to do was to take me house hunting for mansions in subdivisions we couldn't dream of affording. On one such adventure, she quietly muttered, "Don't say anything, follow my lead," as she sweetly looked at the unsuspecting agent and mispronounced our last name, so it sounded like Teperman. The Tepermans were a prominent demolition family in Toronto. Right away the agent snapped to attention and began personally walking us through the home. This game was fun! I caught on fast, and when I began lamenting the pink walls of a very large, very nice bedroom that no one could complain about, he was desperately wishing he had paint swatches to show me.

So hang on a minute. You mean I can just pretend to be someone I'm not? We weren't really lying, not exactly. My mother, with her Polish accent, had simply mumbled our last name, and neither one of us had explicitly corrected the agent. That's okay, right? No one was getting hurt. Was it our fault that he misunderstood?

Is it any wonder that seeing my mother in action was one of the events that propelled me toward acting? I was an extremely shy kid growing up. No one who knows me now believes it, but when my younger sister was born I basically stopped speaking and dropped out of nursery school. That only lasted a few months before I was so bored that I begged to go back, but not speaking in public continued. Even now, if I'm tired or feeling particularly self-conscious, I'll clam up and stand on the fringes of a party.

One day at age thirteen or so, I decided I'd had enough of being shy, so I signed up for Young People's Theater classes. There I was, by myself, riding the subway into downtown Toronto every Saturday morning. My instructor had worked with Keanu Reeves, so naturally she was the coolest person on the planet. Slowly, over time, I managed to come out of my shell. I also learned a lot about acting in the process, namely that I was definitely going "into the theater" when I got older. My leap into this unfamiliar world worked. I currently hold a degree in film, I've been in plays, and I've worked behind the scenes. Most importantly, I'm not afraid to try something new.

When I landed in Vancouver in April 2001 at two o'clock in the morning, Pawel—then my fiancé—was there to greet me and bring me back to our new apartment. He had already been living there for over a month working for EA, a multinational gaming company. As with many tech industry companies, the employees were kept busy from morning until night and occasionally on weekends.

"Huh, what? Where are you going?" I asked at 7 AM when he kissed me goodbye.

"Work. I'll call you later."

Pretty soon, I found myself almost completely alone. For days, I would take long walks around the seawall as I tried to get my bearings and wrap my head around this new situation. This was my first

time living far away from my family and not knowing anyone in a
city. It made for a very lonely existence, so much so that I wound up
gaining weight and catching a nasty case of bronchitis. But not being
able to sit still, I quickly found a retail job. It wasn't glamorous or
even remotely interesting, but it was something to do each day.

At the time I didn't know a lot of my mother's story or either of
my grandmothers' for that matter. Now, thinking back, I can see that
we are all connected by our resourcefulness. While comfort may be
nice, we don't count on it. Put any one of us in a new situation, and
our survival instincts kick in. Of course I have never had to survive
exile, but I can honestly say that those first few months in Vancouver
when I didn't have anyone to turn to only made me stronger.

My first day working at the beauty counter at Shoppers Drug
Mart wasn't very memorable, but over time I found my groove. I do
like cosmetics and beauty products in general, so being around them
all day was bearable. Then one day, while helping an elderly woman
half my size find blue eyeliner, she suddenly looked up and asked me
if I was a dancer. I proudly said I was, and she replied that I looked
like one and that she had been a dancer as well.

That got my wheels turning. I couldn't put my finger on it exactly,
but I knew this woman. Upon further investigation, I found that she
had been coming into that same drugstore for quite a while, and she
always bought the same blue eyeliner.

Finally, one day, while we were discussing makeup, she told me
her name, Rosemary, not a name you hear every day. Then, curi-
ously, she mentioned that she left Vancouver as a child and danced
in Europe. Then it hit me. This must be the Rosemary Deveson from
the memoir *Dancing for de Basil* that I had recently and obsessively

read. She had joined Colonel De Basil's Ballet Russe in 1938 and had quickly become one of my heroes. Of course I had googled her, and I knew she was living in Vancouver. So naturally I almost died when I connected the dots, and when she looked me up and down and said, "You must be a dancer," it took everything I had not to jump across and hug her and then move in with her.

There I was, standing in front of a wisp of a woman I'm guessing 90 percent of Vancouver didn't know existed. At that moment, all that mattered was that we both knew that once dance becomes a part of you, once its essence latches onto your soul and flows through your bloodstream, it will never let you go. I regret not getting her to autograph my copy of her book before she passed away.

Other than that incredible encounter, the drugstore job was not for me, so I set my sights on the local gym. Without much experience as a personal trainer, I boldly walked in one day to ask for a job. The manager asked what I wanted to do, and I responded with "Well, ideally, I'd like to be a personal trainer, but at this point I'll wash your floors." He laughed, and a week later I was installed at the front desk. It wasn't a bad job, and before I knew it, I had expanded their Pilates program from one class a week to eight and, as a result, I'd outgrown the gym.

From there I went to work at a Pilates studio before opening my own in West Vancouver. While Pawel built his career, rising through the ranks of EA, I ran my studio, flipped houses, worked briefly at a car dealership, and finally wound up working for a real estate developer. My studio was a great starting point, with some very interesting clients, but ultimately I wanted more out of life, and I was too curious and ambitious to keep one job.

I think that moving and adapting is in my genes. It's tough to

explain, but I am happiest when starting new projects or jobs. I may
have already mentioned that I am not fond of the word *commitment*.
My life is not unlike my approach to real estate. Anytime I feel that
my life is becoming steady or predictable, it's time for a change.

There were stressors, though, and I struggled with how to handle
them exactly. At the time, for instance, I didn't realize just how unhealthy the North American relationship with healthy food really
is. Of course, I'll never forget the moment when I was thirteen, and
a close friend of the family exclaimed, "Oh, you've gained so much
weight." Like anyone should say that to a teenager, ever. I had been
away for a month that summer, living in an unpleasant situation with
other family friends, and I was thirteen. My body was going through
all sorts of changes. Fast-forward to when I was dancing. Then food,
along with sore muscles, leg extensions, and flexibility, was a constant topic of discussion.

Working at a gym and owning a Pilates studio also made body
image a big part of my life. When you train professional athletes or
actors like Penelope Cruz, you naturally compare yourself to them.
When a gym member looked into my basket at the grocery store to
see what food I was buying, I was so embarrassed that I changed
grocery stores.

Another time, I was out with friends when we decided to stop
for a snack at a trendy Yaletown restaurant. As we discussed food
possibilities, the waiter came over and said, "Remember, ladies,
nothing tastes as good as skinny feels." Needless to say, we promptly
ordered four waters, and he did not get a tip that night. I don't think
I've ever been out for food with friends without having to listen to
an entire conversation about how many calories are in each item,

and how much exercising everyone is going to do after the meal. It's exhausting.

So, yes, our time in Vancouver was marked by personal successes, but it was also shot through with stressful events and attitudes that everyone seemed to take for granted.

Now you can understand why, in Warsaw, the first time I see a girl, walking down the street on her own eating an ice cream, I stop and stare unabashedly. Here is a young woman who isn't walking toward anyone, she isn't posing for a photograph—no, she is simply enjoying an ice cream. How is this even possible? Does she not care that everyone can see her? I see women ordering dessert after a meal, women having something sweet with their coffee. And they actually eat what they order. What is this world coming to?

The shift from Canada to Poland is filled with changes in customs, from momentous things like women eating in the open to everyday courtesies and habits that range from the mundane to the revolting.

"Dzień dobry, kto ostatni?" is the familiar singsong call heard every few seconds in any given waiting room in Poland. "Good day, who is next?" is quite confusing if you aren't expecting it, but it's the way everyone polices themselves as to who is next in line. Basically, you step into the waiting room, do a once-over, give a general "good day," then ask who the last person is. Everyone looks up, murmurs a hello, then someone speaks up, and says, "Me." Almost always, this is followed by a countdown of everyone who is waiting. As I write this, the process doesn't seem that weird, but think about it, how many times have you really acknowledged everyone in the waiting room at a doctor's or a dentist's waiting room? It's all done in a businesslike manner; it's not personal, you just need to know who arrived last.

Now for the disgusting part.

I don't think anyone thinks it's okay or right, but I've also noticed that no one makes a big deal of random men relieving themselves on trees.

I don't know if it has anything to do with the widespread availability of alcohol and the functional or semifunctional—depending on how you look at it—alcoholism that abounds, but it's very common to see this urinating in public. The first time I witness this, I'm shocked and disgusted. And maybe that says something about Canadians being prudish, which we are. But I'm even more surprised that no one else seems to notice. During our four and a half years in Warsaw, I see more men pissing in public than I ever thought I'd see.

One day, I'm walking down the street minding my own business when I see a woman rushing her son. "Quickly, quickly," she hurries him while helping him unzip his pants, then stands back as he relieves himself on a tree. I estimate the kid to be about seven, so, old enough to hold it in for a few minutes. From where I am standing on Kopernika at the corner of Ordynacka, I can see two coffee shops and two restaurants, and I know there are many others just around the corner. We are not in some kind of toilet desert, with no hope of coming across a toilet for hours. We are standing in the middle of the city, and the grouping of trees is in the middle of a small patch of grass filled with pigeons and dog poo.

At least the girl I see who is peeing between two cars one night has the decency to be thoroughly embarrassed before she runs off with her friends.

The other puzzling behavior is smashing the bottle of alcohol after you've finished drinking from it. The upshot is exactly what you would imagine: Glass is everywhere on the street. On one occasion we are sitting outside enjoying an early morning. A bride and her groom are sharing a bottle of vodka since weddings are all-night events. Just as I muse about how nice the couple looks, the groom flings the bottle back over his head. It smashes at our feet, and we are sprayed with droplets of alcohol.

I don't feel bad for cussing them out, but what a way to start your new life: someone telling you that you are an asshole.

Still, even with these unsavory bits, Pawel and I do our best to adapt, and to inject ourselves into society. We're not here as international observers. We want to integrate and learn all we can. So, for example, now that I have been in Poland for just about a year and my health is stabilizing, I am finally ready to start taking ballet lessons again.

The first thing I do is google ballet classes in Warsaw. That goes nowhere fast. Apparently, there are no ballet classes for adults in Warsaw. But that's not possible in such a metropolitan city. So, how to find them? It doesn't occur to me that I need to Google in Polish, balet. The same thing happens when I try to find a yoga class. Who knew that Yoga is spelled "Joga"?

One evening, we come across a music and dance store. I'm thrilled but also silently freaking out because I'm still not used to speaking Polish with strangers. After looking at the pretty pink ballet things, I make myself approach a nice-looking saleslady. "Umm, is there a ballet school anywhere around here?"

She looks at me as if I've lost my mind and points down the street. We are literally standing on Plac Teatralny, aka Theater Square. The National Theater, a grand building spanning an entire block, is right in front of the store, and next door is the National Ballet School that offers evening classes for adults. I take a deep breath and drag Pawel into the school.

The building is imposing, to say the least, with marble steps and grand red velvet curtains. From the chandelier to the two grand staircases, I'm both terrified and in love at the same time. Pixie proves to be the perfect ice breaker, as the ladies in the office are dog lovers. As it turns out, I have nothing to worry about. Pani Maria is sincere and welcoming and tells me that I can start right away, which I vow to do, but after the holiday.

Pani Maria looks like a dancer, everything about her screams "dancer," and I'm immediately smitten. Her hair is pulled back, her back is straight, shoulders down, showing off her long neck. But it's more than just how she holds herself. She speaks with authority and the kind of confidence you only see from people who have spent their life on the stage. Of course, I, too, am a dancer; of course, there is room for me. She tells me not to purchase any specific clothing, it's fine if I have my ballet slippers and a leotard, she simply wants me to come to class, the sacred place for any dancer. I immediately feel like I can belong.

The classrooms, too, are breathtaking, nothing like I am used to. Big windows overlook Theater Square. Each room is a soft pastel color. The warm light of chandeliers illuminates the space. Photographs of dancers grace the hallowed halls.

Now all I need is the nerve to show up.

Weddings and funerals are events that bring people together and separate them at the same time. I had a chance to see both, and to realize that my reactions to both were pretty similar. What that says about me, well, I leave that with you to contemplate.

Living on Smolna 10 and a year later Smolna 18 means Pawel and

I are the lucky uninvited participants in weekend weddings at Villa Foksal. What I mean is that there are weddings there on Fridays and Saturdays most nights from May until September. Polish weddings are not like any North American weddings I have attended.

A Polish wedding is an all-night party, which is fun when you are a guest, less fun when you are not. Villa Foksal is a premium ornate mansion with red accents, set in the park where we take our morning coffee and croissants, in the center of Warsaw. The weddings are lavish affairs, and it only takes a few sleepless nights before we realize that the DJ doesn't stray from their playlist, starting with uptown funk fairly early during the festivities and Cher during the early dawn. My favorite is Leonard Cohen's "Dance Me to the End of Love," usually played, apparently, for the first dance. I can't help but wonder, does the DJ not know the meaning of this song? The song refers to Nazis marching Jews to the gas chamber—not the kind of thing you'd want at your wedding, which is supposed to be one of the happiest days of your life. Is this merely a language barrier? I hope so.

These weddings are a culture shock for Pawel and me. Bad enough that they last all night. That much noise in a residential area would never fly in Toronto or Vancouver. After a year of sleepless summer nights, we join forces with local neighbors to call the police. As expected, nothing much happens, but at least we did something, and that makes us feel better.

Then, finally, we get our very own wedding invitations. My cousin Ela, Zuzanna's younger sister, is marrying her longtime boyfriend. My father also happens to be in town, so we all go together. Ela is a beautiful bride, and her wedding one of the more traditional I have attended. The other contender would have to be my brother-in-law's, held at a Polish Catholic church in downtown Toronto. By contrast, my husband and I were wed in an intimate, immediate-family-only ceremony at Toronto's city hall and threw a huge party for all our friends.

By this point, my wedding was old news, and as I learned, a little unorthodox since we abstained from most traditions. At Ela's, we have some trepidation; churches aren't exactly my favorite place, but we are there to support family. The guests at this modern Catholic church file in, the ceremony starts, and a few minutes in, I am already tuning out. I stand when everyone else stands and sit when they sit, but the priest's droning is meaningless to me until he says, "You aren't truly married unless you've been married in the church."

I glance over at my husband, whose eyes are as glassy as mine. "So does this mean we aren't official? Good to know." The party, at a local resort, lasts all night. When we finally retire to our rooms at two or three in the morning, everyone is shocked that we are leaving early.

A traditional wedding is exactly what Pawel and I wanted to avoid. We'd already been living in Vancouver for months, so even during the planning stages we were clear that we wanted to do things our way. My husband did stomp on the glass as per the Jewish tradition, but our reading was from *A Midsummer Night's Dream*, I'm fairly sure that Santa Claus was the officiant, and we did not have a first dance or a wedding cake. What we did have was a kick-ass party for our friends and family. The space, an old Toronto courthouse with a dramatic staircase covered in twinkle lights, held intimate tables where people could nibble on finger foods, and a huge dessert table complete with champagne truffles from Teuscher Chocolates of Switzerland, which a friend had individually wrapped for us the night before. When my father in-law ran up to me during the party and asked, "Is that all the food you ordered?" I replied, "If people get hungry, we'll order pizza."

A few days later my mother-in-law informed me that their friends had not had a good time, because we hadn't had a sit-down dinner. I shrugged. I knew she was upset because we hadn't implemented any Catholic traditions. Also, I had chosen not to take their last name. Their holding back was obvious, as in, no one from their side even stood to speak. Pawel's father had asked me if he even had to. My answer? "If you don't want to, then I don't want you to."

In contrast to Pawel's family, my father gave a jubilant speech welcoming Pawel to the family, and then jokingly tried to sell my sister off for a Mini Cooper, so at least my side had a good time. No matter, really, since Pawel and I were returning to Vancouver. The point was, we had the wedding we wanted, and we paid for it ourselves.

Funerals are the other events that either bring people together or tear them apart—or do some of both. But a funeral isn't always possible, is it? My father could not attend his father's funeral in Poland in 1979, when the family estrangement and the Iron Curtain were still firmly intact. It wasn't until 2017 when my dad was visiting his brother in Warsaw, and was determined to visit the Wichrzycki family grave, that he and I went together—for me, a first, thanks to the aforementioned family estrangement.

We set off for the Northern Municipal Cemetery, one of Warsaw's big old cemeteries. The day is cold and rainy, and generally awful as we arrive at the entrance to the cemetery, where we stop at a kiosk and purchase yellow flowers, a candle in a covered glass lamp, and matches. As we enter through the big iron gates, a black cat darts across our path. Naturally, we burst out laughing. How perfect. Finding the grave in the vast cemetery is a challenge, let alone navigating the overgrown paths in the pouring rain, until we realize that the hand-drawn map my dad is holding is backward.

I thought this whole thing would be depressing, but for a cemetery, it's actually kind of homey. There's so much history here. I can't help but think, would I have the right to be buried here? In Polish you often hear, "No bo wypada," which translates roughly to "Because it's expected." Would this family accept me no questions asked or because it would be the proper thing to do? Back in Canada my mother's grave is solitary; here there is family, but it's a foreign one. The family grave, when we finally find the large rectangular marble slab, has several names on it. Then it hits me. The only person buried here who I have actually met is Wandeczka, my grandmother. It's a bittersweet moment with sentimental potential that we completely ruin, my dad and I, thanks to our wet matches. We look around for help, but there are no candles on nearby graves that we can borrow. When I see a nearby funeral procession, filled with mourners smoking cigarettes, I nudge him forward. "Dad, go ask them if you can borrow a lighter."

"What am I supposed to do? Chase them down and ask for a light?" he says. We burst out laughing.

My dad and I are like that. We even managed a few inappropriate laughs during my mother's funeral, in March 1995. The first was when a friend of the family decided to admonish my dad for not burying my mother in a Jewish cemetery. I mean, really, who says that? "I'd like to be buried next to my wife one day" was his retort. Then, while we were greeting people, my dad turned to me and asked, "Who is the old Jew whose hand I just shook?"

I'm all of nineteen at the time, numb at the loss of my mother, and still, I can't help but crack up. "Ummm . . . that was Pawel's dad," I say, "and he's not a Jew."

Clearly, my father and I should never be left alone together during a solemn moment.

CHAPTER 10

MY MOTHER: MARYSIA'S STORY

The tricky part about telling my mother's story is that I didn't know her very well. I really only knew her when I was a kid. I lost her in my first year of university, so we never had conversations as two adults. And I only know bits and pieces about her childhood. Of course she told us stories about growing up, but they were the kind of stories you tell your kids. Short episodes, nothing too intense or personal. She died just as I was getting to that age when I could have learned something of substance.

I know that her parents, especially her father, Fryderyk, were strict about her grades, always comparing her and her brother to other kids, as in, "So-and-so got an A+, how come you only got an A?" kind of thing. She used to tell me a story about how her dad once saw her playing hooky, only he didn't recognize her at the time, then back home she heard him talking about the "hooligan youth" he'd just seen.

I love the story about the first day of school, how it found her sitting in the hall next to the principal's office. Every year on the first day of class Marysia would get kicked out because the teacher thought she had dyed her hair. Soon her mother would show up to confirm that the mane of thick red locks on her daughter's head were in fact her own. Again. She didn't even care. It used to bother her, but now it didn't faze her. She was used to the routine.

On Warsaw's Solariego Street, the family occupied an exclusive ground-floor flat with beautiful flower-filled gardens. They had a maid and a personal chauffeur, and they rubbed shoulders with prominent Party officials. On the other hand, the government didn't give them much money: Fryderyk's position was not about financial remuneration but rather about privileges. Those Party officials held all the diplomatic passports.

It's those passports that allowed the family to travel widely. In other words, the family was dependent on the government allowing them to leave the country. On one vacation they sailed from Dubrovnik to Italy, which they did in fourth class, well belowdecks. When Marysia's father, Minister Topolski, was called to join the captain at his table, all Fryderyk had were ragged pants and a few T-shirts. Incidentally, that was the last time Paula would travel anywhere without packing at least one nice outfit.

My guess is that the family's best times were when they traveled. For one thing, it was in summers that they were free to be themselves. No wonder they loved vacation time. A month kayaking on lakes, hiking in the mountains, sailing on a colleague's boat. On vacation, they were just another family, enjoying time together. And knowing my grandmother, she would have packed cucumber sandwiches and hard-boiled eggs to stow in their backpacks and munch on whenever they felt hungry.

One summer, Fryderyk was particularly excited to show them all Mohelnice in Morawy (Müglitz Moravia, Czech Republic), waxing on about the red roofs, the colorful buildings around market square,

the park, the church, and his onetime home in great detail. I imagine
they all had a great laugh when Fryderyk admitted that it all seemed
a lot bigger when he was a kid.

One August took them to Vienna for an official event Fryderyk
needed to attend, and they stayed at the Hotel Edinburgh, a tiny
hole-in-the-wall inn with no running water. Fryderyk had told the
chauffeur to pick him up next door, at the Golden Lamm, but unfortunately the driver came early. The family was startled when a
rather flustered receptionist knocked on the door declaring, "Your
excellency, the car has arrived." Fryderyk was still in his underwear,
washing his hands, KT pouring water from a jug.

So, yes, contradictions. If they roughed it on the road, in Warsaw
the family enjoyed certain luxuries. It wasn't unusual for the official
driver to pick Marysia up from school whenever her parents were
away, which happened often. Fryderyk traveled frequently for work,
whether to Moscow or Katowice, or some other place with coal
mines. As a respected doctor of hematology, Paula attended medical
symposiums and traveled for work as well, although the doctor's life
was far from glamorous. Reality took its toll. Here is an account from
my grandmother about doing rounds in the emergency room:

> I hated it. In Warsaw, there were still a lot of unexploded
> ordinances and often injured children came to the hos-
> pital. I was terribly nervous because I was afraid that
> when several of them came at once, I would not know
> who to take care of first. I remember that once, when
> I was finishing my duty a paramedic brought in a child
> with blood all over its face. I did not know whether the
> child lost its sight. Fortunately, it turned out that it did
> not, but it was a terrible experience. I learned then to
> smoke cigarettes.

Shortly thereafter my grandmother began her final doctorate studies at the Institute of Hematology. My favorite story, one that I would beg to hear over and over again, was from when she was on rotation in the psychiatric ward. She was reading in a small room reserved for doctors and staff when suddenly a woman rushed in and started attacking. "Where are my red slippers?!" the woman yelled at Paula. "You stole my red slippers!"

Some orderlies quickly removed the woman, and my grandmother never saw her again, but she made an impact on us. The end of the story has always remained a mystery, but we spent quite a bit of time talking about the possibility of her having schizophrenia or some other mental health illness. My grandmother admitted that this was a terrifying moment for her and one of the reasons she specialized in hematology.

Then there was the dark side to the culture: this horrible, constant weight of the past that was never talked about. Anti-Semitism after the war was rampant. People actually blamed the Jews for the destruction the Nazis wreaked in Poland.

What are your options then if you're a Jewish family? Let's just say that Marysia was raised in a privileged household by parents who were great at keeping secrets. I'm fairly positive they didn't sit around at night talking about lice infestations, sickness, poverty, pogroms, and miscarriages, let alone the Holocaust.

After all, neither my mother nor her brother even knew that they were Jewish until they learned it on the playground at school. Then, somehow, she got hold of a Star of David, which apparently she also chose to wear. I own a Star of David necklace that I have never worn. I love it, but I have always questioned what kind of attention I would be drawing to myself.

Why was my mother comfortable wearing hers as a teenager but did not wear one as an adult? I can only imagine that perhaps she was exploring Judaism, trying to understand her roots or making a statement. What bothers me most is that despite it being a very big statement, my mother wore her star, but I don't feel comfortable wearing mine. After she died, my father told me a story about how one day a couple of boys dragged her into an abandoned building and beat her up. She never told anyone.

Despite everything—or maybe because of it all, who knows—Marysia grew up to be a gifted artist and incredible linguist, an inveterate traveler, and all-around determined person. On our first mother-daughter trip to Paris, she made sure we hopped a train so she could meet face-to-face with the editor of a journal she wanted to write for. Jerzy Giedroyc was cofounder of the literary-political journal *Kultura*. I played with the chicken in his yard while the two of them spoke. Then, instead of heading off to the Louvre, she took me wandering around cobblestoned backstreets until we found ourselves invited into an unmarked art gallery–museum. My mother is the one person who taught me that straying off the beaten path was mostly, almost always, a good idea.

CHAPTER 11

A TALE OF TWO GRANDFATHERS, AND THE WEIGHT OF POLITICS

As it happens, both sets of grandparents knew each other before my parents ever met. While the two grandmothers tolerated each other, at least at first, the grandfathers seemed to have gotten along. Being high-level engineers, and in the process of helping rebuild the country, they moved in the same circles. Franciszek, my father's father, was several years Fryderyk's senior. But despite the age gap, the two men got on well, even working together at one point, then exchanging friendly letters across continents.

You'd think that those letters, which survived in spite of incredible odds, would be a comfort, and they are. But I also find them kind of eerie. I adored Fryderyk, my mother's father. My father's father, Franciszek, I never knew. For most of my life—and really, before Franciszek's papers and letters came into my possession—pretty much all I knew of my paternal side was through my father's stories.

From the sound of things, Franciszek was a man who followed his convictions and was unrelenting in his beliefs. He was also unflinchingly loyal to the system. I get that being loyal to the Communist Party made life bearable when Poland was under Moscow's thumb, but that same blind loyalty made him push away his youngest son—the man who would one day become my father.

The story of my paternal side, as I'm about to tell it, is riddled with holes. It's a story with political intrigue that resulted in a legacy of family breakdown. It's said that estrangement afflicts a lot of families, and I can tell you, mine is one of them.

That estrangement was sparked by the political and social unrest of late 1960s Poland. I'll say more about that, but essentially things got bad enough on my maternal side—I'm talking shunning and threats—that the young couple, Marysia and Wojtek, were not able to return to their home country, and when they wound up in Canada, they did not look back. Franciszek saw his son's decision as running off, as betraying his homeland. And just like that, it was as if Wojtek no longer existed. From then on, apparently, neither of his parents ever mentioned his name or spoke about him.

It would take decades before my father reconnected with his family, and by then, the only person left was his older brother, Andrzej. In the intervening years, Wojtek had built a life with us—my mother, sister, and me—in Toronto. Meanwhile, Andrzej had lived out his life in Poland, near his aging parents. So, it fell to Andrzej to apologize, decades later, in the early 2000s after both their parents had died, for the family amputation—basically, cutting off all contact with Wojtek. He was right to stay with his wife, Andrzej admitted, and not return to the Eastern Bloc.

Upon hearing that apology, Wojtek, ever loyal, immediately forgave his brother.

I find it remarkable that even though his family disowned him, my father never spoke ill of his father. The most I got whenever I asked about his family was my father admitting that Franciszek had some faults.

Mostly, my dad was proud of his father, and the stories he told highlighted Franciszek's leadership, like about the day in 1951 when Franciszek was the director of roads for Gdansk voivodeship, and he closed the office so that he could be a pallbearer at the funeral of a fellow engineer. The following day, the Communist Party, the iron-fisted government of Eastern Europe, closed Franciszek's office and moved him to Warsaw. They then sent him on to Geneva, to help design traffic signs that would be recognizable in every European country. Franciszek, apparently, looked for projects abroad. That's one reason why my father's early boyhood was lived out in Afghanistan. Franciszek led the Polish team that built the road from Kabul to Jalalabad.

As the story goes, after WWII, Franciszek joined Poland's pitch to rebuild the Hejaz railway from Medina to Damascus, which had been destroyed during wartime. Dressed in traditional garb, Franciszek walked the length of the entire route with his team, plotting out their options. It seems that Poland almost won the contract but were undercut at the last minute by a competing group from Hungary. Franciszek was then asked to join ECAFE, the Economic Commission for Asia and the Far East, to organize roadbuilding in Indonesia. When ECAFE's headquarters were moved from Yangon (then Rangoon) to Bangkok, Franciszek and Wanda moved, and they lived there for the next three years before returning to Poland in 1961.

It's strange. Even once my sister and I were born, our paternal grandparents showed no interest in reaching out to our dad, let alone getting to know us. And yet, long before Franciszek and Fryderyk became extended family, they were not only colleagues, but they were also friendly with each other's families. I know this because I have letters from 1958 to 1961 that document their warm exchanges.

The dozen or so of Franciszek's letters to Fryderyk that I have cover Franciszek's work with ECAFE; his travels through Burma, Thailand, and Malaysia; and their joint work with MetroBudowa, Warsaw's subway and bureaucratic boondoggle. There isn't much about family in the letters, but reading between the lines you can see each man's temperament, their unwavering commitment to their work, and some of what amused them—stamps being one. Every letter mentions stamps. It seems both families were avid collectors. Take the letter below, from Franciszek, when he was working for ECAFE in Bangkok. The envelope included several stamps, which Franciszek had kindly designated for the young Marysia. Decades later, I'm left holding these stamps and can't bring myself to let them go. But what also stays with me is Franciszek's charm, and just how much his writing reveals his sense of humor. He would start each letter like he did below, half in English before veering into Polish.

My dear Fridericus,

I am very ashamed indeed—tak zaczyna się większość listów oficjalnych, pisanych przez mego obecnego szefa, który zawsze jest ashamed i zawsze jest too late z odpowiedzią na listy urzędowe.

[This is how most official letters begin, written by my current boss, who is always ashamed and always too late to reply to official letters because he is always very busy and suffers from lack of time.]

By 1960 Franciszek and Fryderyk had been in similar circles for years—Fryderyk on the building and coal mining track while Franciszek focused on roadbuilding that often took him far afield. Fryderyk would have loved to spend time in the Far East, so the entertaining letters would have at least let him live vicariously.

What I see in the correspondence is how much Franciszek and Fryderyk had in common. Both men were highly intelligent, forward-thinking dreamers who loved building and creating. And while certain character flaws made life hard on their respective families, early on in life these proud Polish men wanted to make the world a better place.

Engineering in Bangkok was rewarding for Franciszek, who apparently relished challenges. One challenge I expect he did not miss was the famously vexed subway-building project he had once led in Poland's capital. The Warsaw Metro build, first begun in 1918, was plagued from the start by economic factors, including the massive disruption of the Great Depression and World War II. With postwar Poland run by Moscow, the Communist Party fired up the Metro build again, only this time, instead of digging shallow tunnels at 15 meters (49 feet), they wanted to dig to a depth of 46 meters (150 feet). Franciszek was a vocal opponent of the plan. Deep tunnels would be a mistake. Given that they would disturb the water table near the Vistula (Wisła) River, it would be impossible to dig that deep.

In addition to this haggling, Franciszek was disillusioned with office politics in general. Afghanistan had been the last place he had been proud of his work: building roads from complete rubble, creating bridges that could bear the weight of entire armies. The sheer audacity of that project had left him with a sense of accomplishment. Yet even then he wasn't sure whether the family would be able to return to Poland. There simply were never any guarantees.

So I understand why Fryderyk would have been an ideal correspondent. Not only would he ship his friend the newspapers and magazines Franciszek could not get in Bangkok, but Fryderyk could also relate, he could commiserate. He had also battled his superiors, trying to get past the bureaucratic bungling, to get things done properly.

In fact, the irony of the history of these men is that at one point, they had faced off over the Metro build. That clash could have led to their breaking off contact and going their separate ways. It happened back when Franciszek was director of the MetroBudowa, the Warsaw Metro build, responsible for the welfare of the workers, including making sure they had food stamps and access to medical help when needed. His position meant collaborating with Fryderyk, who headed up another department that was coordinating the build. One day, Franciszek came to Fryderyk's office to advocate for his workers. Franciszek was pushing for onsite showers so that the men could wash up at the end of long workdays in the trenches before heading home to their families. The ask set Fryderyk off. "We are not here to worry about the cleanliness of our workers," he raged, smashing his fist on his desk.

Being older and more reserved, Franciszek said nothing. The next day, however, he returned to Fryderyk's office. "Yesterday you slammed your fist," he said. "Today I will do the same." With that he smashed his fist on the glass table. "I'm officially resigning from my position and want to be moved to the Department of Building."

It was a bold move. Franciszek could have landed in hot water with that stunt. Instead, he was reassigned, and the mutual respect between the men deepened.

In looking at both grandfathers, I can see how they would have been great friends. Both were engineers by trade, well traveled, able to speak several languages, and loyal communists dedicated to their country. They had their fundamental differences, of course. As fathers, Fryderyk was preoccupied with raising his kids, KT and Marysia, to be the best, while Franciszek valued loyalty above all else in his two sons.

It's important that I understand these men and their motivations, yet frankly this whole subject is painful to write about. Franciszek, despite his letters and papers showing him engaged and curious about the world, remains a mystery to me—a man who made no attempt to meet his own granddaughters. Fryderyk, on the other hand, is the grandfather I knew as a good man who wouldn't harm anyone. And yet, for years, both men associated with a brutal and oppressive organization that did enormous, long-lasting damage to the very country they loved.

Postwar Poland, 1945 to 1948, saw some 150,000 Poles imprisoned by the Polish authorities. Large numbers of the Armia Krajowa (Home Army) and resistance fighters were caught and executed. The Soviet army, which actually occupied Poland illegally until the signing of the Polish-Soviet declaration in 1956, would go on to occupy Poland for another thirty-plus years, until the fall of the Iron Curtain in 1989. Not surprisingly then, in the years leading up to 1956, power struggles within the Polish Communist Party were constant. Some figures were nationalist-leaning, putting Poland first. Some were pro-Soviet communists. Other groups fell somewhere in between, and all factions were shaped by their wartime roots. What was a given was that Soviet "advisers" permeated all branches of the government and state security. These advisers were placed everywhere to ensure that pro-Soviet policies were implemented throughout the country. So entrenched was this infiltration that by 1953, the Soviet-style secret police UB (Urząd Bezpieczeństwa; Security Office) ballooned to 32,000 agents—roughly one agent for every 800 citizens.

The oppressive tactics, betrayals, interrogations, monitoring, and constant undercutting were insufferable. Do I honestly think that my grandfathers didn't know what was going on? No. I can't speak for Franciszek, but I believe Fryderyk chose to turn a blind eye to actual events. Fryderyk knew there were NKVD officers following him. He knew his colleagues were getting fired. His own place in the Communist Party had been threatened several times before things went from bad to worse. Why then did he stay loyal?

Back when he was exiled, living in Tashkent and Moscow, Fryderyk had dreamed of returning to his beloved homeland. And when he finally made it back to Poland, he was eager to rebuild his country. The postwar period was still turbulent as countries struggled to find their positions in the new world order, but people were also exuberant, ready to rebuild Europe in the hopes of creating a new and better world. But as the Cold War ramped up in the 1950s, the very countries that had been ravaged in the war and were still recovering now, once again, had to divert their industries to rearmament. Once again, war was on everyone's mind, and Poles were no exception. Fryderyk was disturbed by all of this and saw a marked change—especially in the youth.

It was the youth who started speaking out, calling out the various governments for lies and broken promises. By the 1960s, young people in Europe, as in America, were openly agitating, fighting for more. Governing parties in turn went on the defensive and mounted heavy crackdowns. Then came June 1967 and the Six-Day War in the

Middle East. The consequences of that war reverberated around the world, fragmenting countries even further. In Poland, where the war divided the population, the Communist Party took advantage of the breach. They identified a scapegoat that would conveniently deflect attention away from the Party's stagnant economic policies and the country's overall decline.

In 1955 over 30,000 participants from 114 countries descended on Warsaw for the Youth Congress, an event that gave local youth the chance to interact with those from noncommunist countries and be exposed to new ideas and new ways of thinking. Not surprisingly, with all this exposure, discontent surged among Polish young people. They, too, wanted more opportunities, access to more food and consumer goods, and better working conditions.

During this time, when Fryderyk was attending meetings with Party leaders in Warsaw, he noticed a disturbing dynamic emerging whenever Władysław Gomułka, general secretary of the Polish United Workers' Party, rose to speak. But it was Gomułka's speech after the Six-Day War in June that was truly alarming.

Simply, the speech implied there were clandestine Israeli sympathizers within Poland, operating within "Zionist Jewish circles." These are what Gomułka referred to as a "fifth column." He said, "We cannot ignore the people who, when facing a threat to world peace and Poland's security and peaceful operation, take the side of the aggressors, the havoc-wreakers and the imperialists. We do not want to have a fifth column in our country. I urge those who feel that these words are directed at them—regardless of their nationality—to draw appropriate conclusions."

While Gomułka's speech was later redacted, his suggestion that subversives were busy undermining Polish national solidarity was

loud and clear. The point was this: Everyone who was counter estab-
lishment, or perceived as disloyal to the government, was de facto
not wanted in Poland. The Jewish population—what was even left
of it—was clearly implicated in this twisted reasoning. Once again,
the scourge of anti-Semitism was gaining traction in Poland, and
Gomułka with all his political influence did absolutely nothing to
stop it.

Events moved quickly after that.

On January 30, 1968, Fryderyk and Paula attended the final performance of Mickiewicz's play *Dziady*, a politically charged piece
first written on the heels of the November Uprising in the 1830s. At
the close of that performance, as the curtain fell, it was impossible
not to notice the intense reaction of the youth to the fact that the play
had in fact been censored.

In February, the Warsaw chapter of the Writers' Union met to
condemn the government's censoring of the play. Świętokrzyska
Street saw thousands of marchers chanting, "Independence without
censorship," "We want Dziady," "Free art, free theater," while heading
toward the statue of Adam Mickiewicz, the playwright, on Krakowskie Przedmieście, near Old Town.

With March came mass arrests and layoffs. These were met by
protests on the streets and at the universities. Meanwhile, much
of the government and military were being "cleansed." On March
8, Fryderyk heard that his son, KT, was not only taking part in the
demonstrations, but he was also part of a large student discussion
that included instigators sent by government security forces. KT was
arrested, and shortly after, anti-Semitic signs appeared outside the
family's door. They later discovered that their home had been under
surveillance.

Two days later, Fryderyk was summoned to a Party official's villa. Piotr Jaroszewicz apparently knew what had happened, and he reassured Fryderyk that everything would be okay. Fryderyk had his doubts, but Jaroszewicz convinced him to keep calm, and not to intervene in KT's imprisonment. Unfortunately, the reassurance was null and void two days after that when the entire Party leadership, including Jaroszewicz, was suspended.

On March 12, the first dismissals were officially published, and as part of the government cleansing, the layoff included three Jews, one of whom was Fryderyk.

The move, although swift, wasn't entirely unexpected. With Paula still employed at the hospital, at first the family hoped that, financially at least, they would be fine. Yet the fact was that their standard of living, which included a well-staffed apartment, was a perk and a privilege awarded by the Party. The Topolski family was not independently wealthy. What they faced now was the stark realization that, at a moment's notice, everything they had could collapse and disappear.

The events of 1960s Poland represented a turning point that, like the Holocaust, shaped the future of my family. Both grandfathers—one Polish Catholic, one a Polish Jew—faced hard choices that would color not only their lives but the lives of their descendants and a family for generations.

How Franciszek felt about the impact of his actions I will never know. I know that the punishing events of 1968 would become ingrained in Fryderyk's mind even more than the war years, and that's saying something. The war years had been influenced by outside forces that displaced and murdered millions of people across Europe and elsewhere. Poland's move in 1968 to purge Jews from the country was something else entirely, and for him, what began as scapegoating that led to outright expulsions was unforgivable. This was his home country turning its back on him.

CHAPTER 12

FINDING MYSELF: AS WARSAW BECOMES HOME

At one point while living in Poland, a cousin e-mails me to ask if Warsaw is "backward." What does that even mean? Not developed I can understand, but backward? Frankly, I am insulted by her question, and for whatever reason I take it personally. The rest of the world might perceive Poland as the old, broken-down Eastern Europe so often depicted on TV, but for the most part the country is modern. Transportation? Easy. You download an app and buy your metro tickets on your phone. Sim card for your phone? No problem. These are easy to buy and a fraction of the price we were paying back home—as in 90 percent less than we were paying in Canada. Day-to-day expenses are lower, too. Only items like cell phones or computers are the same as everywhere else. After all, an iPhone is an iPhone is an iPhone wherever you go.

Old European architecture suggests to some people that everything about Europe is old, but post-communist Poland is only thirty years old. Its roots are old and deep, sure, but there's decidedly a conflict between old and new. In fact, I can't quite put my finger on how I feel about everything—actually, that's not true either. On the one hand, Poland is where I start to feel alive again, but it's also where I grow frustrated by things my local friends find normal and acceptable. Let's start with the insignificant things I can't wrap my mind around.

For example, for any document to be considered official, it needs a red stamp. I'm not joking. In fact, it's the first thing I need to buy when I start my sole proprietorship. In other words, people put a lot of stock in a piece of paper. When I encourage a friend who is considering becoming a dog trainer/sitter to put up flyers around her neighborhood, she says, "That would never work. I don't have a piece of paper saying I've completed my schooling." Another friend informs me that she is a dance professional because she has a dance diploma. Really? The diploma makes you a professional? So there's that all-important piece of paper. It's this stress on the importance of documents that I find totally confusing.

I'm shocked to hear that adding your photograph to your CV is required.

"But how will they know what you look like?" my friend asks.

I choke on my food. "Who cares what you look like? What business is it of theirs?"

"What if they don't hire you because they think you are ugly?" she says. Clearly, she still doesn't get it.

I tell her about my getting hired at a high-end chocolate shop in Toronto, how I was instructed to show up for my interview in a tight black dress, heels, and red lipstick. Would that have made me a better salesperson? Absolutely not. What it meant was that a lot of men felt the need to come on to me. I was young, and I did not stand up for myself back then. Now I know better. I would never put up with that now.

So, yes, there's this gender disconnect.

On International Women's Day in March, when we are all going to be celebrating women, what I see are men bringing women flowers and chocolate. *Really?* I think. *It's all about the men?* And sure enough it is. The dance school where I take classes features only male dancers on their page wishing women a Happy Women's Day.

Get on an elevator with a group of men and make sure you stand against the back wall. Now wait until the doors open and watch what happens. There is this uncomfortable moment when all the men shift, pull in their guts, and just won't move. As a woman, standing at the back of the elevator, I'm expected to maneuver in between them to get out first. How does this make any sense? The first time this happens I am baffled. No one moves, they are all waiting for me. I don't want to touch any of them, but the doors are about to close. My husband comes home after his first day of work and confirms that it's very weird for him, too, and that he may have unknowingly committed this faux pas several times before he caught on to what was expected of him.

It takes me a few weeks to notice that this isn't the only very-new-to-me and hard-to-wrap-my-head-around custom. I am working at OpenBooks, the start-up, when I notice that all the guys shake each other's hands, but no one reaches for mine. When I ask why, they say it's up to the woman to reach out first. So, hang on a minute, let's take five steps back. This is a country where men open doors for me, where men wait until I leave an elevator, and where men bring me flowers on International Women's Day, yet I am supposed to reach my hand out first if I want to shake theirs? How does this make any sense? To be perfectly honest, I don't feel the need to shake everyone's hand every single day, but I feel like they are leaving me out.

From my vantage point, this is a passive-aggressive way of showing women we don't count. It's the classic "boys club," showing the only woman in the group that she is different than them and requires special handling. No matter how men try to explain this away, this is how it comes across. It's isolating, and places me, the only woman, outside their group.

At least only a handful of the men try to kiss my hand in greeting; that trend is slowly going out of style. It's a custom that has always grossed me out. Why do you feel the need to kiss my hand? My mother, when men reached for her hand, always had the best answer: "Just so you know, I don't wash my hands after I use the restroom." I am dying to say that but usually chicken out and smile awkwardly while wiping the back of my hand after the unwelcome gesture. Come to think of it, I may have done a flamboyant curtsy once or twice.

These elaborate gestures toward women are more annoying than anything else. As a good friend put it, "The societies that put women down are the ones that pretend to put them on a pedestal." I agree. These are all empty gestures that do nothing to create equality.

All these things make me crazy. On the other hand, they force me to start finding my voice again. The fitness industry dumbed me down. All those years in Vancouver, I was fighting to grow a business, fighting to be successful, and as a result, I was constantly exhausted trying to reach my goal. I forgot to surround myself with the things that inspire me.

A few months after my initial visit to the ballet school, I gather up the courage to start taking classes again. It has been a long time, and I'm nervous. My first class is exhilarating. My brain remembers the steps, and my muscles do everything they can to keep up. The teacher points out that it's obvious I've had training. Some students smile at me as we silently bond over sweat and exhaustion. This is the only place where your words don't matter because the language of dance is universal. Week after week, I go to class, smile at people, and try to be friendly. Yet even when I'm upgraded to an advanced class, no one speaks to me. This goes on for six months until I finally make friends.

That's right, six months. I know this because I keep track. After class, I walk home at night feeling so lonely, the endorphin high is completely wasted on the dark streets of Warsaw. It isn't until some other expats arrive that I finally have someone to talk to. There are two of them, and they are loud and boisterous, and we start chatting immediately. Another girl, also an expat, joins our little group, and suddenly everyone else warms up to us. We are the loudest people in the class, and what was a quiet structured lesson suddenly becomes an hour and a half of laughter and challenges. Not long after, people start talking to us in the change room. First one person, then another, and pretty soon everyone loosens up. People start smiling more at one another and helping one another out. To me, it feels as if a weight has been lifted; the rigid class energy has finally shifted. Over time, we get invited to outings as well, and soon I find myself surrounded by a wonderful group of people who share a love of dance.

CHAPTER 13

MARYSIA, MEET WOJTEK: A '60S LOVE STORY

I like to think that my love of theater and the stage came from my father. While my grandfather was in high demand and busy and roads in the Middle and the Far East couldn't build themselves, back in Warsaw, Wojtek was spending more and more time hanging out in local bars and cafés or daydreaming in the park, and his parents were getting worried. After a brotherly chat, Andrzej introduced his younger brother to Jerzy Markuszewski, a director working with the Student Satirist Theater, or STS as it was known.

Wojtek joined the group, began as a stagehand, and was immediately hooked. He was also the youngest of the group and completely awed by their forward thinking—unimpressed as they were, to say the least, by the current political climate and determined to make themselves heard. Many were already great artists in their own right. Some would go on to become international household names.

Wojtek started spending more and more time with his new friends, who welcomed him into their midst. Jerzy especially was like an older brother, and on more than one occasion, Wojtek spent the night with his new friends. He also worked on the first show that was banned by the government. Franciszek was less than thrilled about the theater. A strict communist, he was not interested in these new ideas coming from the students and their revolutionary crowd.

Although Wojtek loved and respected his father, in a classic father-son standoff, he couldn't understand Franciszek's loyalty to the Party. He didn't enjoy being a boy scout as a kid, he didn't attend church, and he didn't want to be a part of the Communist Party as an adult. Everything about organized groups like that repulsed him. Unfortunately for Wojtek, his mother and brother also stood by Franciszek, even though they were less doctrinaire. Wojtek's nonpartisanship created a huge divide that before long would have dramatic consequences.

Before learning to speak up to his father, there were some good times. December 20, 1960, found Wojtek and his nephew Alek in Bangkok. Franciszek had been helping to design the AH1, the staggeringly long road system that would join Istanbul to Tokyo. His contract complete, he was ready to drive back to Poland, but he also wanted to use a route that would show my father and Alek, his grandson, another piece of the world. Wojtek couldn't wait to go. He admired his parents' having traveled and wanted to follow in their footsteps. It wasn't that he didn't like Poland, but Poland wasn't enough for him. His big dream was to travel and to see the world.

Franciszek worked out their exact route home, by way of the roads he was in charge of building for ECAFE. Bangkok to the Malay Peninsula, then on to Singapore, then north straight to Burma and over to Bangladesh and India, Pakistan, Afghanistan, and Iran, then on to Turkey and back home, to Europe.

As it turned out, the family was unable to travel to Burma because of insurgents. Instead they boarded a ship, which sailed around the Malay Peninsula to Chittagong in Bangladesh and then on to Calcutta. Along the way, the ship stopped in Singapore, where everyone was eager to debark, but the port authority informed the family that Wojtek and Alek were not allowed off the ship because they carried red passports—communist passports, in other words. Wandeczka and Franciszek had special travel permits thanks to their work with ECAFE.

Franciszek, of course, lost it. He angrily told the port authority officials they were a bunch of idiots, asking if they really thought that Alek, who was seven at the time, was going to start a revolution in their primary schools. The officials wouldn't budge, and the family spent two days holed up on the ship.

Once they arrived in Calcutta, other problems arose, including being presented with huge tariffs to bring their car into the country. The upshot was that they spent two weeks in a dirty, rundown hotel waiting for papers. Franciszek even met with the Polish ambassador to speed the process. Finally, they realized that red tape was something they would have to deal with. After calls to Switzerland, Franciszek was able to present the authorities with a certified letter stating that the car would indeed leave the country. As loyal as he was to Poland, Franciszek kept the family money in Switzerland, where it would be safe.

Meanwhile, as their car sat parked beneath their hotel window with Wojtek and Franciszek taking turns watching it, at some point the lights and windshield wipers were stolen. The old "baba" who minded the dilapidated lot either wouldn't or couldn't tell them when or how the car was robbed.

After three weeks in Calcutta, they drove straight to Delhi. Franciszek was still holding on to the notion of his original plan, but they had to change their route significantly because every country seemed to be at war with each other. From Delhi they traveled to Bombay (now Mumbai) where they stayed with another ambassador who toured them around. Through him they were able to secure tickets on a ferry that would pass through the Gulf of Aden to the Red Sea, to the Suez Canal and the Mediterranean, all the way to Lebanon. After a two-day stop, they went on to Rijeka, Yugoslavia. Once they were on European soil, the road back to Warsaw was quick.

It might not have been the trip that Franciszek hoped for, but the tour left a deep impression on young Wojtek. His experience, good and bad, of other cultures never left him. From that point on, he knew that he never wanted to live in Poland, but he dreamed of moving abroad and traveling the world. I believe that it's also what drove his interest in multicultural foods, and why he brought home delicacies from our local Toronto international markets, even though they sometimes freaked us out. From as far back as I can remember, my father's stories always drew on different cultures and ways of life. He was the one who brought all that into our home.

When Wojtek first met Marysia, she was in her late teens, that rebellious period of life. She gravitated to pants and peplum tops that were in fashion at the time and refused to wear the pretty dresses Paula favored. Marysia knew exactly what she wanted. And why not? She was, at heart, an artist.

In a move both mothers would later regret, Paula and Wandeczka asked Wojtek to show Marysia around the inner workings of the theater. The original introduction was to Wojtek's Student

Satirist Theater group, an outlet for artists and Wojtek to critique
life in Stalinist Poland. Being eight years older than Marysia, Wojtek
had no idea what to do with this kid who wanted to tag along. She
was much too young to bring into the rowdy theater crowd. So at
first, neither Marysia nor Wojtek thought much of each other. He
thought she was a kid who talked too much and thought she knew
everything, so he didn't pay her much mind.

But seeing as their parents were acquaintances, with Paula
working at the hospital with Andrzej's wife, Elżbieta, the pair often
ran into each other at events. It wasn't until the two families planned
a trip to Yugoslavia that he really began to notice her. Wojtek drove
one car, and Marysia and her family were in the other one. It was
either hang out together or with his parents. Marysia, Wojtek, and
KT made for a fun group as they sat out late, drinking and talking.

Upon their return to Warsaw, Wojtek went to finish his studies
in engineering, and Marysia continued hers in fine arts. They kept
bumping into each other at different events, and before they knew it,
they were an item. By then, Wojtek liked having her around. She was
pretty and outgoing and just as eager as he was to explore new ideas.
In fact, she was much more liberal than the views he saw at home.
Finally, one day in the first half of 1966, while sitting together at a
café in Old Town Warsaw, Wojtek looked at his redheaded girlfriend
and said, "So, maybe it's time that we get married?"

Their wedding was held on June 19 at city hall on the corner of
Nowy Świat and Smolna. Wojtek's parents did not attend. They, like
Marysia's mother, were not happy with the union. Paula was posi-
tively showy about her displeasure, whereas Wojtek's parents grew
silent and retreated from the newlyweds.

Paula and Wandeczka weren't exactly friendly to each other either. Wandeczka saw Paula as a conniving woman with disregard

for anyone but herself. Wandeczka, on the other hand, was more the mother lion, the kind whose domain ruled. Regardless of her daughters-in-law, her household was to be the center of all familial gatherings. Wojtek knew to expect the same rules as his brother, and he was certain that neither Marysia, nor Paula for that matter, would accept them.

Displeasure is one thing. Histrionics is another. Paula had been adamant that Marysia move to France to find herself a rich husband so she would be able to take care of her family. When Marysia stood up to her, Paula threatened suicide. She had spontaneous fainting spells and did everything she could to dissuade Marysia from making what she thought would be a huge mistake. Paula even threw the fact that she had lost two babies during the war, meaning that Marysia had survived so much, so how could she possibly leave her mother for this man? This doesn't make sense to me, but I believe that my grandmother was desperate and was doing everything she could to refocus my mother's attention to herself.

Undeterred, the wedding went as planned, with Marysia in a beautiful ankle-length silk skirt with a silver threaded short-sleeved top.

Of course, weddings being weddings, there had to be some drama.

At some point during the evening Paula disappeared. A day or two later, my parents found out what had happened. When KT had returned home to check on his mom, he heard water running in the bathroom. He found his mother in the tub with bloody wrists and a badly scratched-up forehead. He pulled her out and ran to call the doctor. Still, was it all that serious? His mother was a doctor, after all. Had she wanted to slit her wrists, she would have known just how to do it. He suspected this episode was her way of getting attention, and he was right. Paula had used a pumice stone to scratch her forehead, hoping to convince everyone that the toaster had blown up in her face. The paramedics were called, the entire household was roused, and Paula spent the next few days in a private hospital room where she could demand attention from the staff and perfect strangers.

Is it any wonder that the newlyweds might want a change of scene? Three months after the wedding, Marysia fashioned an inquiry.

> Marysia Topolska-Wichrzyczka
> 3 Solariego St. Warsaw
>
> September 1967
>
> Director
> Academy of Fine Arts
> Prof. M. Wnuk
>
> Dear Sir,
> I formally request a break in my studies until the end of the current school year 67/68. I am studying interior design. My request is motivated by the possibility of residing in Paris, which will enable me to study French art and deepen my knowledge before commencing work on my thesis. Additionally, it will help me master my French language skills.
> Thank you for your consideration,
> Marysia

Presumably my mother's application was successful because I also found this note.

> September 18 1967
> Maria Topolska-Wichrzycka
> Warsaw
> 3 Solariego St.

In reference to the application dated the 8th of September 1967, I grant the above named citizen a leave of absence during the 1967/68 school year.

Professor Marian Wnuk

Wojtek, who had already accepted a contract in Iraq to build roads, was happy with the arrangement and supportive of Marysia's dreams of studying art in Paris. Starting out a marriage by living apart has always sounded strange to me. When I asked my dad how he felt about it, and why they decided to do it that way, he merely shrugged. He said it was the way it was. They both had prior life commitments, and this is what they did. I couldn't pull any more information out of him. This is one of those moments when that was okay. They were a young couple starting their lives, they each had an interfering mother, and they certainly did not need their future daughter making her own assumptions about their union.

This is the certificate that my mother would have presented to her school in Paris to confirm where she was in her studies:

The Academy of Fine Arts, Warsaw
Krakowskie Przedmieście 5
No. A-405/69
CERTIFICATE

The Academy of Fine Arts, Warsaw hereby certifies that MARIA TOPOLSKA studied in the Faculty of Interior Design during the period 1962–1967. The above student received a Credit for the obligatory course of five years study.

This document may be shown to relevant authorities.
Secretary of the Faculty of Interior Design: Alina Czerny

Marysia left for Paris while Wojtek was still in Warsaw as his contract had been delayed because of the Six-Day War. Iraq wasn't originally on his radar as a place to work, but an incident at a rally changed his mind. A crowd member mentioned that Fryderyk was a Jew. I can only imagine that it was a derogatory and insulting comment. Wojtek, out of loyalty to his father-in-law, stood up to protest without thinking. His friends from the theater quickly grabbed him and dragged him away. "You need to apply for an out-of-country contract," they advised. "You are going to get into trouble; they will arrest you." Heeding their words, he quickly applied for work as an engineer out-of-country.

When he finally did arrive there, Iraq was not what Wojtek expected, or maybe he didn't really know what to expect. Regardless, one time he was doing his best to socialize with the other engineers. There weren't many European newspapers to be found, and whenever one arrived, everyone gathered to find out the latest events.

Unfortunately, one paper was pumped full of propaganda, and when the young soldier read out that three Jewish government officials had been released from their posts, among them, a Franciszek Topolski, Wojtek, unable to hold in his rage, jumped on a table, his voice trembling. "If you are going to quote events, at least get your facts straight," he shouted. "It's not Franciszek Topolski, it's Fryderyk Topolski, F-R-Y-D-E-R-Y-K, who is my father-in-law, and Franciszek Wichrzycki is my father." With that he ran out of the room, slid into a ditch by the road, and bawled like a baby until a couple of friends came and got him out.

Events leading up to Iraq had been bad enough. At the government office in Poland, Wojtek had been handed a piece of paper and told that in order to get his visa, he would have to agree to spy for

Poland. They would reserve the right to ask him about what he had seen and heard abroad.

Wojtek was stunned. Was this a joke? Was this even possible? In a rage he went home, sure that his family would agree with him. Much to his surprise, his father looked at him calmly and said, "Oh, I've been doing that for years; it's standard procedure."

Wojtek couldn't believe his ears. His father was okay with this? A huge family battle ensued. I believe this was the first time that my father saw his father as a flawed human. There was a lot he could overlook, like political leanings, but this crossed the line. Wojtek finally got up and left to lodge with his theater friends, who eagerly took him in.

Wojtek had been spending more time with his friends than with his family. Still, he needed this job, so a few days later he agreed to sign the documents, with one caveat. He had read somewhere that cursive can be traced back to an individual, but that printing could not. When he came to the spot on the page where he had to add his signature, he printed his name in his best engineer-trained style.

His resistance carried over in other ways. Arriving at his first party in Iraq, he loudly declared, "I am a spy for the Polish government. Please do not say anything in front of me."

Aside from the orally recounted stories, I have a series of handwritten letters that my mother composed. These letters were written in Paris in the late 1960s. I love the way that sounds. It brings up a romantic image of a young woman sitting at a café, fountain pen in hand, dreamy look in her eyes as she signs her name with a flourish. One of the ways I picture my mother is sitting at a writing desk, so it seems fitting that I would find a series of letters that she had written to her parents while she was studying at the École des Beaux-Arts. My dziadzio, Fryderyk, was the sentimental soul who kept them first, and my mother followed suit.

On the surface these letters sound like any other letter written home, but they carry a lot more weight. Marysia, who was living the student lifestyle, would have been somewhat sheltered from the political repercussions her father was facing. She was following her dreams in art school. She was secure in the knowledge that she would be able to return home to see her family and friends. With the luxury of hindsight, I know that the family would soon become political refugees, my father would be estranged from his family, and my parents would never again call Poland home.

When Marysia Z, a friend my mother was traveling with, and my mother returned to Paris, they received the results from their exams at the École des Beaux-Arts. Both passed, but neither one had gained entrance into the exact program they wanted. It likely didn't help that there were thirty applicants per spot. In retrospect, it was okay they hadn't been accepted, because the agency jobs the two were holding down were so demanding. It would be good to find out what was expected of them at work before committing to further studies.

Honestly, letter writing alone kept the two busy. Naturally, the girls loved getting letters from home, and they could count on at least a few each week. At six pages, the record-holding letter to date was one from Nula, Fryderyk's sister. Everyone wanted regular letters, and Marysia felt as if she was writing fifty letters a day. Every once in a while, she resorted to writing one general letter and adding a few personal lines to each recipient. Either way, she could barely keep up with all the correspondence.

[Date unknown]

My Dears,

I'm taking advantage of this moment to write to you, a friend's mother will deliver this letter to you. 1. We aren't going to the grape harvest in Dijon. The weather is uncertain and we are afraid of catching a cold. 2. We found great work with a French (!) agency. Starting Monday we will be making models of a church. The work is interesting and pays well and most importantly it's five minutes from our hotel. The Patron at the agency gave us the use of his studio, space like this is often hard to find.

[Then, a few days later:] Our trip to Dijon was a great success. We visited beautiful castles and some of France's most fascinating wine cellars. Of course the quaint Burgundy villages. We almost made it to Switzerland.

Meanwhile, Marysia was urgently waiting for Wojtek to send her new glasses to replace the ones she'd lost. But he was waiting to send them along with someone traveling to France, since it was expensive to ship the glasses. My mother had astigmatism, and without the proper glasses, everything was unaligned.

Here, she's trying to reason with her mother, the always-anxious Paula:

Mom, please stop worrying about me, I'm doing really well and [am] very happy that I'm here.

I ate blackberries near Dijon all the while thinking of Dad. Thousands of bushes filled with fruit, it was paradise.

I'll comfort you like a mother would, it's not long until the next vacation.

Kisses, kisses, kisses.

Marysia

Knowing my babcia as an adult, I can only imagine that she would have been trying to insert herself into my mother's life in Paris. Paula must have asked about what Marysia was spending her money on, and in a letter dated October 18, 1967, my mother replied with the following:

> Where I Spend My Money:
> Everyday I use the metro.
> We eat in and get invited to friends' homes and several
> times a week Wołodia takes us out but we don't have
> enough money for restaurants for just us.
> Neither of us has purchased any new clothing but I did
> buy two pairs of tights because I could no longer mend
> my old ones.
> We buy nice shampoos.
> We are able to use the laundromat.
> We occasionally buy ourselves an ice cream that we eat
> while walking down the Seine.
> Sometimes we stop for a coffee at a local café.
> For now, we don't have any more needs although I
> admit that I often walk out of my way to walk through
> the art store.

All those lovely paints, the rainbow of inks, and the fancy papers were Marysia's weakness. She knew if she got her hands on a lot of money, she'd probably just buy out the store. As she finished her list, there was a knock on the door. It was the hotel manager standing there, holding her glasses. Someone had found them. What a relief, as buying new glasses would put a serious dent in the little money she had.

Now she had some questions for her parents.

> Why are your letters so depressing? What is going on in
> tata's [Dad's] work? What kind of trouble is he having?
> Now I have some requests, please tell KT that he mustn't
> under any circumstances send any questions or informa-
> tion about that article in *Kultura*. It's true, he is mentioned,
> but he is one of many and in any case, this is not a subject
> that should be discussed in letters or during phone calls.

Distressed about her brother, Marysia hoped KT would come to
his senses and get serious about his schooling.

The family's beloved springer spaniel would later have official papers to take him to Sweden, where he'd stay with Marysia and Wojtek
before heading with them on to Canada.

For now, she missed him dearly and nudged her parents to send
photographs of themselves and the beloved pet. "Everyone is very
excited to see them. Okay, maybe not so much the ones of Żak, but
I'll convince them that he's a regular member of the family."

"It's actually easier to practice speaking in English than it is in
French," Marysia explained to her mother when she asked about
their language studies. The girls spoke English with each other quite
often, and there was a group of Americans staying at Wołodia's
house. "Unfortunately," she continued, "we haven't been to the theater yet, but we have seen some movies. Mostly, however, we go to
every exhibition we can. There are so many galleries that one could
go crazy if they attempted to see all of them."

There was art and socializing, there was news about the weather.
"The weather is all over the place," she noted. "One day it is freezing

and the next there is a heat wave. Sometimes it seems as if it's raining and sunny at the same time. All of these constant changes are becoming exhausting." Not knowing when or how the weather might turn, she dressed in layers and carried an umbrella everywhere she went. That strategy worked. She did not fall ill. If anything, she grew more organized than ever.

> I'm sorry to hear that you have all come down with colds. Mom, imagine that you've taken a break from work and that you are actually resting for a few days. And let's take this one step further and imagine that Dad isn't rowing on the Wisła every day with a stuffy nose. Wouldn't that be a great idea? I'll be waiting for your phone calls on the 23rd and 30th of October at around 20:00. Please also call Wojtek. He hasn't received any of my letters and he's waiting for a phone call on the 23rd and 30th (October) at 20:00. I think he's very upset with me. I think that it's best to try and send letters with someone if at all possible.

Although she was testing her independence, Marysia was very close to her parents and wrote them regularly, even when she was busy. In November she penned,

1.11.1967

My Dears!

I'm apologizing ahead of time; this is a very short letter. Finding a few hours to write is very problematic. I've been working at a large firm since Monday, and I've started working on the model. We [with her friend, Marysia Z] work from 8:30 to 12 and then again from 14 to 18:30. Travel time is an additional two hours during

the day. In the evenings we work a few extra hours because the model has to be finished later this week. Next
week should be easier. Mostly, we are working on let-
tering [typography]. Since the company is French everything is done in French but we are getting along very well.

It's raining all the time and the weather is horrible. We
were able to change our room [in a Polish boarding-
house], it's next to the same stairwell but now we are
near the bathroom and we have hot water. It's much
better now. Now, a request, please send me my papers
translated into French as quickly as possible. I need to
prove that I've taken some courses already. Also, I don't
know if it will work, but it might be possible to get my
French diploma.

Friday was a holiday, which was always a nice break, and they
could finally finish their model after which they dressed up and went
dancing to celebrate their hard-earned time off. Their favorite spot
was in an old wine cellar. It was impossible to know it was there from
the street, and you had to descend a steep stone staircase that went
well below ground level. Other times, when they were with Marysia
Z's brother, Antek, they'd go to the fancier art-crowd clubs.

A few days later, they'd finished their weekly dinner with a family
friend referred to by his last name, Wołodia, who, as usual, spent his
time flirting with Marysia Z. It was a little strange since he was old
enough to be her father, but nothing ever happened other than that
they often ate in very nice restaurants they wouldn't normally be able
to afford, and occasionally he'd try to put his hand on her knee.

It must have been a nice feeling, opening the door to room
number four in their boarding house. Their old room wasn't bad,

but this one was an upgrade, and now the bathroom with warm water was on their floor. No more climbing flights of stairs when they wanted a shower. The room also came with a little black kitten that would visit them on the fire escape. La Mondeuse was after all a nice boardinghouse, where they frequently ran into other artists and sometimes rubbed shoulders with young doctors and other professionals who were just beginning their careers.

One day, Marysia Z walked into their room carrying a package from Poland. The two Marysias were still waiting for the translated documents Paula had promised. Their boss was asking to see their university transcripts. Plus, they would finally be able to get into certain classes, and getting a degree from the École des Beaux-Arts would be a great asset. It wouldn't be easy, but Marysia wanted to work toward it.

Ripping open the brown paper, Marysia laughed when she saw the contents. Three tins of French sardines and some French cheese. How many trips had that food made before returning back to its home country? She appreciated getting the food, but this was a bit ridiculous. It would be easier to buy the exact same food at their local grocery store.

Payday was on November 3, which meant it was finally time to shop. Marysia was in desperate need of new patent-leather flats. Hers were worn through, holes in the soles and all. It would probably be an all-day hunting expedition to find shoes that fit. Marysia's feet were exceptionally narrow, and finding appropriate footwear was always difficult.

Besides, if there was anything Marysia loved other than art supplies, it was shoes.

The weather was rainy and cold, the kind of cold that chills you to the bone. She dreamed of the day when she could head straight for the fancy stores to do her shopping, but for now she had to content herself with the less expensive stores. Having heard of some cute shops in Montmartre, she was dying to check them out. After an afternoon of searching, Marysia finally stumbled upon a tiny hole-in-the-wall with an assortment of high heels. And then in the back, on a shelf midway up the wall, she spotted a pretty pair of ballerina flats with a small heel. Best of all, the less than attentive saleswoman had a pair in an extra narrow size 7. Marysia bought them and celebrated by enjoying a café au lait at a neighboring coffee shop.

Finally, to Marysia's great surprise, her brother, KT, who had been silent up until now, sent her a letter letting her know that he was all right and going to study in Łódź. A few years earlier, he had been admitted to the Warsaw University of Technology because their father had convinced him that every man needed a respectful profession. KT was certainly not cut out to be an engineer, though, and a year in, he had taken a leave of absence, which is when he became more and more involved in politics.

When a leading philosopher, Professor Leszek Kołakowski, was expelled from the Party, the political climate started heating up, and a chain of events began. About that time, Fryderyk stepped in and pulled some strings to get his son into the Sociology Department at the university in Łódź. Marysia knew her parents would be lonely without her brother, but she comforted herself in the thought that they would probably be able to see each other every weekend or so.

But instead of staying in school and out of trouble, KT organized student discussion circles under the umbrella of the Union of

Socialist Youth. Marysia knew that the secret police had him on their radar, but the last straw was when he invited Joseph Kempa, the first secretary of the Provincial Committee of the Polish United Workers Party, to a student meeting in an underground bar in Old Town. Comrade Kempa thought he was going to meet with supportive youth. Instead, he faced a room of angry students ready to fight. His parting words were "We will get even with you."

When she learned this, Marysia told her brother to leave Warsaw immediately. Of course there was nothing she could do from Paris. She was worried that he would be arrested. But by this point, KT was ready for a fight. Many of the professors and intellectuals whom he held in high esteem had already been arrested or unceremoniously kicked out of the university. Meanwhile, in Paris, Marysia was missing her family dearly, but it became harder and harder to get word from Warsaw. They had always been a tight-knit group, and right now she wanted to go back and help. Workers were striking. Students were striking. In other words, all hell was breaking loose not just in Poland but in Paris and throughout Europe. No wonder she was under strict orders from her father to stay away.

By early winter Marysia had settled into her life in Paris. It sounds like the girls barely had time for a social life, but they did make friends, who in turn introduced them to new friends, who introduced them to the owner of the Travexpos-Ranno & Fils. The director of the agency was a nice lady who recognized she had two eager students she could exploit. At the same time, she also wanted them to experience all aspects of putting together shows, so for the next event she made them hostesses. Being a hostess, aka a greeter, at the Palais de la Défense was much easier work than actually building the models. All they had to do was hand out some pamphlets, maybe answer a question or two. For that, they got to work in a heated space, were fed, and received a paycheck.

There are days when I can barely motivate myself to write an e-mail, so it amazes me that my mother was able to keep up with her letter writing, even if it was sometimes delayed by a week or two.

> 23. XI. 1967
>
> I'm writing this letter with a week's delay but this time I don't feel bad about it. The whole time I was thinking that I'm working toward making dad proud. For one, I'm living in a place that, at least by name, sounds like a fancy boarding school. Second, I'm working like a horse, something that always meant a lot to dad (if only I was also going rowing on the Wisła).
>
> Today is a very special day. 1) I arrived in France three months ago. 2) At 5 AM I finished mounting a stand (model). 3) At 9 AM I started working as a hostess at an exhibition relaying information in both French and English.

And now the holidays were coming up. What would they be doing? her mother kept asking. Marysia hoped for a trip to Dijon, but maybe they would just stay in Paris. Marysia Z's older brother, Antek, an architect, was probably coming into town, and he was always fun to party with.

One Saturday Marysia didn't start work until the evening, so she had time to head to the post office. She was annoyed with her brother because he hadn't responded to her letters in a long time. She knew he was seeing someone, and she supposed he was living with her, but the least he could do would be to write every once in a while.

Communicating by mail was an all-around frustrating experience. Letters sent from Poland arrived within a week of being sent, but letters sent from France sometimes took as long as three to six months to get to Poland. Today they were in luck. She discovered a package had arrived from her parents. Only it wasn't the packages she looked forward to. It was the letters! Marysia wasn't able to convince her parents that she and Marysia Z weren't starving.

Opening the package back in her room, Marysia pulled out a loaf of dark rye bread, an assortment of sweets, cheese, and dried mushrooms. There was also a babka kujawska—essentially a bundt cake covered with almond flakes and liquid sugar—that, as usual, had completely fallen apart. She kept telling her mother not to send these. If Marysia felt nostalgic, she could easily get all the same food at the Polish Embassy. Paula, as ever, wouldn't listen.

Even when the girls' funds were running low, they didn't have to borrow money, and their next paychecks always arrived on time. And there was a good chance they might get some better-paying work by way of a full-time job at a big interior design agency. They had already met an architect who was convinced they knew a great deal about the industry; they hadn't yet told him they were completely new. He had refused them the positions of draftswomen, convinced they could do so much more. So far, they had passed a couple of interviews and were keeping their fingers crossed that they might get hired. For now they were still working on the giant model, which, luckily, was interesting work. Two to three times a week they were able to sneak off to take French classes at the Alliance, and as a hostess, Marysia was happy to be able to use her French as well as English.

Toward the end of the first exhibit, the girls found themselves working solely with men, who were very impressed. These Polish girls never seemed to get tired. How, the men wondered, had they ever gotten along without them? My mother cheekily added that to one of her letters home. I'm sure she would have had a good laugh—two attractive young girls and a group of men. I don't doubt that they worked hard and were good at their work, but knowing my mother, I am sure that she would have used this dynamic to her advantage. After all, she had the same charm as her father, my dziadzio.

CHAPTER 14

ON FAMILY AND EXILE: OUR THREE UNCLES

I t's not only the holidays that allow us to connect with family. Our three uncles have become a part of our everyday lives. Back in Canada, Pawel and I only had small family units who we could count on. Living in Vancouver, we had become used to being self-sufficient. Parents and siblings were a five-hour plane ride away and could not be available at a moment's notice. We see our move to Poland as another chance to forge connections with extended family.

All three uncles come from varying backgrounds. Andrzej is a doctor and an intellectual, KT is a businessman, and Marian is ex-military and a farmer, but each in his own way is a survivor of a ruthless government.

Roots go both ways, and we are pleasantly surprised that each uncle shows a strong desire to connect with us. True, it's not always smooth interactions; KT's reasons seem more selfish, but they all make time for long conversations and find moments to impart their wisdom. This is something we feel keenly since we make a point of celebrating our niece's and nephew's milestones in Canada, even though we are so far away.

By the time I meet Andrzej, my father's brother, he is hard of hearing and constantly adjusting the sound on his hearing aids. His eyesight has also started to go, and much of the time his eyes are closed, or I see him squinting. He reminds me of the wooden Lucky Money Man statue my dad keeps in his room. Despite this, Andrzej and my dad couldn't be anything but brothers; they look so much alike. Neither is very tall, and they share a stocky build. They don't ever stop talking and are quick to smile.

Though it has taken these brothers the better part of thirty years, they are on good terms now, having found a way to move beyond their difficult family history and remake a tight brotherly bond. Andrzej is smart, tells great stories, and we get along really well.

By now I've quit OpenBooks, the start-up, and have been told that I am loud. This might not be a compliment in the workforce, but Andrzej seems to appreciate it. He repeats that he likes talking to me. I am not a pushover, and I speak my mind.

What Andrzej doesn't know is that I've read some of his correspondences with my parents. There's a part of me that's angry that he sided with his parents in the family dispute. Why couldn't he see that my father chose his wife over coming back to an oppressive country? Even Alek, Andrzej's son, mentions that he completely understands why my father didn't return.

Andrzej and I never spoke about his relationship with my father and how it all went wrong, but at the end of the day we had a silent understanding that our relationship, his and mine, was free to move forward. A piece of me feels sorry that he spends so much time on his own, so on occasion Pawel and I head over to his place.

"I want the both of you to learn how to make my nalewka," he announces one day, and we can't believe it when we hear these words.

A nalewka is a fruit- or herb-based drink made with spirytus, a 190 proof rectified spirit. After the second shot it's debatable whether you can feel your legs. I know this because one day Andrzej decided I should try all the varieties that he had. I don't remember much of what happened, but I did not pass out, so I am chalking it up to being a success.

Nalewkas are serious business in Poland. You cannot leave a home without sampling one and hearing all about how it was made and how the owner has a secret recipe for their particular version. Of course, the upshot is that you leave slightly drunk, if not blitzed out of your mind. Neither my husband nor I have ever been prolific drinkers, but even we could be found stumbling home on more than one night. In short, getting my uncle's recipe was an important honor.

When I travel to visit my mother's brother, KT, who lives several hours outside Warsaw, I feel like I've been traveling all day, which I have. I am surprised to see KT has come to pick me up at the bus station himself. His lanky silhouette hasn't changed much, except now a cigarette dangles from his lips and his face looks worn. He lost his second wife, the love of his life, a few years ago. Add to that a hedonistic lifestyle—too much alcohol, too many prescription medications, and so on—and it's obviously taken a toll. My stomach churns slightly as I grab my carry-on bag and walk up to his souped-up Citroen. My mother has been dead for well over a decade, and I have only seen him a handful of times in all those years.

For years, in Canada, our families vacationed together and celebrated holidays together, until we didn't. When I was in my early teens, my uncle left his wife and his kids in Toronto and returned to Poland. Another fragmented family.

For years before he left, my mother and my aunt, KT's ex-wife, did not get along, and naturally our families had drifted apart. Once my mother became ill, they reconciled and realized that their rift was because KT had tried to keep them apart. Who knows why exactly, but I can guess that it would have made his life more difficult if his sister and wife joined forces.

When I was younger, I looked up to KT until I realized that he spent his entire life trying to live up to impossible standards set by his parents while pretending to be something he was not. He was the person who was successful in business, something I secretly always wanted. I tried on more than one occasion to get close to him, to understand him, to be family, but in the end I always left his place feeling empty. So I'm surprised to see him there waiting for me at the bus stop. I expected to see one of his staff. We don't say much as he drives, taking the turns at a precarious speed. I haven't eaten anything, and I feel lightheaded and nauseated. I crack the window and take deep breaths. There is no use in asking him to slow down. He is busy showing off, as in, this is how the cool guys drive. I am forcibly reminded of when I was a little kid and he drove me home from a family gathering. I don't remember where my parents were, but he'd been drinking and was driving at breakneck speeds down suburban streets. I can still see the dark green car screeching around corners where children played during the day. I was scared as any child would be. He paid no attention to me.

As we pull into his long driveway, two big dogs come to greet us, acting like I'm the best thing that's ever happened to them. It's a nice welcome.

Dinner is casual. His adopted kids are at the table. This is our first meeting, and they are polite but apprehensive. Who am I barging in on their territory? I understand. They are still young, ranging in age from about eight to twelve. Besides, they have older siblings, my cousins who are roughly my age, whom they barely know. We aren't exactly a close-knit family. The live-in housekeeper is also wary of my presence. It's only later that I find out they expected me to be imperious like some of the other family members.

Right now, I am just as uncomfortable as they are. I smile and offer to help, but mostly try to stay out of their way. This is not my home; I am a guest. We are family, but I am estranged from my uncle. There are bridges to rebuild and new ones to form. After dinner we retire to the cozy living room with a bottle of wine. My uncle instructs one of his sons to bring up a couple of bottles from the cellar. I brace myself for what I'm afraid will be a long night.

As KT settles on the maroon leather couch, a throwback from the '90s, he pours us both a generous glass and lights another cigarette. He has been chain-smoking since I arrived. His dogs settle in front of the stone fireplace, and his parrot makes scratching noises in the giant cage to our left. Darkness has fallen. I can see the stars filling up the night sky. This would be a cozy room if I couldn't feel the weight of its sadness.

Conversation is awkward, punctuated by the occasional parrot squawk, asking for a peanut. My uncle asks about my husband, my sister, and her kids. He tells me that he has always liked her and her husband.

Does he think that I am going to be placated because he likes my sister? He doesn't know that I am no longer interested in learning from him. I am no longer willing to overlook his bad behavior, and I am angry at him and how he has behaved over the years. He left his biological kids in Toronto to start a new family; he has treated everyone badly to feed his ego. As we speak, he does not let me forget how successful he is. He brags that all his kids are geniuses and there are others whom he sponsors financially, who are also all very "accomplished," whatever that means. He is the type of person who couldn't possibly have an average person in his family; it's always all about the image he is projecting. I notice he does not say much about his biological kids. He has nothing to say about my sister or me.

As the wine flows, he begins to reminisce. I'm not sure if I am there to reconcile or to be the audience for his memories. I hear about how he moved to Canada and made his fortune as a serial salesman from cars to exports. If he could sell it, he did. His eyes get misty as he talks about his recently deceased wife.

He starts talking about my mom, his sister, and her untimely death almost twenty years ago. It has been a long time, he says, but he still feels as if it were yesterday. He talks fondly of how she met my father and how they got married. He can't help but make himself the hero of my grandmother's wrist-slitting story. My parents and their special day become incidental. Their big day was clearly all about him finding and saving his mother.

I pretend not to have heard this story. I know she has done worse to try to split up my parents. I don't bring this up. Now is not the time. I am here to make amends. We have not seen eye-to-eye for years. I have nothing to lose, I am not afraid of offending him, and I tell him so, my tolerance for his egoism quickly waning.

When the talk turns to money—a dangerous topic at the best of times—KT asks what my dad did with the money he gave him after my mother died. I had no idea there was a financial gift until I realize that my father used those funds to bring my sister and me to Poland to visit his estranged relatives. I decide not to share this piece of information. In KT's eyes, my father wasn't successful, another sore spot that I have no desire to talk about. My parents might not have been great at making or managing their money, but they always put my sister and me first. By contrast, when my aunt threw my uncle out for cheating, he basically left for Poland and abandoned his kids.

Our mortality had now become a very real subject. The money was used for a monthlong trip for healing and renewal. We had visited KT on that trip, but he and my father can barely stand each other. There has been too much history for a reconciliation. My father hasn't made millions, and money is what my uncle values. He doesn't understand loyalty, which is my father's gift in abundance.

He asks about what my father did with the money again. I don't know why he wants to talk about it. Does he want to show me how much more money he has? He has already alluded to his net worth. He has never been remotely interested in anything I have done or my plans. I can't imagine why he cares so much about the money. Well, maybe I can. I suspect he thought my father would pay off some bills or do something practical with it. The more I think about it, he probably wanted to be consulted before it was spent. I shrug and say, "If there is a choice, I'm always going to choose him over you." It's the truth. He nods and says that's the way it should be. Still, I feel bad because I'm not sure anyone would say that for him.

Now comes the really dangerous part. My uncle gets a dreamy look in his eyes and starts talking about his sister, my mother. He begins by saying she was always much smarter than him. I don't know how to answer. What is he getting at? He begins to cry, telling me that her dream was to be famous, though this is the first I've heard of it, that she wanted to make a name for herself. He laments that he became a success, but she did not. She was never able to make

money, and then he alludes to the fact that my father and our family
held her back.

Now I am getting angry. How dare he say these things to me? I
ask him what success means. She had a loving family while he tore
his apart. She had the love and respect of many while he continues to
have "yes people" surrounding him.

We are now on bottle number three. He is openly crying while
holding my hand, which makes me very uncomfortable. I pull away.
He tells me that he wants me to be in his life, that he wants a relationship. He has a lot of wants. I ask him if he is willing to reciprocate
and call or e-mail me every once in a while. He says he won't.

He opens a fourth bottle of wine and pulls out his dead wife's
dress. It's long and black with a large white collar and cuffs. He gives
it to me and says that I should try it on. I look around to see if anyone
can save me, but the house is quiet. I grab the dress and go try it on,
thinking he won't remember this tomorrow. I step out of the bathroom wearing the dress. I feel like a nun—all that is missing is a
habit. He looks at me and cries harder.

I can't do this anymore. I change back into my jeans and T-shirt.
The clock says 1 AM. I am finished. There is no more talking. I look
at my uncle and say, "I'm going to throw up now, and when I come
back I don't want any more wine. We will put this conversation to
rest." I no longer feel drunk, and my head is clear. My uncle has lit
yet another cigarette and is finishing his wine. He is looking straight
ahead and does not see me.

I say good night. He nods, puts his glass down, and gets up to go
to his bedroom. Our conversation might continue tomorrow, but I
doubt it. I have been let into a part of his soul that he doesn't open
very often.

In the morning, sitting in the living room where my uncle's secrets were spilled the night before, the sun floods the room as I pretend to read my book. I am waiting for my uncle to wake up. At 12:30 PM he finally stumbles out of his room in a white bathrobe. He says good morning and disappears into the kitchen. I hear him making eggs. He asks if I want more coffee. "Sure," I say and grab my cup. I'm a bit nervous to face him this morning, but he says nothing about last night. He tells me that some of his friends will be joining us for dinner. I'm still here for another day, so I'm sure we'll find some time to talk again.

That night I hear many of the same stories I heard the night before. We are sitting on the deck, the scent of geraniums intermingling with barbecue. Somewhere in the distance a dog is barking, stars have overtaken the night sky, and the moon is so bright we barely need the flickering lanterns. I try to join the conversation, but my uncle doesn't let me get a word in edgewise. One of the guests turns to me and asks what I do. I explain Pilates to her, and she's thrilled. It's rare that I see someone so excited to hear more about what I do. She turns to my uncle, interrupting his conversation, and says, "Do you know what you have here? She's a gold mine of information." My uncle half smiles at me and continues speaking about himself.

I get it now. It's like last night never happened. He is more interested in replaying things for his own sake. I am not famous or rich, and I am taking the spotlight away from him. It's obvious to me that he is not ready to move forward.

When I first met Pawel's uncle, it was when he came to visit Canada, and we clicked immediately. I don't have a lot of family in

Poland. There is just one family unit from each parental lineage, so seeing them all is fairly easy. The rest of my family is scattered in Germany, South Africa, and throughout the States. Pawel's family, however, is all in Poland, and he is getting a lot of pressure from his mother back in Canada to visit them. We make time for the local Warsaw people; we never do make it to the country. When there aren't a lot of blood relatives in your life, connections happen in the most unexpected places.

Pawel's uncle, like my uncles, is a drinker. His drink of choice? Vodka shots, but the cheap kind. The first time I tried one, my esophagus burned, and I was convinced that I would die. Each of these uncles, though he has his faults, has something to offer, and when I think about it for a minute, I realize that Pawel's uncle, with his lanky, slightly stooped posture and easygoing smile, looks quite a bit like my grandfather. I like this uncle; we have a great connection.

While alcohol is a constant with these uncles, it is money that sets the three apart. Two of the uncles are well traveled, speak multiple languages, and have cash to spare. Marian barely scrapes by. He is a man who was failed by his country.

In one sense, their lives represent Warsaw's extremes. There isn't, we notice, a true middle class, or very little of it. You either have money or you are struggling. You can shop at stores like H&M or Louis Vuitton. Only a handful of stores sit between the two. I might be exaggerating, but not by much. Our flat, for instance, has Miele appliances and a heated towel rack, a standard in most homes, and yet the entrance to our building is vomit-green, and the dark hallways look as if they haven't been updated in fifty years.

For those, like Marian, who live paycheck to paycheck or on meager pensions, life is hard, and alcohol is cheap. A large beer at every corner store, never mind the twenty-four-hour liquor stores, costs more or less a dollar. A pocket-sized bottle of vodka will run you two dollars. Functional alcoholism is prevalent.

The story goes that in the 1980s Marian vouched for Pawel's family, confirming they would return to Poland when they requested passports to travel to Sweden. At the time he was a junior officer in the army, and he did not know that they were planning on escaping to Canada. When the family did not return to Poland, his career with the army was over. When the communist government fell, he survived by taking on odd jobs.

In 2015 the PiS, or the Law and Justice party, government was voted in on an anti-communist, anti-collaborator agenda. They came down hard on anyone they thought was against them. This meant that Marian was denied his pension. When PiS was firmly entrenched in Polish society, he scoffs at his family in the country: "You voted for them, you get to deal with the fallout."

Marian's the rebel in his family, and I can relate to that. Like KT, Marian is scrappy and a survivor. Like both my grandfathers, he, too, was a true believer in communism. Although he's not technically my uncle, there are common themes on which we can forge a connection.

CHAPTER 15

RACE AND RELIGION: RACISM AND ACCEPTANCE

I happen to like change and excitement, but I'm pretty sure my grandparents thought they'd had enough to last several lifetimes. Although PTSD wasn't recognized back then, they both had to have had it, and from what I can tell, it was passed on to their kids. Here I am, years later, trying to understand even a little of what my grandparents went through and how that shaped their actions. Even now, after retracing their footsteps and trying to decode my family history every which way, I sometimes find that history and its legacy too big to digest.

My grandparents survived the biggest war the world had ever seen. They had witnessed atrocities and narrowly escaped with their lives. What pulled them through? Ironically, it was their complete and absolute belief in communism. They were the proverbial pinkos and commies in the movies. How many times have we heard those slurs? So many people are blinded by religion, and communism was my grandparents' religion. They weren't part of a big conspiracy to overthrow the Western world; they were simply searching for a way to make the world a better place. So I was thinking of my grandfather when I took part in my first march, on Independence Day.

In November 2014, the lease on our flat would be up, and the landlord wanted to raise our rent by a few hundred dollars a month. We have no intention of spending that kind of money. After a quick search, I find a flat eight numbers over, in an old prewar *kamienica*, or tenement house. We check it out, and it's love at first sight.

The cobblestone street, the oversized wooden entrance doors, the courtyard, and the chipped marble staircase with its heavy wooden railing and large arched windows—I'm sold before I see the inside of the flat. It's a small one bedroom, but the ceilings are extra high, the appliances are modern, and there is lots of storage. Never mind the hundred-plus steps it takes to get to the flat. There are much older people living in the same building, on higher floors. Those folks take the stairs multiple times a day. If they can do it, so can we. I'll feel differently a year later when I tear my calf muscle and have to drag myself up those same stairs.

A few days after our move to my dream flat is Independence Day, which we have been hearing about since our arrival. Growing up in Canada, I am accustomed to happy celebrations. There is always an uproar if a city doesn't sponsor Canada Day celebrations, where the day is to be filled with family-friendly events like face painting, food trucks, and games, and to be topped off with an evening of fireworks. By contrast, Independence Day in Poland takes place on November 11, so the weather isn't always cooperative, and the cold gray skies add to the already tense atmosphere. November 11 in Canada is often gray as well, plus it's Remembrance Day. People wear poppies to honor veterans, sober events take place at local cenotaphs, and it's customary to observe one minute of silence at 11 AM to commemorate signing the Armistice for World War I on the eleventh hour of the eleventh day of the eleventh month.

But that's Canada. Polish Independence Day is a very meaningful day celebrating Poland's independence from the Russian, German, and Austrian Empires, resulting in the creation of the modern Polish state. I don't yet know what to expect in Warsaw, but the morning starts off well enough. Different military services in uniforms from different periods march through the streets. The cavalry is out as well, along with vintage and modern tanks that spectators can climb into. There's an old WWI tank that barely works but is a cool piece of history. Marching bands accompany the soldiers and reenactors. Flags are flying, kids are laughing, the atmosphere is boisterous, energetic, and exactly the way a celebratory day should be. My only caveat is seeing little kids running around with toy guns. I'm not against guns; I just don't like the idea of glorifying them.

The afternoon events, however, are terrifying. Rondo Waszyngtona is empty of cars, and foot traffic has moved to the sidewalks. In future years we will learn that most multinational companies instruct their nonwhite employees to work from home on the days on either side of November 11. Today is my first taste of why that is the case.

Even before the massive crowd becomes visible, we can hear their steady rhythmic chanting, not unlike that of a battle cry. Several explosions from flare guns follow; they reverberate on the surrounding buildings. Smoke hangs in the air, making it difficult to see and breathe. Then come the masses, walking shoulder to shoulder, chanting at the top of their lungs. God and glory, hail to our heroes, slogans that sound harmless, but their tone is harsh, they sound like a battle cry. Their leader sits atop a float, with a bullhorn. The crowd waves countless Polish flags, they are the exclusionary patriots. The European Union flag is reserved for the centrist, more liberal crowd who embraces the idea that there is more than one way of being Polish.

Some people, like us, stand off to the side, shaking their heads, but we are by far outnumbered. In the mix we spot skinheads; groups in paramilitary outfits with green armbands depicting a white stylized arm holding a sword, signifying support of fascism; and people you wouldn't look twice at walking down the street. The anger is clear, pulsating through the crowd. There is no mistaking the rage.

This mob is not a happy one celebrating Independence Day. They are going to war. They make their way past the palm tree and toward the Poniatowskiego Bridge that leads out of the city. The road is lined with police in riot gear, an all-too-common sight, and atop the towers at the entrance to the bridge, officers stand with beanbag guns at the ready.

Later that night we learn that the police had to disperse the crowd with water hoses. To no one's surprise, the giant floral rainbow in nearby Plac Zbawiciela (Saviour Square) has been burned to the ground. The next day the general mood is one of resignation with a hint of annoyance. There go the Nationalists burning down the rainbow again because of course that is what they are going to do. In Polish the term *Nationalist* is derogatory; the word is more loaded than what the simple English translation suggests. They seem to wear the term with pride while the rest of the population recognizes its exclusionary undertones.

This isn't even our first experience with riots. When the Vancouver Canucks hockey team lost the Stanley Cup in 2011, we were living just up the street from the stadium. We saw the black smoke rise, we saw noisy crowds march up the street right under our windows, and the next day we stepped over broken glass while passing department stores boarding up their smashed storefronts. Poland and Canada are two very different countries, and of course these events were not the same, but the destructive anger coming from crowds is comparable—so much so that a dozen-plus years later, a documentary film about the riots was made examining why and how they could have happened.

Perhaps the biggest difference shows itself in the following days. In Poland, it's the city crews that clean up the debris. In Vancouver, it's the citizens who show up with shovels and garbage bags to clean up the mess, and leave thank-you Post-it notes on parked police cars. The Vancouver riots left us sad but with faith in humanity. The events of November 11 in Warsaw leave us scared, all too aware of the direction that the country is taking.

The discord is beginning to show where I least expect it. I'm sitting in my stylist's new atelier with a thick layer of hair dye covering my head when she says, "I know, the women don't work or anything, they are always covered, and the government wants to give them ten thousand złoty a month."

Did I just hear that right? I can barely turn my head, but I start listening more closely.

"I'm not racist or anything but we don't even have enough money for our own people." My stylist and another client are talking.

I don't say anything, but I'm thinking, *Are you freaking kidding me? You are totally racist. These people are fleeing Syria. You are horrible and have just lost my business.* But I start to second-guess myself. My Polish is good, but I still struggle with comprehension. What if I speak up in protest, and they kick me out with all this product on my head? Looking back, I sincerely, with all my heart, regret not having spoken up.

Ironically the atelier was located in a place in the city steeped in a history that reflected Poland's struggles. The street, 3 Maya, is named after the date the Constitution was adopted. Many famous people have lived here, some of whom even fought for a better Poland. That was the last time I saw that stylist.

Now, in 2024, I find an article with the headline, "Arabic Signs Appear in Polish Resort Town amid Surge in Tourists from Middle East," I wish I could go back to see if her views have changed. Apparently, the mountain town of Zakopane and the sea resort towns of the Baltic have become fashionable places for folks from the Middle East.

On another occasion, I'm walking with a friend when he makes a derogatory comment about Jews and money. This time I'm ready.

"No, not in front of me, you don't get to say that, and you should know better," I correct him sternly.

I am getting better at speaking out. It still makes me uncomfortable, but I'm no longer going to sit back and listen when people say unacceptable things. I don't believe that most people, ex-stylist not included, are consciously racist, but in my observation, a lot of Poles I meet don't always think before they speak. If anything, a lot of the language they use is a part of everyday speech. Worse still, the folks who hear these slurs and actively despise them but don't speak out in the moment—like me, at the atelier—are inadvertently allowing all this racism to propagate.

This runs counter to how I was raised. Wherever our family traveled, we lived with local people. We'd land in a city, and for the first day or two, we'd run around with a real estate agent looking for a short-term rental. In our family, we like to say that my mother was the first Airbnb-er.

The rental was a cheaper option, sure, but it was also one that kept us away from hotels and other tourists. We had no choice but to learn to communicate in whatever language was spoken in any given city. With no money for restaurants, we shopped at local grocery stores and ate whatever food was available. By living with local people, even temporarily, we were exposed to so much more than we would have had we stayed in hotels. I have drifted apart from my cousins on my mother's side, but I still vividly remember a telling conversation. One of my cousins said, "I like four-star hotels so much more than five-star hotels because four-star hotels still have something to prove, so they try harder." I had no idea what he meant because we never stayed in hotels. Our vacations were immersive. They were never lavish.

My mother stuck to these values at home as well. One day she came home from work to find Pani Irena sitting on the stairs of our townhome looking distressed. She informed my mother that I had brought a friend home from school.

"Well, that's great," my mother said, confused as to why this was such a problem.

"She's Black," Pani Irena whispered, "and I'm afraid she'll dirty the walls."

When telling this story, my mom would always pause at this moment. Then she'd say that she didn't know if she should kick Pani Irena out or cry. At the time, she took a breath and remembered that this was the very early '80s, Poland was still behind the Iron Curtain, and Pani Irena was from a small village and had probably never met anyone who wasn't a white Catholic. She also knew that Pani

Irena was an extremely gentle soul at heart and would never hurt anyone intentionally. So my mother sat down with her and talked. Thus began Pani Irena's education.

After that episode, ignorance was never accepted as an excuse, and for what it's worth, Pani Irena began exploring Canada's multiculturalism on her own. Whenever it was too cold or wet to go for a long walk, we would seek out various religious institutions in our area. On one street was a mosque, a synagogue, and a Chinese Buddhist temple. The last was our favorite, and we often found ourselves burning incense in front of the giant Buddha.

So what's going on in contemporary Poland? This is long after the Iron Curtain has come down. I can't help but wonder how many Poles have even experienced a truly different culture or religion. Maybe it's naive on my part to assume that if they had, this casual racism of rejecting foreign refugees would not persist, or at least there'd be less room for it to flourish.

And yet, for as much as I want to yell and scream and fight, I also feel caught. Pawel and I are living in Poland on Polish passports. We haven't given up our Canadian ones—we would never dream of doing that—but we know very well that if something happens, we might not be able to run to the Canadian consulate. The government of Canada website sums up our dilemma: If you are a dual citizen and travel to the other country where you hold citizenship, local authorities could refuse to give you access to Canadian consular services. This could prevent Canadian consular officers from providing them to you.

All Canadian travelers must obey the laws of the country they are visiting. Dual citizens may be subject to local laws that other

Canadian travelers are not. For example, you may be legally required to register for military service or have to pay taxes in that country.

We try not to dwell on it, but Canada not being a safety net is slowly hitting home. When you live in a country like Canada that prides itself on its multiculturalism, imperfect though it may be, you don't always pay attention to the everyday workings of other countries. This is a mistake because unrest and disaffected youth are like a ripple that travels faster than we might be ready for. It goes both ways. Living in Poland we are not paying much attention to what is happening in Canada. If or when we decide to return, what will we find?

So, yep, for now we are on our own.

CHAPTER 16

PAULA AND FRYDERYK: SECOND IMMIGRATION

Fryderyk sat alone in his wooden rowboat on the Wisla. It was August 21, 1968. Paula had been admitted to the hospital again; his faithful companion and family dog, Żak, was missing; and just that morning the radio announcer confirmed that Soviet tanks were rolling into Prague. At least Marysia was safe in Paris. Still, with his daughter in France, Fryderyk was unable to help her. From the river, Fryderyk would have been able to see downtown Warsaw with its boardwalk on one side and the undeveloped Praga neighborhood with beaches and wild nature on the other. He would have had a clear view of the stadium he had a hand in building.

But the life he was building was changing. I can say with absolute certainty that rowing on the Wisła was my grandfather's escape, his constant when life wasn't. When I think of our hikes and long walks, their even tempo reminds me of oars gliding through the water. Although I never watched him row, it's one of my own favorite types of exercise.

All this time Fryderyk had been hoping that Czechoslovakia would adopt a true people's Communist Party. It had been a few short weeks since KT was singled out in the student protests, and Fryderyk was summarily dismissed from his post. Now it was almost impossible for him to get a well-paying job, so money was going to be tight. The family had already begun selling off possessions to make ends meet. Fryderyk did manage to find work at the patent office until one day, without explanation, the post suddenly "disappeared."

Finally, after much searching, he found a position at the Polish Academy of Science. A month later he was dismissed from that position. It was also a nightmare waiting for KT's sentencing. Fryderyk knew his son would be found guilty, that he was sure of. What then could he do to help? From his own account:

> I wanted to make finding KT guilty as difficult as possible. I hired two attorneys and helped prepare a lot of the defense material. It was very easy to prove that, according to the law, the charges were baseless. Additionally, I found out that the ministry of internal affairs wanted to suspend the investigation and dismiss the charges but it didn't matter because the Party wanted the conviction. At the last minute the judges and the prosecutor were changed. During the actual trial, witnesses were brought in and repeated what they had been told to say. The final sentence called for 18 months of jail time and KT was transferred from the Mokotow holding cells to the maximum-security prison, Strzelce Opolskie.

KT had already been in prison for half a year, and visiting had been a shock, confronting the conditions in Mokotów Prison. The address of 37 Rakowiecka Street was known for the torture and execution of Poles. With every visit to her son, Paula had become more and more despondent. In October, KT was formally accused of treason and spreading false information that could cause social unrest.

In the investigator's office—a small, airless room where the verdict was announced—Fryderyk couldn't help but notice his son's stoic resolve. The sentence would keep KT imprisoned for another year and a half, during which Fryderyk and Paula were able to visit KT once a month. After one year, through the lawyers they hired, they were able to get him released on probation. The Party wanted to conscript him into the army, but Fryderyk and Paula managed to "hide" him in a sanatorium for health reasons.

The "hiding" strategy was another attempt at helping KT. When he was released on probation on March 25, 1969, and conscripted to a special army penalty unit in Orzysz, Paula then had a friend diagnose him with an anxiety disorder—hence his move to the sanatorium in Twórki. Meanwhile, they were working on obtaining a one-way visa for him. "By a miracle," Fryderyk's account says, "there was a substitute on-call judge, who gave KT permission to leave the country."

Some 25,000 Jews left Poland between 1968 and 1970. KT was one of those émigrés. At the end of June 1969, three months after being falsely held in prison, he left Poland for Sweden. Once again, Paula and Fryderyk found themselves alone.

Paula and Fryderyk had no choice but to follow their son, and on September 19, 1969, they saw their first glimpse of Swedish soil from the upper deck of the ferry. This would be the start, again, of a difficult time.

The couple found a government-sponsored apartment in the Stockholm suburb of Täby. During that first six months they attended Swedish language classes every day and received a modest stipend to live on. Having sold everything and uprooted yet again, there they were, once more, in a foreign country, but youth was no longer on their side. And unlike their time in Uzbekistan—at the height of the war, when everyone was just trying to survive—this time their home country had turned on them. Paula and Fryderyk were no longer welcome in Poland, the land they had tried so hard to rebuild. Their whole family had been separated, yet again, and were being forced to restart their lives as strangers in strange lands. They did have some friends to fall back on, but the jobs they had worked so hard to succeed at were gone.

At the end of six months, Paula found work at the hospital as a doctor, and Fryderyk got a job at the Swedish equivalent of the Polish science and technology committee, studying problems with the Polish economy. A number of their friends had also left Poland between 1968 and 1970 under similar circumstances only to find that life in Sweden wasn't exactly what they were looking for either. Fryderyk's work was not very satisfying, and he began reaching out to his many contacts to see if he could find something else.

In November 1970, Fryderyk made contact with a German firm from Sankt Wendel in northeastern Saarland. The firm sent him to Spain to explore investment opportunities. He was tasked with scouting for appropriate lots, where the firm could build hotels and apartment buildings for tourists, and then developing the properties. The company then opened a new division in Madrid, and Fryderyk was appointed their first representative. His official term began on January 1, 1971. Paula, meanwhile, remained in Sweden.

At first, Fryderyk ran the projects from Madrid, until May of that year, when he transferred to Torremolinos, near Málaga. Despite the transfer, he retained a full-time address in Sankt Wendel, and a few years later, in 1974, both he and Paula received German residency papers. By then, life for KT had changed as well. He was busy moving to Canada.

CHAPTER 17

NINE NAILS FOR A COFFIN: MY PARENTS ARE FORCED TO MAKE HARD CHOICES

May 1968 brought weeks of civil unrest, riots, demonstrations, and protests around the world. As a student and an artist, Marysia was in the thick of things in Paris. My parents were still temporarily living apart at this time. I have already speculated about this arrangement, but it's worth noting that there was a big age difference between my parents. Wojtek had completed his studies and was on a career path, and he had too much respect for Marysia to ask her to give up her dreams.

On May 6, the National Student Union (UNEF) staged a protest to reopen the Sorbonne. The crowd built barricades while others threw stones at the police. The only mention I ever heard my mother make of this time was when we were sitting in the Paris metro, and she told me she'd been tear-gassed.

Marysia's last few days in Paris were tense. A group of her friends were planning on sneaking into a tiny hotel room and splitting the cost. About ten of them could easily fit. It was easy enough for the staff not to notice as the friends would walk in at set intervals, lower their heads, and move straight to the elevators or stairs without drawing attention to themselves. It was imperative not to be seen. Their papers weren't quite in order, and the police were arresting foreigners, especially students. Marysia had just been trying to renew her visa. Everyone had their own tactic for visa renewal, and most of these weren't legal. There was a priest, for instance, who everyone knew by sight. If you could register at his prefecture, he would work his connections to get you a visa. As it turned out she didn't have to.

Wojtek and Marysia had been warned about the Iraqi postal service, that it was filled with people who had been specifically educated in Poland so they could intercept and read the mail. Wojtek didn't care. He and Marysia corresponded without censoring what they wrote. And as soon as he found out that she was in a bit of trouble, he wrote and told her to hang tight. As his wife, she had every right to be with him. And given the situation in Poland, he absolutely did not want her to return there. So began the letters to the various ministries to secure her a visa to gain entry into Iraq.

> Wojciech Wichrzycki
> Central Laboratory
> Baghdad
> 18th May 1968
>
> Directorate General
> Of Roads & Bridges
> Personnel Division
>
> Please be so kind and issue the following letters:
> 1. To the Residence Department asking for Entry Visa
>   for my wife MARIA TOPOLSKA-WICHRZYCKA.

2. To the Iraqi Airways for a first-class air ticket from
   Paris to Baghdad for my wife Maria Topolska-
   Wichrzycka. According to the information given by
   the Iraqi Airways the price of the ticket from Paris ·
   to Baghdad is lower than the cost of the ticket from
   Warsaw to Baghdad.

For Marysia, the very act of living in Paris had been so exalted. The young Poles were artists, many also studying at the École des Beaux-Arts, like her, all of them living in the moment. They ate when they felt hungry, often sharing a baguette in the park or a cup of coffee at a local bistro. No one had a fixed address. They couch surfed, often sleeping in chambres de bonnes (maid's quarters) of old Parisian buildings. They felt like the literary figures they read about, elevated above ordinary mortals, the so-called bread-eaters. Whenever one of their friends left, everyone felt the separation, the sudden sense of loss. In turn, the person leaving couldn't help but be jealous of those who could stay on. Paris was the place to be. In Paris, they were a part of history.

Spring 1968 ushered in a different atmosphere, and this time their mark on history felt more transitory. They were no longer youth fighting for a cause. The situation back in Warsaw was becoming more dire, and Marysia dreaded letters frequently informed her that yet another friend had found themselves behind bars. In Paris, in the brief moments between demonstrations, the air was heavy with anticipation. Almost everyone was living on borrowed money, for one thing, since even the few lucky ones who had jobs were forced to strike with the rest.

Marysia in that sense had been lucky. At school, she had been working on her series of floral pictures done in ink, using a pointillism-inspired technique. Based on popular fabrics, the pictures had proven to be very popular. Demand was high, which was good. It meant she could afford to eat. Her family could no longer send financial aid, since her father had been kicked out of the Party. As Marysia spent her last days in Paris, Wojtek received positive news from the Iraqi government.

> Date: 23/5/1968
> > Ministry of Interior
> > D.G. of Nationality
> > Residency Dept.
>
> The Passport Officer,
> Baghdad Airport, Baghdad
> Re: Emergency Visa
> Please grant Mrs. Maria Topperman Wichrzycka, Polish
> Nationality, the emergency entry visa as soon as she
> arrives in Iraq.
> > Sgd. Nassir Abdul Jaber
> > For: D.G. of Nationality
>
> Cc. to:
> D.G. of Roads & Bridges, for information
> Directorate of Military Intelligence, for inform.
> D.G. of Security, raf. Letter. No. 7131 dated 23/5/1968
> from D.G. Roads & Bridges

Eventually, things came together for Marysia so that she could leave for Baghdad. Still, en route to Bourget Airport, her friends Krysia, Olek, and Ania tried to convince her to rethink her sudden departure, even though they knew she had a prominent surname, an overdue passport, a promised visa, and a first-class plane ticket. Her only monetary possession, they stressed, was a pittance. Thirty francs was all she had left after paying her visa de sortie (exit visa) at the pre-fecture. Wasn't it only a few days ago that they weren't even able to take the train for fear of being tear-gassed? Or police checking their papers at every exit?

Every event of that day would deepen Marysia's unsettled feeling of unreality. Only hours before, she'd been walking with her friends in the crowded streets of Ilse-de-France, still in the throes of a carnival-like exalted state. Only a few days earlier, those same cob-blestone streets had been the setting where revolutionary youth and police enacted their battles. The morning after, Marysia had grabbed her small brown suitcase and rushed through the narrow streets so as not to be seen by her manager or, worse, the director of her company, both of whom were aware that she had been refused her passport renewal. Never before or after would Marysia have such a feeling of the absurd as on that mid-June day that she had to turn her back on Paris.

My mother wrote that, as she saw it from the air on her way to Iraq, Europe would never look that beautiful again. First, they flew over the south of France, then the Alps where she could just make out the outlines of skiers swishing gracefully down the mountain. There was Rome and the city of Ostia bordering the azure waters of the Tyrrhenian Sea. The picture-perfect Acropolis shining like a beacon overlooking Athens. A few minutes later, she could see white yachts and ships peppering the blue waters surrounding the Greek islands. Finally, after what seemed like an eternity, the ever-majestic Istanbul presented itself.

The plane touched down for a layover, and Marysia, waiting in the lounge, had just enough time to admire the intricately inlaid fur-niture and to have a glass of water—the thirty francs in her purse would not even purchase a cup of coffee. Only two more hours of flight time and they would arrive in Baghdad.

The pilot's wife, who had sat down next to Marysia, interrupted her thoughts. "Look outside the window, right now!" She was a nice German woman who had been visiting her parents in Munich. It was almost dusk, and they were about to witness the passage from day into night, just before the sun disappeared, where you could see the stars twinkling above Asia and the sun setting over the Dardanelles Strait in Turkey.

The lush green European landscape disappeared. In its place rose the reddish-gray landscape of Asia reminiscent of the bark from an ancient tree. A few minutes later an ink-colored sky filled the window. The plane began its descent, circling the city. Marysia pressed her forehead against the cool window. This, she thought, must be the exact view the travelers witnessed as they flew on their magic carpets in *One Thousand and One Nights*.

The bread-oven heat rising from the tarmac hit Marysia so hard that, without realizing it, she jumped back into the air-conditioned plane. Minutes later, she found herself in the arms of Wojtek, who had impatiently been waiting with a delegation of his friends. Marysia didn't recognize any of them, but she did notice that one older, bald gentleman seemed to take care of the formalities, which included convincing one sleep-deprived mustached soldier guarding the exit to issue her a short-term, temporary visa. That would, hopefully, give her enough time to obtain a resident permit and to force the embassy to handle what should have been a done deal.

And so began her life as an engineer's wife in the desert. As Marysia, with great difficulty, started adjusting to the intense daily heat, she spent time writing letters to family and friends in Poland. She was extremely worried about her parents and her brother. Her mother's unexplained illnesses were also worrisome, and she was guilt-stricken at not being able to get on the next plane. The situation in Poland was impossible. Were she to return home, upon landing, her passport would be confiscated, and there was a good chance that she, like KT, would be labeled a Zionist and imprisoned.

Slowly, Marysia adjusted to Iraqi daily life. Their apartment was nice enough, in a multicultural neighborhood with lots of immigrants and close to the city center. The freestanding villa where they lived was surrounded by high walls and lush gardens. The two-room flat was cozy but spacious.

Marysia kept herself busy by painting and sightseeing. The summer temperatures were so warm, though, it was nearly impossible to do anything during the day. Finally, she was so bored, she called up her landlady to ask if she could paint the door. She then transformed that old wooden door into a beautiful floral garden. The landlady loved it so much that the next tenants were charged extra for the privilege of living with an original painting.

Things didn't always go smoothly, though, which is no surprise to me. My mother was a headstrong woman who would not stand down if she thought she should speak up. In a different way, my babcia was the same. Politics aside, one of the reasons Paula had to wait to get into medical school was because she was a woman, and there was a cap. As we know, that didn't faze her for long. Whenever a man tries to kiss my hand, my mother is the first person I think of. Whenever I find myself in a situation predominantly surrounded by men, I think of my grandmother. True, Marysia was much too independent and headstrong to conform to a conservative society. Once again, her hair got her into trouble.

One night, as they were filing out of a movie theater, Marysia felt someone pinch her behind. She spun around and smacked her presumed assailant. As the man's face reddened, Wojtek quickly winked at him and pinched Marysia's behind. Once again she turned, and this time, she smacked Wojtek, hard, in the face. To Wojtek's relief, the man laughed and went on his way. Later, Wojtek told her he nearly fainted when he saw the man place his hand on his knife. That kind of insolence—her insolence, smacking the stranger—could have gotten her killed.

Even though Marysia's studies were temporarily on hold, and she was now living in Baghdad, her correspondences with her family remained constant.

Baghdad. 5.8 no 5.9

Finally, a second much awaited letter from you! I wrote back right away with a card which I'm sure you already have and now, after a day, I'm responding properly. You probably didn't receive one of my earlier letters, Dad's jealousy made me laugh. Trips! In this heat? Sadly, we can't even think about taking any trips in this heat. It's much too hot and any talk of trips can be thought about in October. I've only seen the Ctesiphon, an ancient vaulted hall made of baked bricks. Its setting is only a few kilometers out of town and we traveled there in the evening with some friends. This isn't a very active place, which is probably due to the heat, this doesn't affect just us but the locals as well. We sleep a lot more than we did in Europe. We try to do some "walking trips," but they are only possible in the evening after the sun sets. I'm still working on learning English but for the time being, nothing has come of it. For fun, I painted the doors in huge colorful flowers. When the work will be finished, we will take some slides and I will send you one. Wojtek's leg is almost healed, he's wearing an elastic bandage, and he is already worried about his efficiency on skis. We have to give it to him. He has a great talent for getting injured. Remember his smashed nose on that ski trip? And now this.

I grew up hearing the story. The reference to the injury is kind of hilarious. Marysia used to wear jeans when they were out walking, so Wojtek would walk along the curb to protect her from the local men, who grew infuriated seeing a woman in casual Western dress. Unfortunately, one time, he didn't notice the missing sewer grate. He fell into the hole right up to his waist and woke up the next morning with a very swollen leg. A month or so later, an official law was passed that all women, even expats and tourists, had to wear dresses with hemlines that dropped at least five inches below the knee.

I was surprised to find that my father seemed to be almost as prolific a letter writer as my mother. He barely likes to write an e-mail now, but back then, he did his share of writing. When I knew the family, Wojtek wasn't close with my grandparents, but as it turns out, he communicated with them regularly.

Finally I managed to shoo Maria away from the typewriter and I can write a few words. Maria, as always, is working hard, with few breaks. When she's not working, she's not, but when she sits herself down at the typewriter she doesn't stop. Today she wrote 5 letters. I've had quite

a bit of work at the office, but I am not complaining because, for a few hours everyday it means one can tear
themselves away from day to day issues and think only
of work. A number of my colleagues in the Soil Department have left for holidays and I am in charge of three
bridges and one very important road in northern Iraq.
Perhaps it will be possible to go north for completely
mundane purposes, i.e. to take soil samples for testing.
But we will go together and we can visit Nineveh and
Nimrud and I really want to visit the village of Tak Tak
(in Polish this translates to yes yes), because the name
is so funny and to not go would be a big mistake. My
dears, it's very late. Marysia is already asleep and so I am
finishing this letter. I wish you many peaceful nights. I
send good wishes to you and all our friends. —Wojtek

PS. Marysia promised to mail this letter tomorrow and
that she will add a few more words. I am leaving the rest
of this page for her private use. Again, sending good
wishes and stay warm, we have too much of this hell.

"Stay warm" is a typical Polish greeting. The two often dropped
into and out of the same letter, to save on time and paper, and to liven
up the stories they were sending home, including the fact that there
was no love lost between them and the local Polish "hierarchy." I can
imagine Marysia sitting down to continue writing the following day.

My Dears! I took a short bathroom break and Wojtek
took over the typewriter. In the meantime, I went to bed
and the result is that it's already tomorrow. According to
official weather reports, the pressure can change many
times a day, that's probably why everyone sleeps and

sleeps. From time to time there is "dust." It's a desert sandstorm that carries clouds so dense that they resemble the fog in the Tatry mountains. The masses of air are so hot that they literally burn. The worst characteristic of the dust storms is that they bring pressure changes. Everyone reacts differently to these changes but no one is unaffected. Some become sleepier, others are more irritated, headaches abound, some are more arthritic, and of course everyone wonders what is going on. It takes 2–3 days for relief to come. Recently it has been almost cool. 40 degrees [Celsius], all joking aside, after two weeks of 50+ degree weather, it's quite a big relief. The humidity has risen 3–4% to about 15%. Time still passes fairly monotonously. I am trying to write letters regularly and to keep in touch with everyone. Other than my correspondences I am trying to simplify my home chores which really aren't my calling. Wojtek, who is used to masterful cooking, has recently asked for seconds of mine.

I have recently taken up counterfeiting works of art. I am drawing and painting Persian miniatures, I will send you some in the next letter. So you see, I have adopted your philosophy about always staying busy. This is the best way to protect yourself from dark thoughts, and the people who never ever, ever have any dark thoughts probably don't exist. I think I wrote previously that, other than very few exceptions, the local Polish colony is not to my taste. They are the worst sort of money grabbers or snobs. Every two to three weeks I have to invite one of those cretins over. Those are the old school customs around here and I am doing my best to conform. Wojtek and some of the others are afraid of the officials but I am choking to keep from laughing when, with a straight face, I bait those cows with idiotic questions which they step into. So now, whenever, I turn to one of the ladies and begin asking, "What do you think of ... ? Or how would you advise ... ?" Wojtek kicks me under the table and the conversation turns to weather. Right now it's fashionable to be envious of everyone. There is a real hierarchy. Now picture this, here comes this snot nosed young woman who, instead of allowing herself to be introduced into society, in a matter of days, knows everyone and has been invited to all the snobby clubs (they are boring), and she doesn't invite any of the Ladies for tea. I have turned down several such invitations and some of the ladies have excluded me. What am I supposed to do with these boring women, some of whom drink alcohol all day, and in all seriousness see it as proof of their emancipation? Not one has yet understood the reason of [sic] their social failures. Almost none of them know any other languages, and only one accompanies me to English classes. From all of them, I only like one lady who is quite a bit older. It just goes to prove that age isn't a factor because most of the crowd is quite a bit older, Wojtek is the youngest specialist. My friend will be traveling to Warsaw at the end of the month, and she promised she'd bring mom a locally made bracelet or necklace. The silver pieces that are made around here are really very pretty. Wojtek gave me a bracelet and ring made by old Kurdish techniques.

Dears! I'm off. You can't blame me for a lack of letters, this one is, at this point worth 6, including the cards I sent earlier. Lots of kisses. Please write, it's the medicine I need for missing you. I miss you all so much even though I try not to think about it. Please send my best wishes to everyone. —Marysia

Often their letters to Poland and back simply never made it. The Iraqi postal service had trained their workers to read in several languages, so they could intercept the letters. Everyone assumed that's what was going on when letters went "missing." It was even more remarkable then that the beautiful amber necklace Marysia's parents sent her made it through security. True, it was an unnecessary expenditure and a slightly foolish one—her parents had no money—but it was a piece of jewelry she would cherish. What she needed were places she could wear it.

One time, trying to get her mind off things, Wojtek dragged her to a work party. Marysia didn't really want to go, but she had just received a beautiful silver medallion necklace from her aunt in Israel. Marysia had an artist's eye, and even though she hadn't brought much with her, she was able to pick up a long blue skirt and structured silver top that worked beautifully with her red hair. Walking into the party, she was an immediate sensation. The women gathered around, wanting to hear the latest from Paris. Marysia had been a poor student—she had no idea what everyone was wearing, and she wasn't following the latest Paris trends. So she looked straight at the women. "Well, for starters," she began, "the ladies shave their legs."

Marysia had no use for the European snobs. And she could not make peace with some of the local customs either. As time passed, she grew more certain that Iraq was not where she wanted to be. One time, walking home with groceries, she noticed a little boy of eight or nine, one of her neighbors, brutally beating a puppy. She ran over, grabbed the boy by the arm, and made him stop. My mother was never one to back down when she saw or heard something that went against what she believed to be right.

As she was gathering the animal in her arms, the boy's mother, a European woman who had married a local man, ran out of her home. Marysia turned to her and lost it. How could she allow this to happen? What was she thinking? What kind of person would look the other way when an animal was being treated that way? The woman conceded that maybe she had let things go too far. She explained that this kind of behavior was encouraged—it was Marysia who'd get into trouble if a man caught her intervening.

But there were highlights, too, and insights into the rich links between Europeans and Iraq. One time, at the souk (market), where they could see jewelry being made or find interesting trinkets, Marysia stopped to examine handcrafted leather sandals. She and Wojtek were speaking Polish back and forth when the man sitting at the kiosk started whistling Chopin's "Revolutionary Étude." He then said (in Polish), "Polish Radio Baghdad here, broadcasting classical music." He had memorized the introduction to the hourlong Polish radio show for expats. When the couple asked him how he knew that, he answered, "There were a hell of a lot of you here during the war."

Wojtek was offered the post of director of the laboratory for the international highway that was being built through the desert. The news was bittersweet. It would mean moving to a new settlement in the middle of the desert, to what would feel to them like some godforsaken area far from civilization, even though it would be furnished down to the last teaspoon. So far there was no word on when the highway would be built. Iraq was building a connection to Europe, and instead of going through Jordan, as originally planned, they were redirecting the route through Syria.

As it turns out, the desert was awe-inspiring, a tricolor ocean of red, white, and black covered in limestone and flint. The settlement, a tent city somewhere between Tel Al Tanf and Ar-Rutbah, meant that while Wojtek went to work, Marysia could take her sketch pad and wander out to draw. Apparently, according to her letters, she did so in a long dress and wide-brimmed hat, which she gratefully accepted from one of the other wives, so she wouldn't burn to a crisp in the desert sun.

To her surprise, she didn't mind the desert as much as she thought she would. Plus, the extra money Wojtek was now making meant they could send a little money to her parents. News from home was worrisome—her mother's episodes were getting more intense. Paula was prone to dramatics, but Marysia could control her and help get her mind off things. In her heart, Marysia was still dead set on re-turning home as soon as possible, but the last letter from her father had been strict. Poland was still too dangerous.

They were hoping to stay in Paris but having steady work was paramount. Wojtek's face said it all, and Marysia had been expecting the verdict: His contract wasn't going to be renewed. With a serious tone, the counselor who broke the news to Wojtek quickly added that he shouldn't treat it as a punishment. Wojtek replied, "But of course sir, who said anything about a punishment? There is no need for one." With that, Marysia and Wojtek left the office and began managing their affairs.

Getting back to Europe would not be easy. One option was to go northeast through Riga Latvia, a route they were hoping to avoid. Another was traveling through the already snowcapped mountains of Turkey—a dangerous undertaking. The closest train, the Orient Express, started in either Istanbul or Ankara, but getting to one of those starting points by bus in December would be suicidal. A freighter would be the best option and stopping so often at ports would mean little time to be seasick. By sea, then, it was. The plan was to stop in Beirut for a few weeks to get their papers in order.

If everything went according to plan, Marysia would soon be a student again and finally finish her studies. "It feels like we are about to begin a new chapter in our lives," Marysia said to Wojtek as they sat drinking tea. "I believe it is going to be the hardest one yet, but I'm jumping in with no illusions."

Before leaving Baghdad, Marysia and Wojtek snuck away for a much-anticipated trip to Babylon. In one letter home, Marysia had written,

> Supposedly nothing much is left of the ancient splendors but I'm still planning on spending some time in awe. From a young age, I read so many archaeological books that I can fill in the magic which may not be there. We plan on spending the holidays "beside" the Casino du Liban. I say beside, because we won't have enough money to stay at this magnificent haven next to which the Lido in Paris pales by comparison. The New Year will fall sometime when we are out to sea. This is not a bad thing because it would be depressing to celebrate it anywhere else.

In general, going to the market was always an adventure for Marysia. Much of the time she wasn't sure what she was buying. She did manage a cooking feat when she had to make 150 dumplings she had promised her neighbors. There was some performance anxiety, and she wasn't making any promises regarding how well they would be digested, but somehow the dinner went off without a hitch.

Ramadan had started, and while Marysia and Wojtek didn't observe it, they did get invited to some nighttime feasts. One day, after several big dinners in a row, she decided that she would only eat fruit for a few days. Thrilled to find a grapefruit, she returned home and proudly placed the giant one-kilogram fruit on the counter. Wojtek laughed and told her that it was actually a pomelo, which is in the same family. He had tasted one in Siam a few years ago. Marysia was surprised to find that instead of a yellow interior it was a red-pink shade.

My mother was never much of a cook. In fact, most of my memories of her consist of her being on a diet. She hardly ate. Of course, she never starved us, and she did have a few cooking wins as well as epic fails. In an effort to convince my sister and me to eat more greens, she once purchased a package of frozen spinach that she successfully managed to overcook to the point of it becoming green tasteless mush. She served it to us in brown wooden bowls. Take a moment to picture that. It was as awful as it sounds. To make it even better, she was very upset with us when we refused to eat it.

Where my mother shone was when she could call upon her creativity. Even after living in Poland for four and a half years, I have never had a meringue that was comparable to hers. In fact, her meringues coupled with her Pischinger torte became legendary—so much so that they were requested for many a birthday. To clarify, that would be many a kid's birthday. Instead of fancy gooey cakes, even kids wanted the chocolate-covered layered wafer cakes.

Wandering around the bazaar, Marysia was looking for some small mementos of her time in Iraq and gifts for friends. Wojtek wouldn't let her buy a giant mortar and pestle set because it was much too heavy and impossible to transport. She knew he was right, but she still really wanted one. On the other hand, they had both gone crazy over the samovars and were desperately trying to figure out ways to transport one back to Europe. Even if it did take up a lot of space, they were authentic and hard to find anywhere else, they reasoned. Then there was the chore of buying new clothing. Everything they had was appropriate for the desert heat and some cooler nights, but they had nothing appropriate for real Paris winters.

This makes sense to me. Our home was filled with many treasures, some of it from this time. I can picture my mother's jewelry boxes overflowing with raw amber necklaces, chunky hammered silver bracelets. Turquoise, lapis lazuli, and malachite were all stones she wore frequently. She was extremely stylish but never trendy. Decorative hand-painted—some by my mother—plates and tiles lined our walls. Even an Ikea table, the kind that can be found in a million homes around the world, was never just an Ikea table. It would be stained and adorned with an ethnic piece, a couch would be upholstered with quality fabric, each piece of furniture looking more expensive than it really was.

I have many letters that Marysia wrote to her parents, and I have a series of letters that Franciszek wrote to Fryderyk but only one letter from Franciszek to Wojtek, written on February 24, 1969. Does this say something about their relationship? I think so. Of course, I don't know this for sure, but from my father's stories and the letters, Franciszek doesn't strike me as the most hands-on father.

The letter is Franciszek's last-ditch effort to have Wojtek come home and would ultimately lead to the family's estrangement. In it, Franciszek wrote to say that on February 23, 1969, he had been hauled into the ministry of the interior because they knew Wojtek's contract had ended on December 10. In other words, where was he? He hadn't yet returned to Poland. Of course, the Department of Foreign Affairs had contacted his father to see what Wojtek was going to do. His last name, Wichrzycki, and Marysia's maiden name, Topolski, still held a lot of weight in Poland. No surprise then that the government was keeping tabs on them both.

Luckily, his father covered for him, saying that the couple had delayed their return due to Marysia's illness. He added that the Road and Bridge Research Institute (COBiRTD) had granted Wojtek an unpaid two-year leave. The powers that be did not accept this excuse. Franciszek was told that Wojtek was not allowed to take a leave unless he had a contract, and that he should have sent in an embassy-certified certificate saying that he and Marysia were remaining in Iraq until she was well enough to travel. Ironically, Franciszek's intentions, while honorable, ended up putting more attention on the situation. COBiRTD and Wojtek's immediate superior would now be on the hook for his father's lie.

Now came the hardest part of the letter.

Wojtek knew his father's views were black-and-white. Franciszek expected his son to come home to Poland, period. For that very reason, Wojtek hadn't communicated to his parents the possibility that they would not in fact return to Poland. As luck, or the lack of it, would have it, a "well-informed" friend of Franciszek's had informed him that Wojtek was in correspondence with his father in-law, who knew all about the plan.

This was a total betrayal in Franciszek's eyes, and Wojtek knew there would be dire consequences. Still, the fact remained that Poland was a dangerous destination for Marysia, as had already been proven with regard to other members of her family.

His father went on to say that Wojtek needn't worry because no one, not Wandeczka or Andrzej, actually believed this ugly story. If, however, the rumors turned out to be true, then Franciszek joked that the nine vintage nails Wojtek had sent them as a souvenir from Beirut were really nails for their coffins and he would distribute them evenly among the family.

He specified that two nails would be for him, two for Andrzej, and five for Fryderyk, my other grandfather. Franciszek was sure that Fryderyk would be harshly persecuted if Wojtek and Marysia did not return. What he did not know was that Fryderyk had already told my parents not to come back.

While this does sound dramatic, and I'm sure Franciszek had a flair for words, the repercussions of Wojtek not returning were very real. The Wichrzycki family could suffer in much the same way Pawel's uncle had when his family did not return. While not literally placed in a coffin, essentially the family could be buried by the government.

The rest of the letter, however, was heavy on the guilt trip—the kind of guilt that would haunt you until your deathbed, complete with overblown dramatics. Franciszek went all out with what would happen, adding that Wandeczka was completely distraught, crying from morning until night. Wojtek's betrayal, Franciszek wrote—his choice to remain with his wife and not return to Poland—would bring such shame on the family that they would all have to quit their jobs and move to small villages where no one recognized them. They were old and would die soon, so this would be worse for Andrzej and his wife, Elżbieta, because they, too, would have to leave their rather lucrative jobs. Franciszek finished his letter by saying that this was a subject no one was talking about, but everyone was thinking about and that he hoped to find a letter in his mailbox letting them know Wojtek was finding his way home.

Still Wojtek didn't have the heart to tell his parents that he wouldn't be returning.

He didn't know it at the time, but the estrangement was a permanent one: Never again would he see his father. In fact, he wouldn't see his mother or brother until the Iron Curtain was lifted some twenty years later and he was finally allowed back in the country.

Wojtek loved his father, but they did not agree on some fundamental issues, the kinds of issues that drove a wedge between them, a wedge that revolved mostly around politics. Where Wandeczka was a lot less harsh in her ideas, and as a mom had a soft spot for her son, Franciszek was set in his ways and difficult to talk to. A staunch hard-line communist, Franciszek expected everyone to adhere to the party line. Following his death on March 5, 1953, Stalin's portrait, complete with black mourning band, appeared on the wall of Franciszek's office, where it remained for several years, even after all the atrocities the Party had committed came to light.

Perhaps admitting that these atrocities had happened would be like admitting that Franciszek had been wrong about the ideology. Or wrong about other things. I wonder, would he have voted for the PiS government or fought their oppressive changes? Would he have marched alongside us or stood on the sidelines?

CHAPTER 18

FAMILY ESCAPES AROUND THE WORLD

I grew up with parents who loved beautiful things. Clothing, furniture, art, architecture, you name it, they loved it and taught us to love it, too. Our home was a cultural haven. Antique cowbells from Afghanistan hung next to an Iraqi rug. A hand-hewn wooden table with chairs and a bench displaying magnificent ram heads, all made by a Swedish artisan friend, centered the living room. Most of the objects in our house had a story, and my parents were always happy to tell it.

Growing up surrounded by treasures from one's travels means that even if you haven't been to a particular place yourself, you gain a connection with it. A print on a fabric tells a story. A piece of jewelry tells a story. Ask someone where a prized piece came from, and right away you slip into another world.

True, languages and misunderstanding cultures can create seemingly insurmountable barricades to the outsider. But, like food, fashion, art, and architecture break down these barriers. My father taught me how to recognize a quality-made Persian rug. Now, when

I flip one over in a shop, the owner is delighted that I've taken the time to understand what it is they cherish. Looked at this way, hard lines between art, architecture, or clothing become blurred. Words like texture, style, movement, and materials become interchangeable. Browse my bookshelves, and you'll find beautiful works on the history of fashion cozied up to those on world architecture. These are things that all belong together.

They say that when the economy is doing poorly, lipstick sales go up. In postwar Warsaw, when nothing was available, the women not only made their own clothing, but they were also so stylish that for a while Poland was known as the Paris of the East. I heard this over and over again when I was growing up. So when Pawel and I land in Warsaw in 2013, I am surprised—and saddened—that this statement is no longer true. The love affair with Paris continues, but with no true middle class in Poland, choice is now limited.

The majority of shopping is either cheap, fast fashion, or high-end brands. A lot of women are crammed into ill-fitting clothing. Most don't wear a full face of makeup. Where, I wonder, is that Polish pride? On second thought, that is a whole other conversation. I realize that what is missing is the in-between shops, with fabrics that are higher quality, so they won't lose their shape or pill right away, with pieces that will still look good a few years down the road.

And then it hits me. Who taught me about clothing and taking care of myself? My parents. My parents, who left the country and traveled, were never depressed by the communist system. Here I am, milling the streets of a country where an entire generation could not cross borders freely. Most Poles my age did not have the advantage of being raised by progressive expats.

When my sister was getting married, my father searched high and low for the right fabric to make himself a bow tie that would match her accent colors. Matching the wedding party showed respect; it meant he was essential to the group. My father had that kind of eye. Ever the engineer, he taught us how to appreciate structural details in buildings.

My mother was the visual artist, the one who could find beauty where others couldn't always see it. A wall hanging that resembled what can only be described as skinned bats made all of us cringe, but she loved it, so it hung on the wall above the stairs. She would shop at designer warehouse sales when we were struggling financially, and pick key pieces to mix and match with items from bargain-basement stores like BiWay. I don't think I ever saw her in sweats. I'm not sure she owned a pair. She was always put together: red lipstick, nail polish, hair done. A T-shirt neatly tucked into jeans and white sneakers were dog-park attire. Tailored clothing, statement earrings, or a necklace were for everyday wear.

Her mother, my grandmother, also had an eye. She especially liked my sister and me to look spotless. When grunge came into fashion, she would sit back in her chair, take a long drag on her cigarette, and make snide comments about our plaid shirts and torn jeans. While that didn't do wonders for our self-esteem, it did make me notice how clothing is made, where it comes from, and what materials are used. Let's just say then that she succeeded in getting us to pay attention.

I learned to pay attention even as a kid. In grade seven or eight, when my mother decided it was cold enough to wear snow pants to school, I protested. "That's never going to happen," I said. "I'm not going."

"You have to go to school, and it's too cold to just wear pants."

"I don't care, you can't force me to wear them."

"Fine, wear something else, but you are going to school."

I chose her old brown seventies-style sheepskin coat, which I loved.

When I was thirteen, and the kids at school started having bar and bat mitzvahs, I wanted one because I liked the fact that the birthday person would receive a piece of gold jewelry embossed with their name or initials. I wanted *that*. My mother, on the other hand, thought the whole idea was tacky.

When it came to style, hers or mine, it was always a battle of wills. Still, at the end of the day, I came to see that my parents viewed clothing not just as an expression of the wearer but as art.

In Warsaw, Pawel and I have settled near Chopin University, along the Royal Route, in an artistic part of town. In the summer, classical music floats through the air, and in the evenings, we are serenaded by students practicing for concerts. This is the museum and galleries route. One street over is Theater Square. The whole experience culminates in Old Town, and a deluge of amber.

The debate about whether Warsaw should be rebuilt after World War II was an intense one. Old photos show the city decimated, a vast wasteland of blasted stone. The idea of leaving that as a memorial was floated, but ultimately the city was rebuilt. While other European cities reconstructed a handful of what had been destroyed, the opposite happened in Warsaw, which is why much of the city looks much as it did before the war. The city is an architectural feat. From the Museum of Cartoon Art and Caricature to the National

Museum to the Polish National Opera, all things cultural are within walking distance of one another, and celebrated.

When my father comes to visit, he can't stop talking about the Poster Museum. He's obsessed with showing me vintage art—a passion that comes from his time in the theater and my mother's time in art school. As I say, I grew up with parents holding art to the highest of standards.

Whenever we traveled, too, we either rented apartments or borrowed ones that belonged to friends. When you're shopping some place where you don't speak the language, you soon shed your tourist's skin. Your vacation becomes an immersive cultural experience.

In late 1980s in Granada, Spain, we had just seen the ruins of the Alhambra Castle when my mother said, "Let's see what we can find down this street"—a street plucked straight from a Fellini film, with an old lady on a stoop peeling potatoes and kids in shorts and tank tops knocking about a football in the street. At least that's how I remember it, and because I can see each detail so vividly, I have to stay true to this memory.

Nobody pays attention to us—tourists probably wander down this side street all the time—and when we come across a set of oversized wooden doors with a small gold cross that indicates a church, we march right in. My mother could never resist churches. The art, the architecture, she loved it all. "Wow!" I exclaim, "This is beautiful." The church is small, maybe big enough for two dozen people. The benches are a rough-hewn dark wood, the walls a stark white. Simple, yes? No. The room is filled with lifelike statues of Mary and Jesus draped in the most expensive-looking cloth I have ever seen. And dripping with gold. As we walk the aisle, my mother points out the fine fabrics used to make this clothing. She knows the name of every one.

When we visit Ronda and Cordoba, my mother, father, and I pile into a car and drive through Andalusia. I was never that girl who dreamed about her wedding or starting a family, but as I stood below the Puente Nuevo (New Bridge, started in 1759), my one and only thought was, this is the backdrop I want for my wedding. Cordoba I remember most. The winding cobblestone streets, my parents helping me pick out a gold bracelet with a classic Islamic geometric pattern, and, most of all, my father's face as he tells me about the unique red-and-white archways in the mosque. He covers the whole history, how the arches were made. Whenever he spoke about architecture, his talk included a breakdown of the structure.

My father had an eye for jewelry, too, and every now and then he would pull out the jewelry he had bought my mother in Iraq. Visiting his brother's home in Warsaw, my father walked me through the treasures once amassed by the family. There is even a collection at the Muzeum Azji i Pacyfiku, the Asia and Pacific Museum, that had been donated there without my father's consent. That was back when he was still estranged from the family.

I take him there one afternoon and on the spur of the moment ask if we can speak with the director. What's the worst that can happen? She will say no? As it turns out, she is very welcoming and offers to take us upstairs to the museum's storage area, where we see the beautiful jacket woven with gold thread that my grandfather had once presented to my grandmother. We are shown old carafes and jugs, sitting in cold storage.

Surrounded by these amazing artifacts, I have another idea. "Would it be possible to include my dad's name on the donor list?" I ask. "These pieces belong to him as much as they do his brother." My father's family has conveniently left him out of the story, but at

the museum, it is immediately agreed that his name should appear
as well.

One of the highlights of living in Poland is that art is so accessible. I realize I've really missed this. In Toronto, I had always been
part of the theater and arts scene. Not so in Vancouver. Although
beautiful, and there's definitely something to be said for living by
the ocean, Vancouver didn't feed my soul. Here, in Warsaw, there
are tiny hidden galleries everywhere, and theater performances are
inexpensive by North American standards. In Canada, going to a
theater or dance performance is a treat. In Warsaw, where fifty US
dollars get you a prime seat, I go as often as I can.

A high point is the STS reunion in October. Seeing the old-timers
act like a bunch of unruly teenagers is heartwarming. No reading is
complete without someone being a smartass. Actors and directors
reminisce about the good old days. My father is clearly in his element. His face lights up, the present is forgotten, and he probably
wouldn't admit it, but I think he forgets about me. The theater is
what saved him when he couldn't turn to his family, but it's so much
more than that. He followed in his father's footsteps and became an
engineer, but deep down he has the heart of an artist, something that
never goes away. When official photos need to be taken, no one is listening or behaving themselves. The next generation, or two, is there
and just as engaged as the originals. They are keeping art and culture
alive. They are, in a word, invested.

In Warsaw, I also see firsthand the kinds of things my parents
prized in their home country. Every time we walk by the art university where my mother went to school, my dad points out the
building. Every single time. And we walk by it a lot. No matter where

they lived as immigrants, they appreciated art and craft. Sometimes it's the quotidian things they cherished. All throughout my childhood, they wore the authentic clogs they'd brought with them from Sweden.

And it was never just about the things from far away. My dad taught me how to sew and embroider so that I could mend my jeans or rips in my sweaters rather than discard them. An embroidered flower does wonders to keep a loved outfit looking charming and new. I can't tell you how many weekends were spent traveling throughout Ontario, searching for antiques. My mother had an eye for them as well. It turns out the best pieces of furniture can be found behind the store with the restored furniture, or in people's barns.

From my mother, I learned to stay true to my own style. I learned to always strive for something better. Best of all, I learned to haggle. The year 1990 brought us to Morocco, where I watched as my mother walked brazenly into a store, picked out some things like, say, a necklace or a pair of earrings, and took them to the salesperson along with a black-and-white handmade bag I wanted. Then she haggled until she got everything she wanted for a fraction of the posted price.

What I remember of Morocco is looking, always looking at all the wonderful things. I remember what I saw even more than I recall the rich aromas of the spice-lined streets.

Five years before Morocco we were in Empuriabrava, Spain, which was filled with things to do and see. Staying in one place wasn't enough for my mom. A relaxing vacation on the beach? It never happened. Sure, we might spend time on the sand, but it was never for long. And because European cities are much closer together than those in North America, it is significantly easier to travel between them. So whenever we traveled, we drove around and explored the region.

After a fairly short but hot drive, we arrived in Figueres—what was probably my favorite city and one that I'll never forget. Salvador Dali still lived there at the time, and I was crazy about him and his work. Dali's painting always spoke to me. The colors, the stories, and most of all the style. I had read biographies and was drawn to his extravagance and his crazy visions. For me, it was love at first sight—his museum with the plant-filled car out front, giant vases tipped on their sides filling a huge saltwater pool that everyone swam in, and taking peeks over the wall into Dali's compound. And then my mother told me that she'd once been invited to a party where Dali was the guest of honor. That's it. No more information. She said it as if it was no big deal, and that changed my world.

While most of our vacations involved a lot of hiking, cultural outings, and some rest, there was always a shopping component as well. Madrid in 1990 stands out. Not for big chains, but for out-of-the-way shops that the average tourist wasn't likely to find. Some of our favorite pieces were found unexpectedly like this. One time, we were returning from almost two months in Costa Del Sol. We'd been traveling through southern Spain, visiting all the small towns we could handle. On our way home, we had a six-hour layover in Madrid. Six hours is a long time but cutting it close when you are on a mission. Which my mother was.

Growing up, I learned from her that every woman should be just a little vain when it came to her appearance. Never one to shop in trendy places, she made sure we passed all the major stores, which is how we found ourselves walking into small boutiques, looking for gold-colored heels.

We were, however, looking for a very specific shade of green-gold heel, and in retrospect, I have a feeling she would have gladly missed our flight home if we hadn't found them. Her relentless search finally led us to a store with a shopkeeper who gave her a knowing look. He motioned for us to follow him into a magical space, where one room led to another, each one filled with different colored shoes and bags. There was a room of red accessories, one with blue, and so on. At last we arrived in a room with row upon row of green and gold shoes, where my mother was thrilled to find the exact shade she was looking for.

We even made the flight home.

The strangest shopping trip of all had to have been in New York City in 2010. That fall, my husband was taking a course for work, and I was tagging along. After all, September 15 was coincidentally our ninth wedding anniversary. Basically, I had told him I was coming to New York with him, or there would be a strong possibility of divorce.

While he was cooped up in an office in the Financial District, I had the whole day to walk and rediscover the city I love. In typical New York early-fall fashion, it was a hot, muggy day. After hours of wandering the streets, I finally made my way through the park, to Madison Avenue and Seventy-Fifth-ish. As I stood in front of Carolina Herrera, lost in the beauty of an expertly tailored white dress, a man walked up to me and mumbled something.

I turned and said, "Excuse me?"

"It's been a long time since I've kissed you, but all that is going to change now," he said in a delighted but forceful voice.

I barely had time to register that he was well dressed. White shirt, tan pants, and a wooden beaded choker.

Ummm, yeah, no, it's not ran through my head as I made a beeline across the street. Over my shoulder I could see him following. Almost all the stores were empty, except the Louboutin shop. With relief I saw they had several salesmen working. *Great*, I thought, as I rushed in.

Within seconds, I explained my situation. Just then my stalker walked into the store. The gentleman who was helping me pulled me aside. "Just pretend you are looking at the shoes," he whispered. A part of me was already calming down. I mean, come on, the shoes are quite fabulous. That was until I felt something go flying by my head and I heard the peculiar sound of a heel hitting a cash register. Everyone sprang into action. I was rushed into the back room, and the store was cleared of all customers.

As I sat in what could only be described as the world's best closet, the manager came rushing in with a tray of coffees. "I only jumped out for a moment; what happened?" I asked. He quickly brought me a glass of Perrier and explained that he had called detectives, because the now-broken shoe rang in at $2,500. I sent off a quick text to my husband and waited.

The detectives arrived just as my husband called me in a panic. In hindsight, texting "a small stalking incident" while waiting for detectives probably wasn't the best thing I could have written.

Being an avid fan of *Law & Order*, I knew exactly whom to expect, and I must say I was disappointed when two "real" cops strode in twenty minutes later. They took down my account of the incident. Then I was left alone, again, with the manager. "So, since you are sitting here anyway, do you want to try on some shoes?"

Music to my ears! Laughing nervously, I said, "Sure, but maybe not the twenty-five-hundred-dollar ones."

"Oh, don't worry," he said, laughing, "it's easy to stay on a budget here." Then he looked me over, turned to a saleswoman, and said, "Bring her the nude sling-backs with the open toe." Turning to me, he added, "There's a two-month waitlist for them."

I knew I was in big trouble, but the whole situation was so surreal that I decided just to go for it and let events unfold however they might. Besides, at this point I wasn't afraid anymore, and my adrenaline was slowly dropping back to normal.

The shoes were everything and then some. They fit like a glove. I swear they were made for me. Even though I was tempted to buy them on the spot, I asked the store to hold the shoes until the next day.

The following afternoon, when Pawel and I arrived at the store we were greeted with air kisses from the manager, followed by a bottle of Veuve Clicquot. There was a long-haired shih tzu complete with red bow running around, and the women, who all looked like they stepped out of a *Real Housewives* television show, turned to see who we were. I spent some time trying on different heels, and as an anniversary present my husband bought me, well, you know, the shoes I'd tried on the day before.

When I told my father and grandmother all about my Madison Avenue adventure, neither asked if I was okay. Instead, they each exclaimed, "Okay, but did you get the shoes?!"

CHAPTER 19

MY PARENTS' NEW BEGINNINGS

I'm not sure that anyone sets out to become a refugee, but that is exactly what happened to my parents. I cannot imagine how that would feel. Wojtek and Marysia said goodbye to Baghdad on December 8, 1969. I never knew the details of this story, no matter how many times I asked. But one day when my father was over for dinner, without prompting, he started to talk. He was surprised that I asked so many questions. This was one of the rare stories not told over and over again. I couldn't get my recorder out fast enough when he started talking.

> The first leg of our trip was by bus. We were supposed to travel from Baghdad to Damascus, but at the last minute they took a detour through Jordan. That added a few hundred kilometers to our journey. We were in a bus traveling along the border, above Israel, which we could see in the distance. It was luck that no one started shooting at us. It was still a few hours before nightfall. Still Ramadan.

Since we hadn't expected to travel through Jordan, we didn't have the appropriate paperwork. We needed visas. We had passage from Baghdad to Damascus. It's the middle of the night, we have been traveling through the desert, there are no cities, no towns, nothing is around, just sand. We don't have permission to be there.

Yet sometimes you can still find some honest help. We approached a policeman who brought us over to a donkey cart. It was about four feet wide, maybe eight feet long, with a donkey. The cart had flaps that lifted, where you would expect to see tourist trinkets for sale. A man with a beard and cloth covering his head. We explained our situation. I pulled out my Bank of America travelers' cheques (yes, really, Bank of America). I had my salary paid out for the year, this was money that would sustain us in Paris for the next few months. The man pulled out a newspaper, looked up the currency exchange. I wrote out a cheque and he gave me Jordanian currency so we could pay for our visas.

Absolute masters of counting. Within a few minutes, our passports were signed and stamped, and we were able to go on our way.

After Damascus, the couple spent a month visiting Beirut, where Wojtek purchased a thin waterproof coat that he imagined would be perfect for Parisian winters. They then boarded a ship headed for Marseilles by way of Naples. And for the next week or so they slept in a small, second-class cabin, not much bigger than what one would find on a train, but the porthole made the cabin airy and bright. The weather was so beautiful as they set sail that Marysia and Wojtek grabbed some blankets and made their way up to the top deck, where they pulled up two reclining chairs. Pretty soon, between the fresh sea air and the rhythmic rocking of the boat, they were lulled fast asleep. As the ferry crossed from the Libyan Sea and into the Aegean, mountainous Crete rose before them. Sailing quite close to land, they could see the lush green landscape. Although they didn't dock, this still felt like a successful first "visit" to Greece. When the ferry hugged the Sicilian coast, Marysia felt she could almost reach out and touch the shore.

The next day they toured Naples, which, surprisingly, wasn't much different from Beirut. Naples had more energy and better weather, but nothing could compare to Beirut's being surrounded by snow-covered peaks. After a classic Italian coffee, cappuccino for Marysia and espresso for Wojtek, they walked along the boulevard drinking in the sea air, then made their way into the city center, where they navigated the narrow streets and the onslaught of bazaars. On a small side street they found a diner, pretty much a hole-in-the-wall, where they gorged on fresh seafood, knowing they wouldn't be able to afford fine food once they got to Paris.

Deboarding the ship in Marseille, it took a few minutes to find their land legs again, but how good to finally be in France. In terms of cities, Marseille was the clear winner of the trip. This could easily be their final destination. Like that of their ship quarters, the berth on the night train to Paris was tight, but all they needed were clean sheets. By morning they arrived in Paris.

They found a charming room at 9 rue Godot de Mauroy, a narrow street packed with small restaurants and tiny shops. For a few francs, they had a room in a second-story walk-up above a restaurant, where the hallways were covered in old-fashioned wallpaper depicting fancily dressed ladies and water fountains. Of course, my mother would note the wallpaper in her letters. The room was freshly decorated, and everything was brand-new. Most importantly, it also had a sink with running hot and cold water. The bathrooms were a level up, on the third floor. This would be short-lived—they did need a stove for the long term. For now, however, their little home was perfect.

They began spending as much time as they could with Marysia's old friends. She was relieved to find that they all took to Wojtek as he did to them, and they enjoyed meeting up in cafés and bars, or scraping together enough money to see a play. They also spent a lot of time at the Louvre. Marysia loved the paintings and explaining techniques the painters had used. They enrolled in language classes at the Alliance Française, an international organization that promotes the French language. Wojtek, admittedly, was a bit lost in Paris. For days he wandered around exclaiming how big the city was. A few days later after trying to get his hair cut, he decided that they didn't know how to cut hair—perhaps because most men in Paris wore their hair long. He was also shocked by the styles, apparently it was anything goes. He even ran into a man wearing a miniskirt.

Marysia had no trouble transitioning back to the city. It wasn't nearly as warm in Paris as in Beirut, but Marysia felt at home. She had missed the arts scene and her friends. The excitement of '68 had died down, and a more somber mood had replaced it. But Paris was still loud and dirty, too much so for Wojtek's taste, but they were safer there, and he could see how much happier Marysia appeared to be.

Marysia loved Paris, and their little hotel room was charming, but the location wasn't ideal and getting around was not always easy. Jumping out for an hour meant actually jumping out for a few hours. She felt as if they were always running around somewhere. Most of the important paperwork for their immigration had already been filed, but there were still odds and ends that needed tying up. Really, she was still hoping they could find a place closer to the Latin Quarter, her favorite part of town by far and close to the Alliance Française, where they took their language classes. The ninety-minute classes took place five days a week and always in the evenings. The commute there and back took forever.

The vibrancy of the Latin Quarter and its many galleries and tiny shops made Marysia happy. She adored the beautiful and affordable fabric shops and spent her free time looking for fabric she could send to her mother and mother-in-law, usually simple, serviceable materials that could be used for three seasons, making them the most useful. Shops aside, finding a new place wasn't easy. One flat they saw had a pink curtain pulled around the toilet, which sat on a pedestal in the middle of the room. Another had a squat toilet with a wooden grate that could be pulled over the hole so you could take a shower. Often flats fell off their must-see list because they simply cost too much.

It was a similar search when it came to their prospective jobs, and by early February, they were both so exhausted by job and house hunting that they decided to splurge by taking in the Grevin Museum, seeing the wax figures, then strolling down the Champs-Élysées—always one of their guilty pleasures. Looking, after all, was free. They could always imagine that one day, perhaps they'd be able to come back and eat dinner on this world-famous street.

Finally, they found another tiny flat and left their tiny hotel for a space that they could call their own. Their budget was 220 francs a month. Renting the flat began with a rather funny moment. They were referred to a very French real estate agent who proceeded to speak very fast and with a lot of intricate hand gestures. Marysia had been working on her French while Wojtek had a rudimentary knowledge at best. Even so, it was all Marysia could do to understand the agent. Wojtek was completely lost. Every now and then the agent would stop and look at Wojtek, who would reply with a "Mais oui" or "Bon, très bon." He had no idea what he was agreeing to, but the agent wasn't any the wiser, and when they finally signed the papers for the place on 97, Rue de L'Abbé Grout in the 15th arrondissement, the agent shook their hands. "Madame speaks French very well," he said, "but Monsieur, Monsieur, c'est magnifique." Even Marysia, who prided herself on her ability to speak numerous languages, had to laugh.

They settled into the flat nicely. True, their bed took up most of the space, but it was their own space, and they loved it. Plus, Wojtek, who had been working at an entry-level job as an engineer, got Marysia a job at the same office, so they finally had some money coming in. Even at that they could only afford a one-way metro ticket and one cigarette a day, but at least they were safe. And spring finally began disrupting the winter cold. Marysia could at last put away her heavy sweaters and replace her woolen coat with a favorite suede one. There would still be a few cold days, but Paris was already hinting at spring. Trees were on the verge of blooming. Some days, the couple could even share a coffee outside. Marysia then received word that her parents had managed to join KT in Sweden, which must have been a huge relief. Everyone was safe.

Sometime around then, Wojtek and Marysia left the Alliance Française with a feeling of relief, having both passed the monthly exam. Their language wasn't perfect, but Marysia was managing well enough. She was even reading a difficult novel that she hadn't already read in Polish. It was going surprisingly well, although she did need to check in with her instructor every now and again just to make sure she understood everything.

Sadly, their life in Paris was short-lived. Marysia loved the city, but even she had to admit that it was difficult to live there if you weren't Parisian, as she shared in a 1970 letter to her parents. My father was vague about the details of why they chose to explore their options of leaving Paris. I have more questions than answers, but from what I can surmise, Paris was expensive, and foreigners weren't overly welcome, especially if they did not speak French well. Wojtek was having a difficult time finding a permanent job, and her family was pressuring her to join them in Sweden. Her dream life in Paris just wasn't in the cards, it seemed. At least not for the time being. Wojtek wanted to move to Italy, but in the end, her family won out.

On Tuesday, January 20, Marysia and Wojtek got up early and made their way to the Swedish consulate to apply for a visa. A nice woman welcomed them and informed them that they didn't officially need a visa since they were living on a Titre de Voyage, but as they were applying for an open-ended stay in Sweden, it was a good idea to apply officially. There was no telling how long the process would take. Marysia was getting cold just thinking about the weather in Sweden. What about moving somewhere warm like California? But, no, her parents were in Sweden, so Sweden it was.

In the process of applying, the couple received a surprise "gift" of a three-year permit to stay in Paris. That meant they could travel and cross borders freely while still officially having their address in Paris.

Then, in five years, they would receive French citizenship. Marysia knew it was probably closer to fantasy than reality, but she nursed a secret hope that this would work out in their favor, especially after speaking with other Polish expats for whom it had been a success.

In the meantime, she still needed to arrange certain matters with her parents. There were all the books, for instance. What had been given away for good? There were a few titles she knew she'd have a hard time finding in France, namely, Polska Plastyka Teatralna. Hopefully someone would be willing to bring the books over during one visit or another. Also, what had happened to their beloved books by Proust, Sienkiewicz, and Żeromski? So, yes, the books.

But from her mother, Marysia needed more obscure information, which meant that yet another letter home was necessary. What was the possibility of giving birth in a London hospital and paying for it directly? Could this type of thing be arranged? Her friend's due date was fast approaching, and getting the right paperwork was proving to be quite the challenge. Her friends were set on having the baby in London, so the child would have UK citizenship. Usually, these kinds of things could take years to organize, but Marysia knew that Paula knew people, and that sometimes things could be expedited.

At this Marysia pulled out the letter she'd been working on. It was too late to type, the clicking noise was too loud, so she wrote her postscript: "Please extend my love to my crazy brother who is apparently too busy being in love to write back but let him know that I'll send him some medication for his obvious penophobia." She sealed the letter and left it on the table. She would send it tomorrow.

But things did not prove simple at all. Just as their lives were beginning to settle down, the office where they both were working was restructured, and Wojtek was laid off. Worse, he was asked to resign, so the company could pay out a lower severance. The job was in a construction company that built prefabricated slabs that would then be made into subsidized housing in newer areas of Paris. Unfortunately, there were just enough of these companies that there wasn't always enough work to go around.

For some time now, Wojtek had been sitting at work with nothing to do. He already thought the whole thing was a waste of time. On the one hand, it certainly wasn't his dream job—and nothing compared to what he had worked on in Iraq. Still, a job meant money coming in, and they certainly needed the money. Plus, the prospects for a Pole who did not know French finding other work in Paris were slim.

Wojtek was shaken by the news of the layoff, and Marysia suggested that they go to a movie to get his mind off things. A seemingly small gesture, but one that would have been a big expense and a rare treat. He was still getting paid for another month, so they weren't starving. But clearly it was time to get serious about that Swedish visa, yet that would have to wait for a few more days.

The couple had been invited to the Great Synagogue of Paris for a commemorative service in memory of the twenty-fifth anniversary of the liberation of Auschwitz. Wojtek had purchased a small hat in Beirut that resembled a kippah—at least it was close enough that he could wear it on what would officially be his first time as an honorary Jew. Wojtek sat with the men, and Marysia sat in a separate area with the other women. First the rabbi blessed all those gathered, then France, then the rest of the world. In later years, we would laugh that my dad was often an honorary Jew at events. In fact, whenever we had a question about Jewish holidays or traditions, he was our first point of contact.

As their emigration to Sweden drew nearer, Marysia and Wojtek found themselves running around Paris gathering supplies. The trick was to buy expensive, high-quality things for cheap, and Marysia was good at finding deals. She found a beautiful sheepskin coat and already had her eye on one for Wojtek. She had made peace with the fact that she wasn't returning to Warsaw, but Sweden felt like a move to Antarctica—she wasn't used to real winters, and most of the winter clothing she was finding were thinly lined woolen coats. Still, she needed to stock up on as much warm clothing as they could afford.

She was also having a very difficult time parting ways with Paris.

From the start, her parents had put a lot of pressure on her to move to Sweden to be with them. A part of her missed her family and wanted them all to be together, but Paris was in her heart. She vowed that if she ever had "too much" money, she would buy a pied-à-terre in Paris.

Soon she and Wojtek would land in Sweden. She sent one more letter to her parents, saying that, really, she would not be in the mood to meet with all their friends and relations upon arriving in Stockholm. It was a thirty-hour trip, and she wanted to wash her hair and clothes and maybe get her nails done. Appearance meant a lot to her; it always did.

While Paula was convinced that even distant friends became closer, Marysia thought it was the opposite: that when you are an immigrant, close friends become distant. The friends you left behind carry on with their lives while you work at creating a new one for yourself. Marysia didn't know exactly, but it was a topic that she wanted to explore. I don't know if my mother ever did follow up on this thought, but I have found that while a connection remains, close friends become distant when you move away. Those friendships aren't built around the extra communication it takes to keep them fresh. By contrast, I have long-distance friends, who have always been long-distance, and both parties put in the same amount of effort to communicate with each other.

But for now, their move was all about pragmatics. So much was up in the air, like the question of a car: whether to get one in Paris or in Germany, or to wait until they arrived in Sweden. Marysia was getting frustrated with her parents and their lack of correspondence. I think she was also expecting them to be more enthusiastic about the family's reunion, and more involved with her and my dad's travel plans.

What she probably didn't realize was what her parents went through. My mother and father couldn't return to Poland; her parents had effectively been kicked out. Once again, they were being forced to start over. They would have to find new jobs, learn a new language, and make new connections. Sweden was no one's first choice. Their natural destination could have been Israel, but my grandfather was still convinced that communism was the ideal system. He had plans to get a visa for Yugoslavia, which he had been advised to apply for from Sweden. With their lives so up in the air, I think that they can be excused for having lukewarm responses to my mother's letters.

Marysia and Wojtek, however, needed real details about what they could expect to find in Sweden. It was all fine and good to make plans, but now they had to either execute them or just stay put. Something was going on, she felt, something that she and Wojtek weren't yet privy to. Didn't her parents realize that leaving Paris was not an easy choice for her? Didn't they realize that timing would be everything once Wojtek stopped getting paid? If her parents would only answer, she would know how to proceed.

March arrived in Stockholm as expected—cold, very cold, and very gray. My parents arrived by train, having decided not to buy a car, which meant they could afford to book a direct couchette from Paris to Stockholm, arriving at their new home midday. Marysia was happy to see that her parents had respected their wishes not to have to meet all their friends and family at the station. She wanted the day to get herself together before having to be social.

A curly black ball of fur came running out to greet the couple. Marysia was so happy to see Żak, the family springer spaniel, she sat on the floor and cried.

They decided to celebrate that night, and the whole family gathered—for the first time in two years—at a local restaurant. Marysia was thrilled except for one thing. She could not get warm, no matter how many layers she added. She ordered a glass of warm milk, hoping that would warm her up. The milk placed in front of her was cold, so she sent it back. Unlike in Sweden, milk in Paris was always served hot. When the milk came back to the table, she realized the glass had simply been placed in warm water. The contents were still cold.

Next to the weather on the adaptation scale was the language. Every country they had lived in, language was an issue. Wojtek and Marysia immediately enrolled in Swedish language classes.

Within a few weeks of their arrival, all hell broke loose when Fryderyk announced that he had found a job in Spain and that he was leaving. Wojtek was furious. So, this was the plan? That Paula would live with him and Marysia while Fryderyk fled to a new life?

After some of the initial emotional response died down and after much discussion, the upshot was that they agreed to sell the parental flat and Paula moved out on her own. Fryderyk, meanwhile, had re-lented and promised to bring her to Spain when he settled. Until then he traveled back and forth.

Meanwhile, Marysia and Wojtek found a one-bedroom flat in the suburb of Taby. It was a bright, sunny space overlooking a large mall with a zoo. And being right on the train line, they could easily get to Stockholm whenever they felt the need to immerse themselves in city life. I am hazarding a guess that my parents didn't want to be swept up into family drama. That would soon change, but for now they could mostly ignore it.

But if it sounded promising, in all honesty, suburban life was boring, nothing like the vibrancy of Paris life. What saved them from complete boredom were their friends. They found the Swedish people very welcoming and open to starting friendships. One group of their friends lodged in a type of commune. There were four or five couples, some with kids, all living together and sharing household chores. Marysia and Wojtek went up there often to swim and spend time roasting in the sauna. Being around all these healthy Swedish families made its mark in other ways as well. Wojtek and Marysia decided they really wanted to grow their family.

As soon as the weather thawed, they started taking road trips to Finland and Norway. Once, when Wojtek was driving their VW sedan, they arrived at a fork, and he asked Marysia which way to go. "Well," she said, "if you go right, we will cross the Russian border." They turned left. This was a symbolic turn, a turn for their future. For two families who had run from Soviet Russia, going back would not have been a good option.

With twenty-four-hour daylight and awe-inspiring landscapes, the couple could finally catch their breath after all the family drama.

The air was pure, and the flora was lush. They both wished they could stay in the wilderness forever—except, of course, wilderness has its own drama. Once, when they let Żak out for a quick pee break, he turned gray from all the mosquitoes covering him. Then there were the Norwegian seagulls. Somewhere near the Arctic Circle, without thinking, they accidentally left Żak's food bowl outside. Within minutes, the birds had swooped down, finished the food, and pecked holes in the metal bowl. What a Hitchcock moment that was.

These kinds of trips were a lifesaver for my parents. Up until this time they had spent little time together. Mostly, though, the two settled in and worked at adapting. Wojtek found himself at a construction company again. Marysia enrolled at the local university, in their business program, and went on to become one of only two non-Swedish women to graduate.

But while Marysia and Wojtek did their best to assimilate, my grandparents had a harder time of it. They were revolutionaries, and there were thousands of them, and for as grateful as they were to have been taken in by Sweden, they were not given preferential treatment. That held true even for those who had held prestigious positions back in Poland. Fryderyk, for instance, was given some sort of archival work to do, and Paula was left to assess disability insurance. She hated her job, although there was one minor consolation. She was able to exact a small degree of revenge against some of the past agents of terror. Many of the men coming forward to claim more government money were ex-German soldiers who had been injured in the Wehrmacht.

The war had left its mark in strange ways, on countless people. The family was no exception. Paula, for example, seemed to suffer in ways that were outrageous, and that made her inflict more suffering on others.

The exact date and timeline is unknown, but roughly a few months later, everything finally came to a head. The family agreement was that Paula, still in Sweden, and Fryderyk, now living in Madrid, would meet in Toronto, Canada, for KT's wedding, then the two would leave together for Spain. Instead, word came that in a matter of hours, Paula would be landing in Stockholm. The reason given was that she needed to pick up her winter coat.

Of course, Wojtek and Marysia knew that was made up. It was a perfectly crafted story to make it seem as if Paula had made the decision to return. Once again, Fryderyk was dumping Paula on them.

Marysia couldn't take it. She could not be her mother's keeper.

Up until now, when Marysia was away during the day taking continuing education classes, Paula would frequently call Wojtek, make gagging noises, then hang up. He'd send friends over to check if she was okay, thinking she was about to hang herself. By now, he'd had his share of her bad behavior and decided that the situation was no longer tenable.

Waiting for her to arrive at the apartment, Wojtek called Fryderyk. "Your wife will be on the next plane to Spain. We're done," Wojtek continued. "You deal with her." The next call was to the travel agency for a plane ticket. Now, all there was to do was wait.

When Paula arrived at the flat, Wojtek flat-out refused to give her Marysia's address. In return, she flew at him, fists flying. Wojtek held firm. He would not let her come between him and his wife again. Paula's behavior was abhorrent, and while he was sorry that her life hadn't turned out the way she planned, he was not going to take responsibility for that, or her. He had said as much to Fryderyk the last time they spoke.

In fact, it was thanks to that conversation that Paula was moving to Spain, permanently. And if she didn't know that before then, she did now—the plane ticket had just been purchased. We know that it didn't turn out quite this way, and that my grandmother's presence would once again infiltrate their marriage, but it's comforting to know that my father stood his ground that day. His wife came first.

CHAPTER 20

ROADS, MAPS, AND GRANDPARENTS: THE FAMILY TRAVELS AROUND EUROPE

The summer of 1987 saw my family in Europe again. While my friends at home were off to camp or cottages, we were busy flying overseas to see our grandparents. Mostly my mother traveled with my sister and me while my dad remained at home in Toronto, so it was just the three of us, and that summer, when we went to Frankfurt, I was excited to finally be treated like a grown-up. For one thing, my mom had decided to take me to Paris. But before our trip, we met up with cousins on a different trip they were taking with their parents. So, yes, there was a lot of family, and a lot of excitement in general.

At this point, I was also getting an allowance and had my heart set on a Swatch watch. My first grown-up accessory, and at a whopping sixty dollars, it wasn't cheap. One day my older cousin and I set out to shop for the watch. There were so many to choose from, but I knew exactly the one I wanted. It was subtle, interesting, and different from the rest, with a clear strap and a see-through face, so you could see the mechanism working. That watch stayed with me for years, long after the band had yellowed. I was so sad when it stopped working.

In any case, Paris. Our travel there by train was delayed thanks to a mudslide that blocked the tracks, but I didn't care. I was finally going to Paris, a place where I belonged—my mother always told me that the correct pronunciation for my name was with a French inflection. Once, when she had still been a student, a fortune teller had stopped her in the street and told her she would one day marry a man with dark hair and move overseas, which is pretty much just the way it happened.

The way both my parents talked about Paris infused us with dreams of a magical place. It was the last place where my parents really had the ability to be carefree, to explore the world with innocence and curiosity, and without being bogged down with the responsibilities that would later dog them. The paintings my mother made as a student there hung in our home, and she and my dad were always telling us stories about when life was tough but happy in Paris, about the art, and the ways of Parisian culture. So, naturally, when it was finally time to travel there, I was chock-full of romantic anticipation.

We arrived late at night, and my mother was immediately at home, despite the fact that she didn't pull out any maps or puzzle over road signs. It had been seventeen years since she had set foot in the city, and she still knew where she was going. We took the metro, where we were serenaded by a less-than-sober guy looking to make a few extra francs. He sang some Madonna songs and then passed around an empty pack of cigarettes. Once on the street, the first taxi driver wouldn't even talk to us. His cab was facing the wrong way until he snorted, mumbled something incomprehensible, and pointed to a different cab. We crossed the street, and the other cabbie took one look at us, drove us around the block—we were in the cab for all of two minutes total—and delivered us to our friend's apartment.

It took us ten minutes to figure out how to get into the building. Very simply, there was a button in the middle of a large brass square inset into the wall. Very obvious if you know to look for it, but for two exhausted travelers, it was impossible to see.

It all ended well, though, because in the morning we awoke to hot baguettes and fresh-from-the-farm eggs and honey. To this day there is nothing I like more for breakfast. Our hosts had a farm just outside the city, and their pantry was well stocked with farm-fresh fruits and vegetables.

This was my mom's first time back to the city she loved, and I think she was excited to show me around. For the next four days we spent every waking hour visiting every sight we possibly could. We didn't have a lot of money or time to stand in line for the Louvre, so we ventured off the beaten path. Is there a better way to get to know a city? When we got hungry, we'd stop and buy a fresh baguette with some salami, sit by the road, and people-watch.

This was before the giant lineups at Notre Dame Cathedral, so of course we headed there, except that when the doors opened, we found ourselves at someone's wedding. Oops! We caught a quick glimpse of the longest train I've ever seen, turned around, and left just as the guests had turned to look at us.

In the evening, we met up with an old friend of my mother's who treated us to dinner on the Champs-Élysées, where we drank twelve-dollar Cokes and used the bathroom with purple velvet sofas at a fancy—very fancy—Burger King.

Day after day we walked. I'm fairly sure we hit up every museum in Paris. It was the most exhaustive and exhilarating trip, and my mom laughed that she had nearly died on the day I made her climb to the top of the Eiffel Tower. I couldn't help it, I had the energy of a teenager, and I wanted to see everything.

In me, she finally met her match when it came to exploring cities. Even now, whenever I travel, I try to channel my mother. Who wants to lie around on a beach all day when they can explore every inch of a new city? The trick is to get lost, and never follow a map if you can help it. This is the way my mother was able to immediately eliminate some cultural barriers by immersing herself in a new place and its people. We always have preconceived notions, but when you step away from the tourist traps and the community you know, assimilating into a new place becomes easier.

For my mother, our trip had an added purpose. It wasn't simply leisure, or a mother-daughter rite of passage—it was that and more. She was on a quest to speak with Jerzy Giedroyc from the monthly *Kultura*. She was a visual artist at heart, but she also dabbled in writing. After her arrival in Canada, she was a regular contributor to CBC Radio for a show that was broadcast back to Poland. She would write and read her work on air. Her most fascinating project was a biography of a good friend of ours who had survived World War II. Three times he had a Nazi gun pointed at the back of his head, and three times he managed to survive. The piece was ready to go to print when our friend got cold feet and was afraid to have the story printed. That's what my mother and Jerzy were discussing at his home in central Paris while I was left to play with his cocker spaniel and pet rooster.

Paris, la Ville-Lumière. The city of lights. Marysia's dream. Although she didn't know it at the time, moving to Paris in 1967 was effectively her goodbye to Poland. The next time she returned was in 1991 with my father. What was supposed to be time at a new school and maybe a work opportunity turned into permanent political displacement when her home country turned on her. In return, she turned her back on Poland.

I remember all this as she and I walked rue Bonaparte, in the Latin Quarter. I never heard her speak of Warsaw the way she spoke of Paris. Even seeing the school she once attended brought with it a surge of emotions. This was the place of possibilities—her honeymoon, if you will—before reality forced her to swerve off course.

Since Poland was never again home, she was unable to complete the final component of her degree. For a family who put so much stake in education, this was a sore spot and never spoken about. I only know because I heard it mentioned in passing. Now here we were—in her favorite spot in all the world.

A little over a year into our move to Warsaw, Pawel is working on building his virtual reality business, and I've jumped into full-time blogging. I've been promised a trip to Paris, and we decide to sneak it in before my in-laws come in June for a six-week visit. Besides, Paris in the springtime is a thing.

Where Poland is my connection with my father, Paris is my connection to my mother, and I have a not-so-secret mission with this trip. But when we find ourselves standing at 97 rue de L'Abbé Groult—one of the first places I dragged my husband to on our first trip to Paris—I'm disappointed. I am determined to see where my parents lived and to retrace some of their steps. Only 97 rue de L'Abbé is not the same place anymore. My father is positive that it's the correct address, but the building is too new. It's disappointing, but we rally. We are in Paris, so a lot can be forgiven.

We retrace my mother's steps in the Latin Quarter and pay our respects to the École des Beaux-Arts, where I spend a few moments hoping to see her ghost. Then we wander the streets, turning down every street that captures our imagination. We take time to notice the architecture, we peer into narrow galleries, and I pull out her old letters to try to figure out which boardinghouse she might have lived in. Of course, a trip to Paris isn't complete without a visit to the Louvre, where I connect with my father in the present, one of the engineers who worked on the glass pyramid covering the entrance.

When we return to Warsaw, my in-laws arrive and then promptly leave for Władysławowo, on the Hel Peninsula. We decide to join them and rent an apartment overlooking the Baltic. Even though it's nearing the end of June, the weather won't cooperate. It's so cold, I buy a sweater. We might be at the beach at the start of summer, but the winds are unforgiving. On a clear day, here on the northernmost tip of Poland, you can see Sweden. Despite the weather, we spend time on the beach and are thrilled to finally pinpoint Pixie's coloring: She blends seamlessly into Baltic sand. Then it hits me. This is where my grandparents met. This, *this*, is where this story started.

Roughly two years after we arrive in Warsaw, PiS (the Law and Justice Party) gets elected. People living in the country and in small towns are elated while those in the big cities mourn. Tension in the country had been growing. This election takes it over the edge.

The protests begin almost immediately, pushing back against the reactionary agenda of the new government. Apparently a lot of people don't necessarily believe in those good old Christian values, meaning they don't like migrants; they don't like anyone who isn't a white Christian, preferably Catholic; and they don't like anyone who is part of the LGBTQ+ community. Period. I realize that spelling all this out means risking my Polish passport, but at least I'll be in good company. As much as I hate the current Polish government, a part of me really enjoys participating in protests, feeling that powerful energy emanating from the crowd.

Shortly after they come into power, PiS takes over the television station and starts trying to control the media, and the moment I find myself standing on Plac Powstancow Warszawy in front of the Polish Television headquarters in Warsaw with a crowd of angry people, protesting their right to free speech, I burst into tears. My grandfather would be proud of me, wouldn't he? I wonder what he would think of me living in Poland. I think he would want me here.

I think the only person who would object would be my mother.

There is a lot you learn in retrospect, and those are things you can't forget. They will forever color your memories. Moments you didn't notice before will suddenly fall into place.

My parents were very careful not to let me and my sister know about our grandparents' issues until much later. So, for a long time, we had no clue that there'd been affairs, or that Fryderyk had tried to leave Paula, and so on. My babcia and dziadzio were the best grandparents in the world. Where they were lacking was as parents. We had an uncomplicated view of things for quite some time.

Now, of course, things are different. Now that I've read the letters, I have some notion of just how bad things got, and over the years my father has been more forthcoming with his stories. Still, I have the fondest memories. I adored the long hikes with my grandfather or sipping coffee on the beach with my grandmother—the moments when they imparted their wisdom and became coconspirators when we wanted to do something my parents wouldn't have approved of. After he and my grandmother moved to Toronto, my grandfather would take me walking through the local golf course in North York, where we'd dodge flying golf balls and get yelled at by the golfers. He'd just laugh and continue on his way.

Some of my fondest childhood memories are of family road trips. Whether it was a short drive to a local cottage with my parents or a cross-country trip in Europe with my grandparents, as long as we were in the car headed somewhere, I was happy. Now I think that my mother must have felt the same all those years ago in Poland.

I suppose from the outside, our vacations looked exotic, but they weren't. Our car was always filled with provisions, clothing, food, whatever we would need. Wherever we went, we were a self-sufficient group.

A family trip to Switzerland in 1982 was no exception. While Fryderyk drove, my grandmother sat in the front with the troll doll who was in charge of the sugar-covered candies, and my mother sat in the back with my sister and me. In an effort to keep us entertained, she had bought us joke books, and I was in charge of the jokes. There was one we told over and over again in which the teacher asked a boy named Bobby to make a sentence using the words *defeat, defense,* and *detail*. Bobby thinks for a moment and comes up with, "Defeat of the dog went over defense before detail." If you aren't getting it, read the joke out loud. Days later, we were still repeating that joke, and years later each one of us could repeat it.

But even telling jokes and eating cucumber sandwiches couldn't keep us from appreciating the narrow, twisting road that seemed to go straight up the mountain. On one side the rough rock face, on the other a straight drop down the mountain blocked only by a metal barrier. Every time we'd pass a precipice, my sister and I would shout gleefully while my mother and grandmother would grab at anything to keep us all from driving over the side of the road.

When we weren't telling jokes or eating, I loved staring out the window and making up stories in my head. These usually involved my doing great extravagant things or traveling to exciting places. All these things made the act of simply going somewhere as exciting as the destination.

Our destination was Torgon, a small resort town at an 1,100-meter altitude in the French part of Switzerland. As we drove into town, we could see three large, triangular-shaped residential buildings that mirrored the surrounding mountains. Our apartment, in the central building, belonged to a friend of my grandparents who was away for the summer. It was a cozy but bright apartment with a balcony and lots of green, green plants. We settled in and spent the summer hiking the Alps, learning who has the right of way on steep mountain trails (spoiler: it's the hikers going uphill, since they have less of a field of vision), and getting to know the local wildlife. Have you ever petted or scared the hell out of a ram? We did! He was guarding a pristine *Heidi*-like cottage surrounded by green grass, dotted with colorful wildflowers. When he came over to the strange people—that would be us—without a second thought my grandfather grabbed him by a horn and lovingly shook his head.

When we weren't hiking or sightseeing, we hung out at the pool, filled with unheated water straight from the glaciers. No one over the age of fifteen ventured within ten feet of it, but my sister and I loved it. Who cared if the water was a little chilly? The mountaintop roller coaster, however, was a whole different beast. I've since seen the ride on my other travels, but this was a time before safety was a priority and everyone lived in fear of being sued. My mom, my sister, my grandmother, and I decided that it would be a ton of fun to go careening down the side of the Swiss Alps. We packed ourselves into small two-person carts, strapped in by a simple seat belt and with a hand brake to control the speed.

My babcia and I, the two musketeers, naturally went together. As we turned a corner and found ourselves on the edge of a precipice, she pulled as hard as she could on the brake and the whole ride stopped dead in its tracks. I was mortified. I mean, there were teenagers on that ride as well, my grandmother was furious, and my mother was laughing her head off. My grandmother and I made it to the bottom of the ride at a snail's pace with the brake screeching the whole way down. No amount of my yelling could get her to speed up. She not only ruined the ride for pretty much everyone, she was disgusted by the whole event and refused to talk about it. In retrospect, I love that she stood her ground and wouldn't succumb to all our pleading.

Travels with my grandparents were always about living in the moment—creating memories that we could bring back to Canada. One of the traditions they started, in Switzerland, was buying us hand-carved wooden canes made specifically for hiking in the Alps. Then in every town we visited, we'd buy a small metal tag to nail to the cane. The goal was to have a cane covered with images of various Austrian and Swiss cities and towns. My grandparents had finally settled in Bad Homburg, a few kilometers outside Frankfurt, at the base of the Taunus Mountain range. Because they were extremely social, they had friends everywhere we went. Then when I was about thirteen, my mother convinced my grandparents to relocate to Canada so they'd be close to us.

These trips are fragmented memories; some merge as images, and others stand out. They are not, however, passing anecdotes. I see them as a map of my grandparents' loves, interests, and personalities. The homeland that they would have introduced us to wasn't open to them. They could not show us where they grew up, but they could introduce us to the world they knew. Both my babcia and dziadzio loved the mountains, so Switzerland was a natural choice. They had lived in Spain, so of course that was also a natural destination.

The first time my sister and I flew alone was to Germany in 1985 when our parents dropped us off at the Toronto International Airport, and we were shuttled into a room packed with other kids waiting for their flights. One girl had been there for hours because a bird had flown into the engine of her plane. The room was filled with junk food, meaning it was a lot of fun. There was probably an adult in the corner somewhere, but for the most part we got to run around without much supervision. Little did any one of us know that history was being made in the world that day.

I don't remember much about the flight except that we had our own private flight attendant and got extra candies, which they used to pass around on a big tray right before landing. I kind of miss those days. For some reason, unbeknownst to us, our plane landed far away from the terminal. Huge stairs were brought up to the exits, and we took a shuttle to the terminal. As we arrived, who should come barging through the doors but my grandmother? Today she probably would have been tackled and arrested on the spot, but security was more relaxed back then. Plus, she was a Jewish grandmother on a mission, and you don't get in the way of that. It was only later that I found out that my mom was also worried sick back in Toronto. That day, the day she'd put her daughters on their first solo flight, all eyes of the world were on Frankfurt, destination of the hostages from TWA Boeing Flight 727.

I say that my mother was worried sick, but that sentiment can't be strong enough for what my family must have been going through. Briefly, Flight 727 had a scheduled route from Cairo to San Diego with several stops in between. The flight was hijacked by two Lebanese men, who threatened and beat the passengers and separated anyone with a Jewish-sounding name. The plane crisscrossed the skies for two weeks landing in places like Beirut and Algiers before finally touching down in Germany.

Canada and Germany were safe places for my family, and this was bringing the horrors of the past into the present. Thinking back, I can see how this, and getting beat up in the abandoned building when she was young, would have a lasting impact on my mother.

My grandfather always held Poland near and dear to his heart. I have to say that his loyalty and devotion to the country are the kind of attachment I don't quite understand. Still, I wasn't surprised when in 1987 he offered me whatever I wanted if I learned to read in Polish. Challenge accepted.

This was way too good to pass up. Someone gave me a Polish *elementarz* called *Ala ma kota* (Ala has a cat), and I taught myself to read. It wasn't that hard once I learned the basic letter combinations for each sound. Nothing like explaining why enough is actually pronounced eenuf.

When I saw him a year later, I proudly read aloud the first three pages from a book about Piłsudzki, under whom both my grandfathers served in the army.

"Well, what do you want?" His easy smile and twinkling eyes were expecting me to ask for a new dress or a toy.

"A trip to Italy," I replied.

To his credit my grandfather came through. That summer we were off to a small town on the bank of Lake Garda.

These are the good memories. While I'm more than aware of the fact that my grandfather Fryderyk wasn't perfect, I have to say that in my books, only my good memories of him prevail. Then there's Paula, my grandmother.

As I say, for a long time, she was my best friend; we connected on every level. We could talk about anything, and one of our favorite topics was fashion. She liked the fact that I was always conscientious about how I dressed. She was also my go-to person when I wanted a break from my parents. On walks we would speed ahead of the group and gossip about everything imaginable. I think it was on the Italy trip that we were sitting at a café on the beach while the rest of the family was swimming. She ordered a cappuccino con panna (coffee with cream, very, very good and yummy cream). She offered me a sip, and I promptly emptied the whole cup. She laughed, ordered herself another cup, and instructed me not to tell my mother.

She was like that. With her, there weren't a lot of rules, and she was always open to me. She spent hours teaching me canasta, chatting about clothing, and supplying me with props when I staged plays in her home in Bad Homburg, which she tirelessly watched.

I'm not sure why that all changed.

My first glimpse of what my grandmother *could* be like was when my grandfather died in 1989. Naturally she was grieving, but when she moved in with us, she immediately became the boss of our household, with my mother bending over backward to make her happy and fulfill her every whim. My parents even began looking for a home with an in-law suite. Meanwhile, my grandmother made herself more and more at home at our house. I've already mentioned the "forgotten" empty pot and the fateful trip to Fort Lauderdale where she spent the whole time drinking cognac in her room. It was more than just those two incidents.

My grandmother inserted herself everywhere and always made sure that she was the center of my mother's attention. Slowly, systematically, she began creating a wedge within my family unit. I do not want to disparage my grandmother; this is the complicated part of who she was. It was simply that my mother was the only person who would give her all the attention she craved. Years later my mother apologized for allowing that to happen. I accepted the apology, but it came too late. I never saw my grandmother the same way.

When my mother entered the hospital for the final time, my grandmother stopped bathing or taking care of herself. Was that in protest? I don't know, but the fact was that by that point someone had to be hired to take care of her. Once again, she controlled everyone's attention. My mother became the secondary character— she was in a hospital room being taken care of, after all—so we could all focus on my babcia. I remember my father wanting nothing to do with her, and my uncle KT being forced to step up and handle the situation, probably for the first time in his life. Up until then it was my mother who corralled their parents on an emotional level.

My babcia's drama built up for about three months with her culminating moment being at my mother's funeral, when she tried to throw herself into the grave. I wound up riding in the limo with her and my uncle instead of my father and my sister. Her behavior was once again out of control. I was afraid my father would relive their time in Sweden, but that this time, he would finally snap and kill her.

During the reception, held at our home, where she was holding court, she declared that she would never enter our house again because that is where her daughter died. She did enter, but to the best of my knowledge she never went upstairs.

Then she started threatening suicide again, but as far as I know, only to me. In retrospect I can see that this was true to character, but at the time it was gutting. Is this the way a grandmother should behave? Was I stepping into my mother's shoes and chosen as the receiver of her whims? I don't know. What I do know is that this wasn't the designation I wanted. I loved my grandmother, but my attachment to her wasn't the same, and I certainly did not have the same guilt complex toward her. One day I had finally had enough.

"Go, jump. I promise I won't stop you," I said, pointing to her balcony.

She looked at me in shock. She never brought up suicide with me again. I did, however, hear, "You shouldn't be as sad as I am. Kids should expect their parents will die." Sadly, that's what became of my grandmother—the woman who made my mother's death all about her.

This was shortly before my uncle moved her back to Poland. Not once did she gather us into her arms so we could share in each other's grief. Not once did she check to see if we were okay. Come to think of it, I don't remember a single adult reaching out to my sister or me during that entire time. My father did his best, but he was also grieving. My mother was the love of his life, and I can only guess that without the support of his family he must have felt very alone.

It sounds strange to say, but if I had to pick the one moment when I had truly become an adult, it was when I told my grandmother that she could jump off her balcony and I wouldn't stop her. Shocking, I know. Not the kind of memory you want to say is your coming-of-age story. But it's true. That was the moment I realized that respect goes both ways, and that everyone has to earn it.

So, lots of change over the years, and a lot of growth, too, so much so that when I arrive in Poland in 2013, I decide I'm going to make an effort to be nice to my grandmother and maybe even reconnect. But once again, somehow our efforts are deemed insufficient.

Even though Pawel and I try to go up to the lake region where she's living with my uncle, it's never enough. And there is zero appreciation of the fact that those trips are tough emotionally and physically—emotionally, because I never truly reconnect with my grandmother or my uncle, for that matter. All our conversations feel like they are for show, as if we are being filmed for a reality program. Our conversations are formulaic, and again I am left with the feeling that my grandmother doesn't really care about anything but herself. I don't have the energy to confront them, to bring up family history, but I notice that they never call me. They never check in on me, and never ask even the easiest question: How are you doing? It's a one-sided relationship in which I am expected to do all the work.

Even the travel is taxing, although that doesn't seem to matter to them either. First, we either need to rent a car, which is expensive, or we need to take a bus, and taking a bus is a whole other process. Buses are the backbone of the transportation system, and getting one is a crapshoot. Sometimes you get lucky with air-conditioning and plush seats, but we've also caught buses that seem to be relics from communist times. The actual route, though, is quite pretty.

We pass one small town after another. The towns all feel old and worn, and some are bigger with grocery stores and a restaurant or two, and others are just a few houses. Little chapels, *kapliczka*, stand at the end of winding driveways. Some are old, some are new, some are elaborate, and others are a simple box attached to a tree, but each wayside shrine is steeped in traditions. Each has a Madonna, candles, and a specific prayer. In between are farm fields. Rows of trees line the narrow two-lane highway. If you are lucky, you will see storks perched on their great stick nests on the towers that dot the flat landscape. Every country has small towns. In Vancouver and Toronto, many are recognizable by their roles in Hallmark movies. In Poland, the towns have a village feel, with some, like Pułtusk, dating back to 1257. Each town is a self-sufficient microcosm where modern-day consumerism collides with a romanticized history. It's yet another study of contrasts. I love this drive. All I can do is stare out the window and daydream. The drive up north is a way to decompress before we arrive.

We visit my babcia sparingly until one day two years later when I have a strong urge to go. Mazury, or the Masurian Lakes Region, is pretty, not unlike cottage country anywhere in North America. The biggest difference is that it's peppered with quaint small towns that have a lot of history. It's not unusual to see remnants of buildings from the 1300s. Szczytno is a town of about 30,000 and can get quite busy, especially during the summer season. Many of the buildings have red roofs, there is a lake, and best of all there are small statues, *pfajdok*, causing mischief all over the town. From here we have a little farther to go to get to Romany, a village founded in the fourteenth century.

Finally, after a winding drive, we arrive at my uncle's compound, which consists of a barn and three white houses with brown and red accents, typical of the region. Today, at the beginning of July, I think we are visiting my grandmother. I say, "I think," because I have blurred out some of this time. Driving up, I have much the same feeling as I did years ago when my mother was in palliative care.

On the day my mother died, I was a student sitting in the large main hall of York University in Toronto, when suddenly I knew that I needed to see her. I can't explain it: The moment just swept over me, and nothing was going to stop me. At the hospital my mother was under the effects of morphine, my father was sitting with her, and their favorite piece of music, *Misa Criolla*, was playing quietly. My mother recognized me and pulled off her oxygen mask for a moment. I didn't stay long. Later that night my father came home and told me she had died.

We haven't been in Romany in a while and have been mostly out of the family loop. When we do arrive, my grandmother is fading in and out of consciousness. Although she does recognize me, I can't get over how small she is. She was always a petite woman, but now she is downright tiny. From many years spent lying on her side with bent legs, she is stuck in that position and can't completely straighten out. My uncle had physiotherapists who came to work with her until at some point she refused their help.

No one has called me or let me know how she has been doing. There are plenty of people around. KT is away for a few days, but my babcia has a full-time caregiver, there is a couple who runs the main house, and another family that lives on the property. Every one of them has my phone number and the ability to call me. Although I am her only blood relative, I have been relegated to a distant acquaintance. I simply sit with my grandmother, and my uncle arrives shortly thereafter. She is in a lot of pain, and one of his staff manages to procure morphine. We know this is the end.

Over the next few hours we sit with her as she gets smaller, and her skin begins to grow blotchy. That's how you know the end is near, the person stops looking real.

We open a bottle of Metaxa and toast to her. My uncle drips a few drops into her mouth. A few moments later, it's over.

Several days later, one of my uncle's yes-men contacts me to let me know that my grandmother's will has been changed, and they think I should know that. When I tentatively ask my uncle about some of my grandmother's things that were promised to me, I hear, "I bought her those things, so they are mine."

I am not surprised; it's true to form.

In November 2015, Pawel and I decide to take another trip, this time south, to Cracow. We haven't been in several years, and it is a historical and arts hub, something I always crave. Not too far from Zakopane, the mountain region, I know it's a place my grandparents loved, and I am always on the lookout for connection no matter how good or bad our relationship is. In Cracow the smog is so bad that random people yell at us to get off the street. They aren't wrong either. On city outskirts and in poorer neighborhoods, people often burn garbage in their fireplaces. During the winter months the air in Poland is so thick you can taste it. The smog is compared to places like Beijing, and taking a deep breath is near impossible.

On our last day there we are approached by a well-dressed couple frantically looking for someone who speaks English. Standing beneath a lamppost, looking slightly agitated, is an aging British soldier who is barely able to walk. He is wearing a white T-shirt and khaki slacks with the left pant leg half tucked into his unlaced boot. He seems relieved when he hears that we speak English and proceeds to ask us if we know about any perfume stores nearby. The only one

I can think of is a Rossmann drugstore that I'm sure has a perfume section. He can barely walk, and I have no idea how to get him there.

As we stand on the street corner, he explains, in a heavy British accent, that he was part of the liberating army and has always wanted to see the camps before he dies. The day before, he had been to Auschwitz, and he'd be leaving tomorrow, so he wants to buy some perfume for his wife, Anna, back in England.

At this point I am thinking there isn't a chance in hell that we aren't going to get this man some perfume. We finally convince a tour guide in a glorified golf cart to take the soldier, Pawel, and Pixie. For me to join them would be an extra thirty złoty, the equivalent of about ten dollars, so it's not as if we can't afford it, but I'll be damned if we pay the tour guide even more. We are already paying for his services, which amounts to carting them around the block.

The last look Pawel and I have of the soldier is of him standing in his hotel lobby, holding Anna's present. He's inviting us up for a drink. We don't go. We have a train to catch.

I can't help but think of what he witnessed. If in fact he was part of the liberation, his stories would have been invaluable. The more I participate in marches and do my best to oppose the family-values crowd or the Nationalists, the more I believe that stories of survivors and witnesses need to be told. The world is slowly forgetting, and humanity's mistakes will be made again. I will always regret passing up the invitation.

CHAPTER 21

SIX MONTHS TO A CUP OF COFFEE: MY FIRST FRIEND IN POLAND

I want to talk about friendship. Over the years I've learned to make friends quickly. A smile, a cup of coffee, a few words, and we can call ourselves friends. With some people you just know that you are immediate friends; with others it takes longer, but the word we use for the relationship is the same. I've never heard anyone being referred to as my friend-in-training or my almost-friend or my wait-and-see friend. Even the jump from acquaintance to friend can happen quickly. It doesn't always take years.

So it is a shock when the concept of friendship in Poland is first explained to me. With some exceptions, most people never jump from acquaintance mode to friendship mode. My theory is that, because people here don't move as much as they do in North America, their friends are the people they grew up and went to school with—the people they have known for years. The rest of the people you know fall somewhere on the acquaintance spectrum. It's not that you can't become friends with someone—I did. It's just harder to break into the fold. Once you do, however, you are in for life.

On the flip side, it isn't uncommon to see something like this: *Drogi Facebooku! Potrzebuje ekranu do rzutnika na przyszlą sobotę i ewentualnie dobry mobilny internet jeśli ktoś dysponuje.* (Dear Facebook! I need a projector screen for next Saturday and possibly good mobile Internet if someone has it.) This happens all the time, and I guarantee someone will come through. If I check back on this message in a few hours, a bunch of people will have responded. Want to raise money for a cause? Don't worry about going through official channels; your friends will jump in and repost. I have never seen anything to this extent among my friends in North America. People actually going out of their way to help one another? Not this much.

Even so, Pawel and I pick up on the deep feeling of mistrust many people seem to have. The ladies at our local food market are guarded. They barely make eye contact and never engage in small talk. New friends are guarded, the people in our building are guarded. . . . I can only blame this on a generation that grew up under communist rule and passed the guardedness on to their kids. For many years following the war, neighbors couldn't trust neighbors. Life was regulated, from fixed prices to freedom of speech. People spied on one another, and they knew that at any moment they could be reported to the authorities for real or imagined crimes.

There will always be some people who are forward-thinking about the future, but when you grow up in a society that mistrusts one another—and that values getting a job and keeping that job forever—it must be hard to break out of that mold. Most of the people we meet are well traveled, much more so than most of my North American friends, and well educated, and they speak several languages. Yet very few are natural optimists, willing to take risks.

One night a couple of my friends drive me home after a get-together. They are a brother and sister who are related to my cousin.

Just as I'm about to get out of the car, the brother turns and asks me what I think of him changing directions and taking a new job.

"That's fantastic! Totally. Go for it!" I reply enthusiastically.

He looks sad. "But don't you think that people will think badly of me? This isn't the first time that I've changed jobs. Won't they think that I'm unreliable and unsuccessful?"

He's asking the wrong person. By this time I've already worked at a library, taught rock climbing, worked at a drugstore makeup counter and in a gym, taught Pilates, owned my own Pilates studio, sold aftermarket automotive upgrades, then sports insurance, worked for a real estate developer, then sold everything and moved to a different country, where I am currently a copywriter. He grew up in a culture where you go to school, graduate, then get a job you keep, if not forever, then for most of your adult life. I cannot imagine that as a way of life. Already, I have been working at all kinds of jobs since I was fourteen years old.

His sister then chimes in to say that her boss at the bank, where she works in marketing, is heading up a new department and wants her to come help run it. Again, I'm thrilled for her. She's a few years younger than I am, and this sounds like an amazing opportunity to get ahead and grow in her field.

She does not look happy. This is extremely stressful for her, she explains. "Well, I've been in my position for fifteen years, and what if that doesn't work out, what if I can't do the job, what will people think?"

Who cares what they think? This is your life, not theirs.

Before I get out of the car, they tell me they specifically wanted to discuss these job situations with me because they knew I'd have a positive outlook and be supportive of them no matter what.

There is a saying that no one is poor in America; they just haven't made their millions yet. That mentality is the complete opposite of what we encounter in Poland. We are going to visit my uncle, and I've decided to bring a bottle of wine. His favorite, Sangre de Toro, is a readily available Spanish wine. We walk into a liquor store to ask about the wine.

"No nie, nie mamy. Chyba pani nie znajdzie. Może Pani takie inne chce?" (Well, no, we don't have any. I don't think you'll find any. Maybe you would like to try another one?)

"Dzienkuję nie, pójdę gdzie indziej." (Thank you, no. I will try someplace else.)

"Nie uda się, no nie możliwe." (It won't happen, it's impossible.)

This is a typical conversation I have over and over again during our entire stay. Basically, whatever "it" is—whatever you're trying to do—is impossible and will never work. Every excuse as to why is brought forward. Only later things do get done. This is a classic case of lost in translation. The tone of that conversation is bored and dismissive, and it's always said in a long drawl.

For the record, the next liquor store ten doors down had an entire case of that wine in the window.

This dynamic makes me think of my family, and how different we are. I'm sure that my mother never knew the meaning of "it's impossible"; her brother certainly didn't. They were two people who spent their entire lives worried about appearances, but it was about making themselves look better in the eyes of strangers. This is the complete opposite. I wonder, does the store clerk care that I roll my eyes and leave without them making a sale? I can't see that happening in North America. I have Polish friends who think that North American salespeople can be overly friendly, so much so that they sound fake. In turn, many North Americans find that Polish salespeople sound abrasive. What is the midway point where we can meet?

These kinds of interactions make it difficult to break through societal barriers. Always being told that something is impossible or can't happen is exhausting. Even so, three years have passed faster than we expected, and by 2016, we have settled in quite nicely. I am taking regular classes at the ballet school and loving every minute of them. My dad has been making an effort to visit his brother each year as well, to rekindle that relationship. Our flat is too small for him to stay with us, so he lives with Andrzej when he comes to Warsaw. I do, however, try to plan fun trips while my dad is here.

In 2014 we went to Prague for a week, but this year we decide to stay closer to home and take the train up north, to Gdańsk and Sopot. This trip is a big deal for my dad. It has been fifty years since he was last there. The last time was when the family moved back to Warsaw. Walking up Mickiewicza Street, we watch as he becomes a young boy again. He laments the fact that the neighborhood fence he used to run around to steal fruits and nuts is no longer there. He describes his old house before the new addition and points out those where friendly neighbors used to live.

Although I'm sad when my dad leaves, I see him again the following month when we land in Toronto. It feels like no matter how hard I try to leave, my hometown keeps pulling me back. Time and time again, since moving away in 2001, Pawel and I find ourselves giving up holidays only to return for an event we cannot miss. I have always dreamed of living overseas, but family comes first. This is mostly a business trip for my husband, but a bright side for us both is meeting our newest niece, a cuddly ball of smiles.

It's June and sweltering. I am waiting for my friend to show up in the *patelnia* (frying pan), a common meeting spot in Warsaw. With no shade in sight, the name is fitting. Pawel is in Israel for a work trip, so I've invited my friend to come along with me to the Parada Równości. Two hours later we are on the Google float in the Equality Parade, aka Pride Parade. When we lived in Vancouver and I worked at Denman Fitness, I participated in many Pride Parades, always a giant street party.

Today, here, is different.

Yes, people are in costumes, albeit tame ones, and there is music and an abundance of rainbows. Interestingly, I see people taking our picture. Do they think that two females together automatically means we are lesbians? There are also two rows of police in full riot gear flanking the floats, and a procession of sixteen police vans trailing them. The main arteries of Warsaw are packed with a mostly joyous crowd having fun, dancing to the music blaring from the floats, and so on. But somewhere along the route I see protestors dressed in black, faces covered, carrying fascist and neo-Nazi signs.

The grim effects of the PiS government are beginning to show, and much of it comes to a head later that year in October when women (and men) all in black walk out in protest about the proposed ultra-restrictive abortion law. Black Monday, the English-speaking papers call the Czarny Protest, the day when thousands of progressives take to the rainy streets to listen to speeches and to march up the Royal Route to Old Town. The government reports just a few thousand participants, but the aerial photographs say otherwise. The voices are so insistent that the government finally backs down, and the proposed law that would have criminalized women who had to terminate a pregnancy does not pass. It will in 2020, but for now a small victory has been won.

By now we are used to the protests and marches; there is one every weekend or so. More often than not, I'll pass one in the evening on my way to ballet class. It's easy to tell which side of the street I should walk on. The people holding EU flags are like-minded while those with Polish flags are usually the church-minded nationalists. On the way back from class on any given night, I'll have to pass a group of people praying in front of an oversized white cross erected in front of the Presidential Palace. They will place memorial candles on the ground and pray. It takes me a minute to figure out what they are praying for. Ahhh, right, this is related to the Smolensk tragedy. On April 10, 2010, a Polish aircraft carrying ninety-six government officials crashed near the city of Smolensk, Russia. There were no survivors. The event made headlines around the world and became an unbearable constant in Poland. Half of society thought the accident was just that, an accident. The other half was convinced that the downing of the plane was a Russian conspiracy.

Of course, everything in Poland seems to revolve around it.

To complicate the situation, Poland's president, Lech Kaczyński, was on that flight. His twin brother, Jarosław Kaczyński, is the current leader of the PiS party. As a result, instead of being a national tragedy that brings people together, the Smolensk incident has become a theatrical farce, complete with a monthly memorial. The foundation of the government has been built on trauma. When the previous government tried to move the cross into the adjacent St. Anne's Church, that group of Catholics began bringing the cross out in public every single night. When PiS comes to power, there is even less standing in their way; now every month there is an overblown memorial to the victims of the crash.

On the yearly anniversary, the roads are blocked. The day is messy, loud, and fraught. And protestors, speaking out against this tawdry nationalistic drama, are also in the streets. As a consequence, many older adults are hauled off by the police. These are the people who have lived long enough to know what life will be like if there is not a separation of church and state. Dissolution between the two is exactly what is happening. The Catholic Church is slowly sinking its teeth into the government, and into the everyday.

So, friendship, right. Close ties versus the long shadow of mistrust. Who is friendly? Who can you really trust? That remains a very Polish question.

CHAPTER 22

ANOTHER SHIFT IN FAMILY DYNAMICS

Secrets don't stay secrets for long. I don't understand why my dziadzio didn't leave my grandmother. Having one foot in his marriage and the other decidedly out wasn't doing anyone any favors. All that he successfully managed to do was to drag everyone into his marital problems. I try to imagine my grandfather digesting the letter his good friend Karol, someone I never knew but who was a confidant of my parents, had sent him. Fryderyk's letter to Karol had been a fairly honest description of his current situation with my babcia. I picture my grandfather preparing to read his friend's response, with a cup of coffee and a slice of bread in hand—his standard breakfast.

> I'm sorry but your situation is serious enough that I feel I have to respond. I hope that you don't think that I'm overstepping boundaries but it's dire enough that I must write to you. Let me start with the facts, how I see and understand them. 1. Paula has better days and worse days but she's far from returning to a healthy norm. While she

did go to see a psychiatrist, she's against any continued systematic help with the exception of pharmaceuticals. Her claims, which are supported by the doctor, Marysia can tell you more about this, is that she is in such a bad state because she doesn't feel safe or secure, she is in a constant state of uncertainty and feels completely lost by the situation. This is linked directly to your new "friend" and Paula isn't even hiding it. She doesn't believe that your work is what is keeping you apart and she is convinced that you are purposefully keeping her at a distance and that you have deposited her with the kids and have sentenced her to isolation. This is how she's describing her complete apathy, her reluctance to return to work or to find another job. Not only that but she's also talking about committing suicide.

That sounds exactly like my grandmother. She would say she was suicidal many times over, even when I knew her. Clearly, the strain on the marriage when Fryderyk went to Spain was another one of those times. Karol continued,

Now, even if those threats are solely to put pressure on you, it's still proof that she's mentally unstable and that can be a dangerous situation. In her state anything is possible. 2. Marysia and Wojtek are taking care of Paula with sincere care and dedication. Deep in their hearts they don't feel that it's fair that all of Paula's care has fallen on their shoulders and your financial aid is far from enough. They believe, similarly to what the doctor is saying, that the uncertainty of her situation is what is keeping her in this form of limbo. Marysia and Wojtek don't doubt that it is you who needs to step in and handle this situation and immediately, the current affairs keeping you in Spain or Germany notwithstanding.

I have to add that their current situation is not a happy one as they did not arrive in Sweden to the stability and family unit they expected to find. Right now, they want to live their own normal lives, which is normal. Although they haven't said anything, they feel that they are unwilling victims of their parents' misunderstanding. It shows up more in Wojtek's behaviour as he is more explosive and less tied to you. He married Marysia after all and not her family. He's also living with a very difficult break up of his family. Neither his brother nor his parents have forgiven him for not returning to Warsaw and they are refusing contact. Even if they both agree to continuing with the current situation, things are bound to change when Marysia finds a job. If she's occupied during the day, there is no way that she will be able to take care of Paula virtually all day every day. Neither one of them will be able to focus on work if they are expecting that Paula might try to commit suicide. And what if they find jobs outside of Sweden or even Stockholm, what will happen then? I can't confirm, but I wouldn't be surprised if they aren't thinking about returning to Warsaw, where they can expect a fine and possible jail sentence for extending their time abroad. I know I haven't painted a very optimistic picture, but it is very close to a realistic one. I'm not going to offer you any advice or to tell you how to act next in such personal and complex issues. I just don't want you to be surprised by any development of events or for you to find yourself in a situation where you have lost control. I'm simply fulfilling the role of a good friend, a feeling I have toward your entire family. Your last letter felt like an authorization to "intrude on your personal affairs. . . ."

I was shocked when I found this letter. I could not believe that someone had stood up to my grandfather. I remember my grandfather as being mostly silent. Sure, he took me for walks where he spoke to me, but a lot of our bonding was also done without words, simply being in each other's presence. I can picture him boarding a plane, not telling anyone he was leaving, and just disappearing for a given period. This is largely how my grandparents' relationship was throughout my childhood. No one spoke of it; therefore, it did not exist. I hadn't really realized growing up—really, not until I read this letter—the extent of the burden on my parents, or what their options actually were in Sweden: Returning to Warsaw and imprisonment would be better than staying in the hellhole of taking care of Paula. It was all so much to process. I can't imagine going through that with a parent.

I don't believe that my grandfather thought ahead or thought of the implications that his affair and disdain for my grandmother had on the family. He was living his life the way he wanted to, and he was going to continue to do so. His tall frame, his long gait, placing one foot in front of the other, that was my grandfather. When he arrived in Spain he simply adapted, like he had always done. He had learned to speak Spanish and immersed himself in his work. There was nothing not to love when it came to Spain, which he compared to heaven on earth. The history, the people, the culture was everything he could have asked for. Still, let's be frank.

At this point, it's fair to assume that he wasn't in love with Paula and that he hadn't been for a long time. As we know, she had been pulling these stunts for years, even more so when she didn't get her way. Being a doctor, she could easily fool others in her field, and she had already convinced someone that she had cancer. Fryderyk's life would have been so much easier had Paula remained a few countries away, but after a rather uncomfortable conversation with Wojtek, Fryderyk knew he'd have to send for his wife.

When Paula arrived in Torremolinos, a small town just east of Gibraltar, they stayed in a cliffside boutique hotel, overlooking the sea. It was an idyllic spot, where Paula could sit and sun herself all day. She had not adapted well to Sweden. There wasn't enough sunlight for one thing, although there was one amusing incident at the Stockholm Opera that made her laugh every time she thought of it. The theater seats were fixed, and their neighbor was a friendly, extremely polite, older gentleman. Whenever they ran into him at the coat check, he always let them go ahead of him and often helped Paula with her coat. Later, they were told he was the king of Sweden. I remember my grandmother telling this story, as it's one of the few she told. Much like my grandparents' stories, their relationship was also heavily curated. It was presented to the family in the same way it was presented to the public. Everything was for show. It's easier to act as if everything is great, and when no one asks questions, you don't have to have tough conversations. A throwback to communist days, perhaps?

With Paula gone, Marysia and Wojtek settled into their new lives in Sweden. Wojtek was enjoying his job at ELU, an engineering and construction firm in Stockholm, working as a structural engineer, calculating and creating shop drawings in preparation for bridges and industrial projects in Sweden and Eastern Europe. Marysia had completed her studies at the Swedish Retail Federation's School of Retailing, where she got top marks. Her dream was to make window displays. Between travels and having friends come to stay, Marysia and Wojtek kept busy.

Sweden was expensive in 1975, and big trips were out of the question, but there was no reason not to take mini-vacations. They also made a point of walking every evening after work. Now that they were finally on their own, having a family became a priority. Żak would always be their first "baby," but it was time for some human kids as well. The problem was that Marysia couldn't seem to get pregnant. So, without letting on to their parents, the two began to speak with an adoption agency.

Fall of 1974 brought with it ideal conditions for mushroom picking, and every weekend was spent driving out to Uppsala, where they found a plethora of fungi. Wojtek got to work as soon as they returned, making rich stews, then drying and pickling the rest. By the time the holidays rolled around, Marysia couldn't bear to see another mushroom. But life was looking up. They had been approved as adoptive parents. It would still be a process before they could meet their child, but they didn't care. They were ready to be parents.

Sometime that year they even made the trip to Malaga to see Marysia's parents, KT with his new wife, and their firstborn son. The warmth and sun of Spain did everyone good. They looked at the land that Fryderyk was studying for development. While her relationship was solid with her father, Marysia was able to reconnect with Paula, even though relations remained somewhat strained.

Then, good news upon their return to Sweden. They were matched with a baby. The adoption would proceed.

Sometimes life has a way of coming at you from out of nowhere. Just as Wojtek and Marysia were preparing to sign the final papers and meet the child, Marysia discovered she was pregnant. Then came the tough decision, realizing that the baby should go to another home.

After adjusting to the shift, Marysia and Wojtek began preparing their flat for their new addition. Then Marysia sat down to write a very awkward letter.

> September 11, 1975
> Dad,
>
> I'm sorry to put this on you but I'd rather that Mom not come on her own, without you. Can you make something up? I'd rather you do it because then it won't be as hurtful but if you can't or won't think of anything, I suppose that I can make an excuse. My intention really isn't to hurt Mom but I don't think I'll be able to handle her here if she's on her own. You remember all those problems we had with her two years ago and honestly, she still puts me on edge. If you can't say anything to convince her not to come, then please let me know and I'll try to break it to her as gently as possible.

As far as I know, my grandmother was not present at my birth, and we did not meet until I was three months old. I have a vague memory of my babcia telling me that she came immediately after I was born. At first, I was shocked when I found this letter but after my experiences with my grandmother, I am not that surprised. I can believe that my mother would have been thrilled to be a new mom and didn't want her mother overshadowing the moment. Again, the underlining family tensions were suppressed for the sake of appearances.

Throughout this drama it's easy to forget that my parents were still considered displaced. They left France before getting their resident cards and presumably had to spend a certain amount of time in Sweden before making their status official. The year 1975 was drawing to a close when my parents were finally able to apply for Swedish citizenship. I was already in the world as Caroline-Joanna Wichrzycki, with immediate Swedish citizenship, and a dog tag giving me a spot in a bomb shelter. It was after all still the Cold War, and the threats were real.

My dad was running into all sorts of problems with his name. Wojciech Władysław Wichrzycki was nearly impossible to spell, never mind pronounce, so my parents decided to change the family name. Swedish rules around last names were tricky. It was possible to change your name as long as no one else already had it. Marysia and Wojtek wanted something short, international sounding, and easy to pronounce. They originally tried using Wicher, a shortened version of Wichrzycki, but Wicher had already been taken. Their fallback was Toperman, Fryderyk's last name before the war. The name was approved, but the Swedish authorities suggested that they add a second "p."

Toperman became Topolski, Gottlieb became Gotlicka, and Wichrzycki became Topperman.

When I was born, without thinking, my father hyphenated my first and middle names. This has caused problems like you wouldn't believe. Some government institutions are okay with Caroline

Topperman. Others want my official name. Somehow, it manages to be a problem no matter what I do. I've had government officials ask if they can drop my middle name because it doesn't fit on documents.

While my parents were settling into life in Sweden, my grandparents must have come to some sort of understanding, probably an unspoken one, because they finally settled in Bad Homburg, where Fryderyk continued his work as an engineer and Paula as a doctor. Eventually, Marysia and Wojtek realized that Sweden was not a fit for them. Wojtek wanted to stay in Europe, but Marysia was dead set on America, with California her first choice. She finally won, but as a compromise they chose Toronto, to be near her brother. Like their parents had before them, Marysia and Wojtek would start their lives in a new geography, once again. This time, they chose a place that was neither warm nor sunny, nor at the time, art filled, or particularly stylish. What it was, was home.

CHAPTER 23

HOME IS WHERE THE COMPASS LANDS

Smolna Street has served us well. When we landed at Smolna 10 four years ago, I didn't realize that I would be connecting to my family's footprint. The street I randomly picked to live on is one where my family lived, and where my parents were married. I have no idea why no one told me this when we first got there. I would have taken more pictures and maybe done some more digging into the history of this street.

Even though we know our time in Poland will eventually end, I am convinced that we have one more move left in us before we leave. My love affair with the stairs and the character of the building is waning. I'm sick of staring at our partial view of the park but more so of the peeling concrete wall, and truthfully, I'm a little afraid of the balcony. Pieces of the one above us regularly fall onto ours, and I can't help but think that must be true of ours falling on the one below, and this leads to thinking that perhaps our balcony might not be as sturdy as it could be.

It's time for something more modern. Up to now, I've never really been a renter, so the whole concept is still new. But I quickly find a place across the park from where we are. In fact, an American Polish friend lived there before she moved back to the States. The second I walk into the thirteenth-floor flat, I know we will move here. Never mind that the building is a '70s-style block, and that the entry is old, complete with peeling paint and zero character.

"Check out these light fixtures," the agent gushes.

"Sure, they're great," I counter, "but have you seen the views?" I have no idea what is so amazing about the light fixtures, I have no idea what they even look like. The views, however, are another story. Two balconies on opposite sides of the penthouse-level flat will give us almost 360-degree views of Warsaw. To my left is a small but brand-new kitchen with an open living space. From one balcony there are expansive views of Old Town, Theater Square, and the Vistula. In the distance, I can see the church where my father was baptized. To my right are two rooms joined by antique pocket doors. One room will be our bedroom, and the other a sitting room with a large stone fireplace. From the second balcony there are sweeping views of Plac Zbawiciela, Powiśle, Pałac Kultury. I know immediately that these balconies need to be covered in plants. They will be my oasis in the sky.

Right after we move in, we fly to Paris for a few days. This is me, in a nutshell. I love this kind of lifestyle. I don't want to be tied down or expected to stay in one place for too long. When I travel, I am always sad to go home. I live for the unknowns of new neighborhoods and winding side streets, preferably with cobblestones. By this time, I have lived in seven different homes, and keeping the possibility of moving to a new place is important to me.

The seventh anniversary of the Smolensk disaster falls on April 10. It's a Monday, and I am on my way to ballet class. It's hard to explain what I encounter. Nowy Świat starts out like it does every day, a busy downtown street. About a block before the Bristol Hotel, the road is pretty much barricaded, and I can't get past. I take a left and head toward the Tomb of the Unknown Soldier, thinking I can cut across the open square. No such luck.

The whole area is teeming with robed priests in all their splendor. I can feel their animosity as I squeeze by, only to find myself staring at rows of military units lining up in formation. This doesn't feel like people preparing for a memorial; it feels like a war of wills and beliefs.

Feeling desperate, I look around for the people carrying European Union flags, but they aren't yet grouping. By the time I make it to class, I'm exhausted, sweating, and thoroughly frustrated. Every protest, not just on this day, is bigger and more violent.

It's June, and Pawel is in Warsaw for the Parada Równości, which literally translates to Equality Parade but is essentially the equivalent to the North American Pride Parade. We decide to board the Google float again. We want to be part of the message. This year there is less police presence and more participants, but the route has significantly changed. We head away from the best parts of the city, away from the crowds who probably need to see the support that the LGBTQ+ community has, and squeeze down a quieter, less visible street. It's as if the city has grudgingly given permission but only if Pride's voice is tempered. The protestors, however, are still out in full force with their megaphones spewing hate. The police keep them in an orderly pack, but they are allowed dangerously close to the revelers. That much hasn't changed.

In July, President Trump drops in for a visit to very mixed reviews. American soldiers appear on the streets, and it's rumored that supporters are being bused in from nearby small towns. I don't believe this. Then I see groups of Polish citizens carrying American flags, filling a dozen buses parked along parts of Ordynacka and Kopernika streets where we live. Poland, I realize, is not unlike most North American cities where the city people are more liberal, and suburbs more conservative. PiS still has its stronghold on the majority of the voters, and if they collaborate with President Trump, the voices of the far right's path will be wide open.

We need a break from all this and decide to run away to the mountains for a week. What should be an easy train ride proves to be a grueling journey. There has been an accident on the tracks, and the train comes to a halt in the village right before our stop. It's the end of the line. We climb a steep concrete staircase that looks like it has been in place for the past one hundred years and cross the tracks to the station, where we are informed that buses will be arriving shortly to take us the rest of the way. There are several hundred people waiting as a gentle mountain mist rolls in. A few taxis arrive, but the drivers want 100 złoty to take us. At the time we decide that it's much too much, but two hours later, when we are still waiting for a bus, we regret that decision. When we finally force our way onto a bus, the driver notices Pixie in her bag.

"Oh no, absolutely no dogs."

"Yeah, I'm getting on this bus and if I have to stall its departure I will."

Luckily he doesn't hear me and doesn't notice me barging on. Our double-decker bus is overfilled and likely breaking a dozen safety laws. My little terrier in a bag won't make a difference.

As soon as we arrive in town, we catch a cab. Why am I shocked that the driver feels the need to make rude comments about my accented Polish? I want to tell him off, that I'm not from Poland, but I'm exhausted after the long journey and not eager to start a fight. These reactions are unexpected. My father says it's because I am clearly a foreigner, and the thinking is, how dare I come back and flaunt my riches? True, there is an element of envy, but I believe that part of the clear disdain is that they feel I don't respect the culture and language enough to not have an accent.

The pull between the good old days of classic Poland and the outside world is ever present; even though the borders haven't been closed in decades, people travel widely, and many speak multiple languages. Besides, we are in the mountains, and this is where I feel closest to my grandfather. I can't wait to climb Giewont and hike the same paths my grandparents once took.

In a very different way from what my grandparents and parents experienced, just as my life becomes even-keeled, something happens to knock me off my course. October finds Pawel working out of the Silicon Valley headquarters for his office, and me working in a sunny apartment in Mountain View.

It's so nice to be out of the cold gray Warsaw weather, but a text from my friend Emily interrupts the good vibes. *What is going on there?!* She has included an article link from the *New York Times* titled, "Nationalist March Dominates Poland's Independence Day." I turn on my news app and read *The Independent*:

> Fascists and other far-right extremists are set to assemble
> in Warsaw tomorrow for a march that has become one
> of the largest gatherings in Europe, and perhaps beyond,

for increasingly emboldened white supremacists. The march, held on Poland's 11 November Independence Day holiday, has drawn tens of thousands of participants in recent years. Extremists from Sweden, Hungary, Slovakia and elsewhere now join Polish nationalists in a public display of xenophobic and white supremacist views, since the event began on a much smaller scale in 2009.

I sigh deeply. It's the same story over and over again. Countries like Germany have outlawed this kind of behavior, but Poland seems to welcome it.

Meanwhile, I can't tell my friend about our situation since we've been sitting on a secret. Shortly after we arrived in Silicon Valley, Pawel was offered his dream job. It happened quickly and unexpectedly, but until Pawel signs his official contract we are sworn to secrecy. He doesn't want anyone in his current job to find out, and we don't want to have to manage family expectations quite yet. For now, it's our secret, a moment in time that we can plan and organize on our own. This is how we've always made plans; we have learned that too many consultations only muddle the situation. Even I don't know all the details. Of course I want to be supportive, but I am of two minds. On the one hand, the situation in Warsaw is getting more and more uncomfortable. On the other hand, I don't want to go back. It feels like I'd be going backward. I hate all the bad political and religious things about Poland, but I'm also comfortable there. I like my life in Europe.

We arrive back in Warsaw toward the end of December, and in early January we start to tell our closest friends that we are leaving. It happens quickly; neither one of us has time to process it. Our friends and family are shocked, but so are we. There's a position in Canada that needs to be filled. By now, four years have passed, world politics has taken a sharp turn, leaving Warsaw deeply affected, and a lot of ugliness has begun to surface daily. Nationalism, fascism, and racism are on the rise, no longer in the shadows, but coloring the mainstream. There are times when we no longer feel comfortable walking down the street. Not a week goes by without a protest or a rally. Poland is a part of us, but we aren't sure it's the place we want to fight for. We aren't prepared to give up potential careers to stay in Warsaw.

Our last few weeks pass in quick succession. Between packing, saying goodbye to friends, and trying to secure a place to stay in what will be our new city, we don't have time to stop and breathe. On January 10, my friend and I are walking home from ballet class when we are forced to take a detour. This is unexpected. Where there would usually be a protest in front of the Presidential Palace, there is a police barricade. Police trucks are in a neat row, officers standing shoulder to shoulder in riot gear.

It's a terrible sight, and a flashback to our very first days in Warsaw. It's as if we have gone back in time. Many passersby, me included, document the scene with our phones. The riot police don't stop us. It's clear that the political shift is solidifying. While the monthly protests were disruptive, they gave the public a place to be heard. Now, no one is allowed near the Presidential Palace. The public's voice has been silenced. There will be other marches before we leave, one in particular, that brings out tens of thousands standing for women's reproductive rights. But this feels different: The government has placed a physical barricade between themselves and the general public. Again, I can't help but think: *Is this the country we want to fight for?*

We are due to arrive in Canada on March 1, meaning there is still some time for a trip or two. Pawel and I travel to London for a few days, then a friend convinces me to go to Vilnius, Lithuania. She is determined that I see her country. The heavy hand of communism remains present everywhere, which in turn makes this city the perfect soil for artistic expression.

Vilnius is a city that celebrates its arts scene, which is especially highlighted in the self-declared Republic of Užupis, a neighborhood in Vilnius where out of the 7,000 or so residents, at least 1,000 are artists. Walking through the tiny republic feels like one is entering an open-air museum where anything creative goes. I am there in winter but still see baby grand pianos placed randomly on the streets, including one by the rushing river, and random statues on every corner. As the tourism minister was quoted in a BBC article, "If you cross the bridge, you can become yourself. You don't play any social role, you don't belong to anyone, you belong to yourself. You can think about who you are and you can live without being part of that mad race that all of humanity is involved in."

Nearby, in Old Town, is the Literature Wall, with a few hundred plaques dedicated to writers. I pause to read the names and recognize many of them. The dream is to have my name or names—Topperman for my mother's family, and Wichrzycki for my father's—on that wall one day. It's the icing on the cake of my European education.

The past four and a half years have opened my eyes to so much of the world. I've burst out of the bubble I didn't know I was even in. I've never liked being in a box, but the bubble I couldn't even see. I think that living in North America made me complacent, and I was shielded from much of what the world was going through. The vastness of countries like Canada and the United States means its residents are often disconnected from the wider world.

By contrast, there are forty-four countries on the European continent, and each one is easily accessible. This makes sense if migration paths are considered. Using the example of Syrian refugees arriving in Germany, their route was straightforward and didn't include a lengthy and costly flight across an ocean. Even a country like Poland, which rebelled against bringing in refugees, is still more connected to the wider world.

I have also learned to fight, to be vocal about the things that I believe in. I have come to realize that the people who don't step up and participate in some sort, any sort, of protest are the people who scare me the most.

I am on the move. We are packing up our belongings and dusting off our Canadian passports. One-way tickets mean that in a few short weeks, we will land in the True North. I don't know how I feel about this, really. While my connection to Poland has strengthened, I still don't feel that I am Polish. Only now that we are going back to Canada, I can't say I feel 100 percent Canadian either. What I am is a migrant, a traveler, an adventurer. What I am is like my family.

ACKNOWLEDGMENTS

This journey started when I first mentioned that I wanted to write a book and my no-nonsense, get-things-done friend Emily Levenson told me to go for it. Thank you to Amanda Filippelli and Lindsey Smith for seeing the vision in the original version of this book.

Susan Scott, my mentor and cheerleader, I will forever be grateful that you did not run away when I showed up with a bag full of old letters and photographs. I could not have written this book without your guidance. Andi Cumbo, your enthusiasm is exactly what I needed to bring this project to completion. Darcie Abbene, your input has truly been invaluable. Thank you for taking a chance with this story. Thank you to the entire team at HCI Books, you have been wonderful to work with.

My deep gratitude goes to my husband, who gave me the space to write, helped with research and translations, and has stood by me through it all.

I would also like to acknowledge the family that isn't here, both the people I knew and the people I didn't. The more I researched, the better I got to know many of them. For all their faults, they were people who lived through more than many of us will in a lifetime. I can only hope that sharing their stories will help preserve their memories.

ABOUT THE AUTHOR

Born in Sweden and raised in Canada, in 2013 Caroline Topperman returned to her ancestral roots in Poland to live, and to explore her love of traveling and experiencing different cultures: from sampling authentic Neapolitan pizzas in Naples to photographing a piano frozen in a river in Užupis, an independent artist's republic in Lithuania, to pitching poutine as a great comfort food to a local French baker in Poland. She speaks fluent English, Polish, and French. Caroline holds a BFA in screenwriting from York University (Toronto). Her book credits include *Tell Me What You See: Visual Writing Prompts for the Wandering Writer* (One Idea Press) and a complementary guide to her blog, *FitWise: Straight Talk about Being Fit & Healthy*. Caroline has written a column for *Huffington Post Canada* and was the beauty editor for *British MODE* magazine.